Network Infrastructures

Infrastructures are complex networks dominated by tight interdependencies between technologies and institutions. These networks supply services crucial to modern societies – services that can be provided only if several critical functions are fulfilled. This book proposes a theoretical framework with a set of concepts to analyze rigorously how these critical functions require coordination within the technological dimension as well as within the institutional dimension. It also shows how fundamental the alignment between these two dimensions is. It argues that this alignment operates along different layers characterized successively by the structure, governance, and transactions that connect technologies and institutions. These issues of coordination and alignment, at the core of the book, are substantiated through in-depth case studies of networks from the energy, water and wastewater, and transportation sectors.

ROLF KÜNNEKE is Professor of Economics of Infrastructures at the Delft University of Technology. He has a long research record on the restructuring of the energy sector.

CLAUDE MÉNARD is Professor of Economics at the Centre d'Economie de la Sorbonne, co-founder and past president of the International Society for New Institutional Economics (now SIOE), and a former co-editor of the *Journal of Economic Behavior and Organization*.

JOHN GROENEWEGEN is Professor Emeritus at the Delft University of Technology. He is past president of the Association for Evolutionary Economics (AFEE) and past general secretary of the European Association for Evolutionary Political Economy (EAEPE).

Network Infrastructures

Technology Meets Institutions

ROLF KÜNNEKE
Delft University of Technology, The Netherlands

CLAUDE MÉNARD
University of Paris I (Panthéon-Sorbonne)

JOHN GROENEWEGEN
Delft University of Technology, The Netherlands

CAMBRIDGE
UNIVERSITY PRESS

CAMBRIDGE
UNIVERSITY PRESS

University Printing House, Cambridge CB2 8BS, United Kingdom

One Liberty Plaza, 20th Floor, New York, NY 10006, USA

477 Williamstown Road, Port Melbourne, VIC 3207, Australia

314–321, 3rd Floor, Plot 3, Splendor Forum, Jasola District Centre,
New Delhi – 110025, India

103 Penang Road, #05–06/07, Visioncrest Commercial, Singapore 238467

Cambridge University Press is part of the University of Cambridge.

It furthers the University's mission by disseminating knowledge in the pursuit of
education, learning, and research at the highest international levels of excellence.

www.cambridge.org
Information on this title: www.cambridge.org/9781108832694
DOI: 10.1017/9781108962292

First published 2021

A catalogue record for this publication is available from the British Library.

Library of Congress Cataloging-in-Publication Data
Names: Künneke, Rolf W., author. | Ménard, Claude, author. | Groenewegen, John,
   1949- author.
Title: Network infrastructures : technology meets institutions / Rolf Künneke, Technische
   Universiteit Delft, The Netherlands, Claude Ménard, Université de Paris I, John
   Groenewegen, Technische Universiteit Delft, The Netherlands.
Description: Cambridge, United Kingdom ; New York, NY, USA : Cambridge University
   Press, 2021. | Includes bibliographical references and index.
Identifiers: LCCN 2021024922 (print) | LCCN 2021024923 (ebook) |
   ISBN 9781108832694 (hardback) | ISBN 9781108965460 (paperback) |
   ISBN 9781108962292 (epub)
Subjects: LCSH: Systems engineering. | Industrial organization. | BISAC: BUSINESS &
   ECONOMICS / Labor / General | BUSINESS & ECONOMICS / Labor / General
Classification: LCC TA168 .K865 2021 (print) | LCC TA168 (ebook) | DDC 620.001/
   171–dc23
LC record available at https://lccn.loc.gov/2021024922
LC ebook record available at https://lccn.loc.gov/2021024923

ISBN 978-1-108-83269-4 Hardback

To our families for their patience and support
throughout the years this book developed

Contents

List of Figures and Tables   *page* viii

Preface   xi

Introduction: Lifting the Veil   1

Part I   Conceptual Framework   13

1   Network Infrastructures: From Coordination to Alignment   15

2   Institutional Embeddedness: A Conceptual Challenge   43

3   Technology in Three Dimensions: Economics Meets
    Systems Engineering   76

4   Bringing Together Two Worlds Apart   93

Part II   Empirical Explorations   123

5   Structures: Unraveling the Energy Transition   125

6   Governance: A Tale of a City's Water and
    Wastewater Network   148

7   Transactions: The Many Challenges Faced
    by Self-Driving Vehicles   177

8   Taking Stock, Looking Ahead   206

Glossary   237

References   240

Index of Names   256

Subject Index   259

Figures and Tables

Figures

I.1 Our alignment framework: first insight *page* 4
I.2 Our framework with its key components 10
1.1 Features of network infrastructures: the
   alignment perspective 41
2.1 Institutional layers 47
2.2 Dimensionalizing macro-institutions 62
2.3 Dimensionalizing micro-institutions 68
2.4 Dimensionalizing meso-institutions 71
3.1 Technological layers 78
3.2 Features of the architecture of network infrastructures 85
3.3 European high-speed rail system 86
3.4 Features of the technological design of
   network infrastructures 88
3.5 Features of the technical operation of
   network infrastructures 90
4.1 The European gas network (2017) 94
4.2 Dutch state revenues from the exploitation of
   natural gas 103
4.3 Dutch gas transportation network 105
4.4 Layers of alignment 107
4.5 Control systems engineering approach to the
   safeguarding of critical functions 109
4.6 Smart gas grid 117
4.7 Our extended alignment framework 120
5.1 Deployment of renewable energy sources required to
   meet Paris climate objectives 126
5.2 Alignment between architecture and macro-
   institutions: structure (layer 1) 126

5.3 Indexed cost reductions in intermittent
    energy technologies   129
5.4 Architecture of traditional electricity systems without
    renewable energy sources   133
5.5 Architecture of traditional electricity systems with
    marginal renewable energy plants   134
5.6 Architecture of contemporary electricity systems   136
5.7 Future energy systems, with integrated energy
    conversion technologies, serving different sectors   142
6.1 Alignment between technological design and meso-
    institutions: governance (layer 2)   151
6.2 Reuse and desalination capacity in Singapore as a
    proportion of daily sales   156
6.3 Key technological layers of the Singaporean
    water system   157
6.4 Nodes and links characterizing the Singaporean
    water network   161
6.5 The hybrid status of the Singaporean Public
    Utilities Board   166
6.6 Overlapping roles of the MEWR and PUB as meso-
    institutions   169
6.7 (a) Main properties and role of governance, (b) with
    application to Singapore   176
7.1 Alignment between technical operations and micro-
    institutions: transactions (layer 3)   179
7.2 Aircraft and automobile software codes compared   191
7.3 Control system for automated vehicles   194
8.1 Alignment framework   214

Tables

2.1 A synthetic view of institutional layers   *page* 74
3.1 A synthetic view of technological layers   91

Preface

This book is the combined result of the expertise on network infrastructures developed by the three of us over decades. Notwithstanding some specialization among us on more specific networks, the book has been written by all three hands. Each chapter started with a draft extensively (and often passionately) discussed and rewritten several times by way of a back-and-forth process substantiated by regular meetings. This meant that we now jointly assume full responsibility for the challenging ideas hereafter submitted to the reader.

The challenges arise from complex and highly sensitive issues. Network infrastructures concern all citizens. They are also currently going through extensive technological changes and profound transformation in their institutional environments, which put them at odds with traditional approaches. In this book, we develop a framework based on concepts that intend to capture the different dimensions of the issues at stake. In doing so, we are not building on sand! Besides our own experience of and expertise in network infrastructures, we take into consideration the work of economists and social scientists well known for their contributions to a better understanding of technology, innovation, and institutions; and also of engineers who have developed sophisticated models of technological systems, often with a glance at their societal dimension. References included in the different chapters register our debt to these contributors.

The analysis hereafter submitted has been under construction for several years, which has allowed us to benefit from presentations of different versions of our chapters to numerous international conferences and seminars, and in many different institutions around the world, addressing a wide variety of audiences, from economists and engineers to social scientists and philosophers. We are hardly able to overemphasize all that we have learned throughout the entire process. We have also capitalized on extensive discussions with several cohorts of students in our respective universities and in the various institutions we have visited. Being challenged by these young researchers has been a source of continuing pleasure, stimulation, and improvement for our project. We also gained immensely from discussions and insights provided by colleagues and operational managers, who willingly agreed to share ideas and/or their specific expertise in relation to different aspects of this book. Although we cannot name them all, for which we apologize, we owe a particular debt to (in alphabetical order): Aziza Akmouch, Eduardo Araral, Marine Colon, Claire Delpeuch, Michael William Dowdle, Robert Gibbons, Paul Joskow, Cheryl Long, Gaetano Martino, William Melody, Paul Nightingale, Douglass C. North, Alessandro Pacciani, Shivani Ratra, Annie Royer, Sylvia Saes, Pablo Spiller, Daniela Toccaceli, Hakan Tropp, Wijnand Veeneman, Bert van Wee, and Oliver Williamson. Last but not least, we are most grateful to the following colleagues, who contributed in very special ways by providing inspiration and/or spending time to read, comment, and make suggestions on advanced versions of specific chapters that fell within their domain: Aad Correlje, Theo Fens, Matthias Finger, Olivia Jensen, Chrys Mantzavinos, Andrey Shastitko, and Mary M. Shirley.

At the end of the journey, we hope that the book resulting from this long process of intense interaction provides stimulating ideas for the reader and a different way of looking at the profound transformation going on in the world of network infrastructures.

Introduction
Lifting the Veil

This book is about network infrastructures. We consider network infrastructures as socio-technological systems characterized by the interdependence and complementarity of their two dimensions: institutions and technology. Relying on a combination of nodes and links, these infrastructures require coordination along both dimensions, in order to fulfill functions hereafter identified as "critical." Critical functions determine the capacity of a network to deliver expected services in line with societal values. Thus understood, network infrastructures cover a wide range of sectors, from energy, water and sanitation, urban transportation, to telecoms and internet. These networks provide the backbone of economic as well as social activities. The key argument underlying our analysis is that alignment between the two dimensions, institutions and technology, is central to the fulfillment of performance expected from these networks. Misalignment can generate discrepancies or gaps challenging the integrity of a network and its capacity to meet its goal. The so-called New York blackout is a good illustration of this.

I.1 In the Dark

At 16:00 EDT on August 14, 2003, the most widespread electricity blackout in North American history paralyzed the city of New York and a wide corridor all the way up to Detroit (United States) and Toronto (Canada). All in all, about 50 million inhabitants were deprived of electricity and thousands of businesses were shut down, some of them for over a week, with a total loss estimated to range between USD 4 billion and USD 10 billion.

The causes of the outage are now relatively well known, thanks among other contributions to the detailed report from the US-Canada Power System Outage Task Force created after the event

(US Secretary of Energy, 2004).[1] According to this report, the Cleveland-Akron area was highly vulnerable to voltage instability problems, largely because a private operator "had not conducted the long-term and operational planning studies needed to understand those vulnerabilities and their operational implications" (US Secretary of Energy, 2004: 23). This was the case because the company did not fulfill the standards and practices codified by the electricity industry through the North American Electric Reliability Corporation (NERC),[2] a behavior warranting dismissal apparently shared by other parties to the network. Indeed, according to the task force report, several operators in the Midwest consistently under-forecasted load levels the days before the blackout, with the institutional mechanisms of control (in this case delegated to the NERC) not perceiving the problem early enough and/or not responding adequately to the problem. So the cause of the outage would be "the inadequate understanding" of how the system worked and/or the inadequate performance of the tasks assigned.

Following the public outcry the outage caused, along with much associated media coverage, the American Congress promptly reacted in adjusting the regulation and in 2005 adopted the Energy Policy Act, which delegates to the NERC the responsibilities for drawing, implementing, and enforcing reliable standards throughout the US bulk power system. However, this rapid adjustment may not have fully taken into account the far-reaching technological changes that had already transformed the conditions of production and transportation of electricity and the significant institutional changes following the deregulation and liberalization of the sector since the creation of the NERC (in 1968). The new legislation, adopted in 2005, might well have underestimated the impact of these changes as a source of misalignment between institution and technology that weakened the system by challenging its coherence.

I.2 This Book in a Nutshell

Notwithstanding its specificity, the complex combination of technological as well as institutional flaws that created the greatest ever

---

[1] *Final Report on the August 14 Blackout in the United States and Canada: Causes and Recommendations.* US Secretary of Energy, April 2004. Available at www .energy.gov/sites/prod/files/oeprod/DocumentsandMedia/BlackoutFinal-Web.pdf
[2] The NERC is a nonprofit organization created by the electrical industry in 1968 to coordinate norms and standards in distribution.

disruption in the distribution of energy in North America points to the much more general problem of the potential misalignment between these two dimensions and its consequences.

Indeed, the New York blackout, more appropriately identified as the "Northeast blackout," provides an excellent illustration of the problem explored in this book: what are the sources of alignment (or misalignment) between the technological requirements and the institutional rules that shape network infrastructures and determine the success or failure of their organization? Blackouts in electricity systems, repeated train accidents, disruptions and delays in underground transportation, and faults in communication systems of self-driving vehicles all provide examples of failures in technological coordination or institutional coordination or both, and flaws in the alignment of these two dimensions.

Our analysis of this interdependence between institutions and technology, and of the resulting successes and failures in network infrastructures, is framed around the concept of *criticality*. "Critical" in this book is understood as pinpointing factors that can provide indispensable support, but which can also obstruct or even derail the fulfillment of functions we refer to as "critical functions." These functions, to be specified and discussed extensively in Part I of this book, are at the core of network infrastructures. The challenge they pose comes from the need to simultaneously coordinate and secure complementary technological and institutional entities and devices. On the institutional side, meeting this goal requires to define, allocate, implement, and enforce rights. On the technological side, it requires to identify, design, implement, and monitor the physical artefacts instrumental in providing expected services.

In the coming chapters, we explore how these two dimensions, the technological one and the institutional one, are interdependent and have to be in alignment in order for a network infrastructure to meet its assigned role. More precisely, we shall argue that the performance of network infrastructures depends on their capacity to fulfill four fundamental functions: capacity allocation, system control, interoperability among components, and interconnection between segments of the network. Figure I.1 summarizes this first insight into our approach.

I.3 Our Core Question and Hypotheses

Our driving motivation in developing this framework can be expressed as a quest to answer the following question:

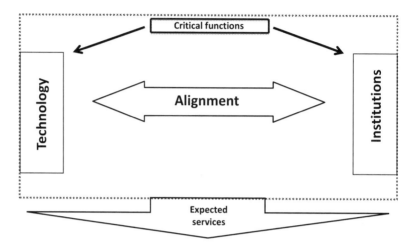

Figure I.1 Our alignment framework: first insight

What features can align the institutional and technological dimensions of network infrastructures, in order to obtain performance that meets societal expectations?

In pursuing this goal, the challenge we face comes from connecting the complex engineering systems of network infrastructures to their institutional embedding. What we are looking for is those institutional features needed to support specific network infrastructures; and, symmetrically, those technological requirements needed to make a specific network operational. We assume, and will substantiate in the coming chapters, that both the technological dimension and the institutional dimension need to be aligned in order to fulfill the requirements imposed by the critical functions, thus giving a specific network the capacity to deliver expected services. In exploring these issues, and notwithstanding differences across network infrastructures, we assume the existence of certain regularities; that is, the presence of reproducible and transposable patterns, which we aim to unravel. While elaborating on our theoretical framework in Part I of this book, and in order to better substantiate its empirical significance, we refer to examples from different network infrastructures, mainly the energy, transportation, water, and information sectors. In Part II, we explore the relevance of our theoretical approach through in-depth analysis of specific cases from a variety of network infrastructures.

More specifically, our analysis relies on the hypothesis that alignment operates differently but in complementarity along three interdependent layers: (1) a layer that defines the "structure" of a network, connecting its technological architecture to general norms and rules embedded in laws, customs, and other institutional settings; (2) a layer that models the "governance" of a network infrastructure, relating its specific technological design with the specific institutions that transform general norms and rules into customized ones and delineate the conditions of their implementation; and (3) a layer that corresponds to the planning and actual implementation of "transactions," providing support to the transfer and usage of rights and related resources in a way that makes technical features operational.[3] The central characteristics associated with these layers can be summarized in the following four hypotheses, and are substantiated in the theoretical analyses and empirical explorations developed in the coming chapters.

> H1: *The structural alignment (or misalignment) between the technological architecture and the general institutional set of rules and norms in which network infrastructures are embedded conditions their existence and frames their properties.*

We identify this structural level as the macro layer. For instance, networks can have a centralized or decentralized mode of operation. Centralization (or decentralization) is heavily dependent on the technological architecture of the system and the general rules framing its usage. To illustrate, in most countries electricity networks have for a long time been built and developed through an architecture that imposes very tight constraints on the production, transportation, and usage of power, thus resulting in a strictly centralized system. At the opposite end of the spectrum, the internet owes its success to the widely decentralized characteristics of its architecture and conditions of access.

---

[3] With respect to this distinction between layers, we found initial inspiration in the scheme proposed by Williamson (2000: 597), who made a distinction between "Institutional Embeddedness" (Level 1 in his terminology), the "institutional environment" (Level 2), the level of "governance" (Level 3), and the level of "Resource Allocation and Employment" (Level 4). However, we transformed Williamson's scheme to deal with aspects his typology did not capture, particularly his "benign neglect" of the technological dimension.

H2: *General norms and rules must be translated and embedded into context-specific ones linking specific protocols and guidelines with context-specific technological features through modalities of governance.*

We identify this intermediate level as the meso layer. It involves entities and devices developed at the intersection between the structural features (rules and architecture) and the level of transactions at which the network becomes operational. For instance, following the Northeast blackout, the Energy Act of 2005 delegated to the NERC, a nonprofit corporation, the role of securing the critical functions for the North American electricity transmission networks. To meet this goal, the NERC operates as a private institution in charge of the definition of "reliable" standards and procedures, their implementation, and their monitoring.

H3: *Ultimately, rules and norms and their technological counterparts must be implemented through the organization of transactions that interconnect specific institutional arrangements and specific technical requirements, allowing a network to operate.*

We identify this operational level as the micro layer. This is the layer at which transactions must be carried out through the coordination of relevant agents within organizational arrangements that must meet and satisfy the technical requirements of the technology/technologies adopted to deliver the expected services. For instance, once a producer of electricity has been allocated rights of access to the grid under conditions established at the macro layer and its capacity to meet the technical procedures of access agreed by the entities and devices through which the governance operates at the meso layer, this producer must still organize transactions, for instance through contracts with providers of coal or uranium, in order to meet the standards of the technology chosen.

H4: *The alignment (or misalignment) along the three interdependent layers of structure, governance, and transactions determines the capacity (or failure) of a network infrastructure to deliver expected services.*

We shall argue in the coming chapters that the capacity of a network infrastructure to meet these requirements along the three layers, and to secure the alignment between the technological side and the institutional side, is central to the delivery of expected services by way of modalities that are economically sustainable and socially acceptable.

I.4 Underlying Premises

Our structuring question as well as our working hypotheses are built on the premise that network infrastructures share common features that make them different from other economic activities; for instance, the centrality of interconnection through nodes and links that impose challenging requirements with respect to coordination. Although it is the purpose of this book to substantiate this statement through the development of a conceptual framework and empirical tests, some initial insights might provide a useful guideline throughout the book.

First, we consider network infrastructures as socio-technological systems. Infrastructures are engineering systems that function in a specific social context. They perform intended functions, for instance, the safe and reliable provision of energy to households. Human agents purposefully design these systems; they monitor and adjust them in order to meet expectations that encompass values. To be sure, not everything in infrastructures is purposefully planned. Technology develops according to path-dependent trajectories. That the Netherlands has one of the most developed gas networks in the world is an important condition for the smooth transition to the use of biogas in residential areas, following the political decision to close down the Groningen gas field. However, the interest of farmers in providing biogas can certainly not be planned in every detail, and the willingness of consumers to adjust their behavior or of environmentalists to accept the fundamental changes in agricultural practices that biogas requires cannot be predetermined.

Second, coordination within each dimension, technology on the one hand, institutions on the other, is essential to the existence and running of network infrastructures. The different components of an infrastructure are not operating in isolation, they are interdependent. The local production of energy needs to be attuned with the technological properties and the capacities of the grid, the required energy quality, the limited possibility of storage, and of course the needs of final users. There is the necessity to implement institutional entities that will allow the coordination of the required technical features, in order to produce and deliver the expected services. Access to safe, drinkable water is a case in point: "safety" refers to parameters of quality that evolve over time and vary according to societies, the implementation of which also depends on available technologies or innovation. Coordination of each dimension is required and provides the alignment (or misalignment) that conditions the performance of the network.

Third, critical functions that characterize network infrastructures must be fulfilled for expected services to be delivered. System control must be implemented to make the network operational. For gas, this would be a certain calorific value and chemical composition, for electricity voltage (230 volts) and frequency (60 hertz), and so on. Capacity must be allocated and managed in a way that balances production and delivery with the actual demand. For electricity systems, this physical balance (called "load balancing") is a central feature, otherwise the system might collapse. In the railroad or airline industry, scheduling and monitoring the allocation of "slots" is a determinant factor for a secure system. Interconnection among segments of a network is needed to improve the technical functioning of the system, in order to benefit from externalities associated with the delivery of expected services. For instance, the reliability of rail transportation depends on the existence and quality of interconnection between the local, regional, national, and even international networks. Last, interoperability among different parts of a network requires that they are technically equipped and institutionally monitored in a way that fits the technical needs of the system. For instance, solar panels need to fulfill certain technical requirements in order to be connected to the electric grid; signal systems on board trains need to be tightly coordinated in order to secure passengers' transportation.

Ultimately, our main concern when exploring these properties of network infrastructures and the interdependence between technology and institutions that characterize them is about the outcome. How can network infrastructures be technically reliable, institutionally feasible, and perform satisfactorily thanks to the proper alignment between these two foundational dimensions? At this stage, our approach remains static. We consider the alignment issue at a certain point in time. Although we may refer occasionally to dynamic aspects, for example, the impact of innovation on the organization of electricity grids, we do not develop a dynamic model. In that respect, we are aware that criteria other than alignment could be introduced to assess performance, for example, sustainability (which refers to co-evolution) or affordability (which refers to pricing strategies and financial considerations).

What we do explore in this book is how the factors commanding the interdependence between the macro, meso, and micro layers identified above shape the capacity of specific networks to meet expectations and fulfill the objectives they are assigned. For instance, in the railroad industry passengers expect trains to be on time, to be safe, to provide a certain level of comfort, and to make connections easy. These expectations translate into substantial technical requirements as well as rules implemented and enforced in a way that allows transactions to be accomplished efficiently.

I.5 Outline of the Book

Based on this introductory discussion of our core concepts, which will be extensively developed in the coming chapters, we can reformulate our initial figure, in order to better capture the hard core of our framework.

Figure I.2 summarizes and somewhat anticipates developments explicated in the coming chapters. These chapters are organized in two parts.

Part I ("Conceptual Framework") is analytical. It develops our core concepts and explores in some detail how they are interconnected, thus defining an integrated and coherent approach to network infrastructures. Chapter 1 examines the features identified as typical in the literature on network infrastructures and points out substantial flaws, particularly when it comes to taking into account the societal values involved in the determination of institutional rules and in the choice of specific technologies. As well as the introduction of key concepts, we emphasize how value-loaded is the domain of network infrastructures when understood as socio-technological systems. Chapter 2 focuses on the institutional dimension of our framework. Building on contributions coming mainly – although not exclusively – from the new institutional approach, which has its own flaws, particularly when it comes to the analysis of technologies, the chapter provides an in-depth study of the characterization of institutions as composed of interdependent layers identified through specific concepts. The chapter emphasizes the different institutional modalities through which value-oriented network infrastructures are ruled. Chapter 3 turns to the technological

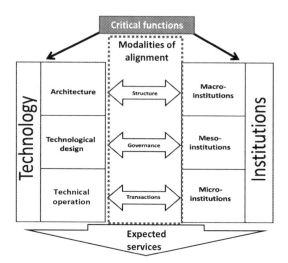

Figure I.2 Our framework with its key components

dimension. Paralleling the previous chapter, it identifies distinct but interdependent layers through which the technological architecture of a network infrastructure is translated into technological features that need to be made operational. Building on engineering approaches, it emphasizes the modalities through which the technological dimension of the critical functions can actually be fulfilled. Chapter 4 puts together these elements to deal with the central question of our book: what conditions regarding the alignment of institutions and technology of network infrastructures must be fulfilled, in order to meet the critical functions that determine the capacity of these infrastructures to deliver expected services. The chapter emphasizes the sources of alignment (or misalignment) between the two interdependent dimensions of our framework.

Part II ("Empirical Exploration") delivers analyses through which our framework is mobilized to assess factors of alignment or misalignment of specific network infrastructures. Chapter 5 takes stock of the complex transition toward sustainable energy systems to show the structural factors that make macro-institutional rules and norms and the architecture of energy networks interdependent. The emphasis is on the tension between the existing centralized arrangements and the emergence of alternative technologies that support a radically different structure. Chapter 6 focuses on the critical provision of water services to a major city, and draws lessons from what is considered to be a success story to illustrate how modalities of governance have been implemented that allow the appropriate alignment between meso-institutions and the technological design of a system based on four substantially different technologies. The emphasis is on conditions that made the alignment appropriate, but also on factors that may plague the governance of an otherwise successful network. Chapter 7 discusses the ongoing technological changes in urban transportation through the case of the introduction of self-driving vehicles. It shows how the modalities through which transactions are established and monitored impact all three layers of our framework because of the societal values that such emerging technologies challenge. The emphasis is on the interdependence of layers exhibited by technological changes that require the transformation of existing social norms.

Chapter 8 concludes by pointing out the novelty of our approach, its relevance for the study of specific empirical cases, and also the directions in which new developments could enrich the conceptual framework. The chapter also comes back to policy issues raised by our framework and the different cases explored. In doing so, we also discuss some limitations of our analysis, thus opening up room for future research.

Throughout the entire book, our focus is on identifying and characterizing the different and interdependent layers that shape the institutional as well as the technological dimensions of network infrastructures. Our goal is to provide conceptual tools for assessing the conditions under which the alignment or misalignment of the two dimensions and their internal coordination determine the performance of specific network infrastructures.

PART I

Conceptual Framework

Providing expected services requires alignment between technology and institutions of network infrastructures such that critical functions are fulfilled and safeguarded. Although there is an abundance of literature on specific network infrastructures, for example, the energy sector, railways, road transportation, etc., there is a fundamental lack of knowledge about how such complex engineering systems are connected to their institutional embedding. In this Part I, we develop a general approach that could capture this novel field of research. The following chapters elaborate on the building blocks of a conceptual framework that intends to fulfill this goal. This framework provides a set of coherent concepts and it explores their complementarity, thus delivering tools to understand and analyze the interdependence between technologies and institutions that characterizes network infrastructures. It does so with an emphasis on the coordination issues among components from each of these two dimensions; and on the modalities of alignment or the sources of misalignment between these two dimensions. Ultimately, this framework intends to show that the capacity to fulfill the critical functions at the core of network infrastructures depends on this mix of coordination and alignment, which conditions the capacity of specific network infrastructures to provide expected services.

More precisely, Chapter 1 identifies what we consider key features that make network infrastructures specific. It is argued that there is a need to develop more comprehensive and subtle concepts than those provided by the leading paradigms dealing with this issue. Using that perspective, Chapter 2 provides a deeper understanding of the institutional dimensions of network infrastructures. We differentiate between macro-, meso-, and micro-institutions, and provide concepts to capture the essence of these three layers. Similarly, Chapter 3 analyzes the technological features of network infrastructures related to the technological architecture, technological design, and technical operation characterizing network infrastructures. Chapter 4 brings together these worlds which have largely remained apart, providing concepts to capture the interdependent technological and institutional dimensions for each of the three layers. The resulting inclusive framework allows us to develop the multifaceted features of alignment and to provide tools relevant for an analysis of the interdependence and alignment (or misalignment) of institutions and technology in network infrastructures.

One last remark about what we mean by "framework": in using this term, we follow the distinction made by Ostrom (2005: 27–29) between framework, theory, and model. A framework identifies the most general set of variables or elements (and their relationships) to be considered for understanding the features and elements of a general research problem. Theories target specific components of a framework: they *"make specific assumptions that are necessary for an analyst to diagnose a phenomenon, explain its processes, and predict outcomes."* Finally, models specify a limited set of parameters or variables that allow formalized research methods. All the coming chapters clearly relate to the first notion. They develop a framework that identifies and delineates the various features of alignment between institutions and technologies in network infrastructures.

1 | Network Infrastructures
From Coordination to Alignment

1.1 Introduction

In the opening chapter, "Lifting the Veil," we briefly outlined our perspective of alignment between the technological and institutional dimensions of network infrastructures. We consider these networks to be socio-technological systems in which the technological dimension is subject to physical laws, whereas the institutional dimension of norms, laws, and organizations frames and organizes the production and consumption of the services delivered by network infrastructures. In what follows, we shall further elaborate on the issues of coordination and alignment mentioned in the opening chapter by discussing the special features of network infrastructures. What makes network infrastructures so special that coordination and alignment are considered crucial with respect to their performance?

Analytically, we represent the two dimensions of our framework as layers, starting at the top with the generic technological architecture that is interdependent with macro-institutions. The intermediate layer is concerned with technological design specific to a time and place that is interdependent with meso-institutions. The lowest layer of specification in our alignment framework refers to the technological operations that are interdependent with micro-institutions, which coordinate transactions. This is the layer at which the concrete services should be delivered by the network infrastructure as expected by society.

In this chapter, we shall use examples from road transportation infrastructure to illustrate these two dimensions and three layers. The technological architecture consists of a network of roads (highways, urban roads, secondary roads in the countryside) connected by crossings, tunnels, bridges, and the like. Passenger cars, transportation trucks, and buses all use the roads simultaneously. A number of means of technological communication are used to guide the drivers of these vehicles – also cyclists and pedestrians – such as traffic lights, road signs, and information panels. The technological architecture is inter-dependent with the macro-institutions of norms, laws, and regulations providing general rules regarding how to behave on the roads (e.g., driving on the right side, priority of traffic coming from the right).

Technological design at the second layer of the road network example is concerned, for instance, with the creation of specific lanes on the roads that are only available for public transport buses. This is the case when government policies aim to stimulate the use of public transport by making it more efficient compared to private transport; the creation of specific lanes in crowded areas offers buses the oppor-tunity to bypass private cars that are locked in traffic jams. In terms of contextual technological design, the lanes need to be equipped with specific technical components such as traffic signs and radar systems. This is necessary for monitoring and controlling the use of specific lanes by dedicated vehicles only. The corresponding meso-institutions (e.g., traffic control authorities) translate the general macro laws and regulations into more specific ones designed for the traffic in these designated lanes; they monitor the use of the lanes and intervene when necessary.

The third layer of our framework concerns the technological oper-ation of the road network infrastructure. For instance, in order to increase safety, both the infrastructure and vehicles have been equipped in recent years with driver assistance technologies that help drivers avoid drifting into adjacent lanes or making unsafe lane changes. Or the vehicle might brake automatically if a car ahead stops or slows down suddenly. These technologies at the operational layer use a combination of hardware (sensors, cameras, and radar) and software to help vehicles identify certain safety risks, so the driver can be warned. The operational technology is interdependent with the micro-institutions that coordinate the transactions at the micro layer. In the institutional dimension, transactions should be organized through micro-institutions (such as contracts, vertically integrated firms, public–private partnerships), which fulfill the technological safety requirements. This will be further discussed below, and more specifically in Chapter 7 of this book.

These examples highlight some of the core characteristics of the road network infrastructure. Underlying these characteristics, societal values such as the general need for mobility, efficiency, and safety permeate the three institutional layers already identified, largely determining the kind of services society expects to be delivered by the network and orienting technological choices accordingly. In the technological dimension, different complementary components are involved that require tight coordination, in order to perform their functions well. Strong interdependencies exist between the components of the technological dimension and the institutional dimension at all three layers of our framework. A central hypothesis underlying this framework is that alignment between the two dimensions is crucial for network infrastructures to deliver expected services.

In Section 1.2, we discuss the specific features of network industries from this alignment perspective. The line of reasoning starts with the desired performance of the infrastructures: What are the services societies expect the socio-technological system to deliver? Network infrastructures have to provide clean water, remove waste, support safe transport, assure a reliable electricity supply, etc. In Section 1.2.1, we discuss how the expected network services are related to the values of the society in which the network infrastructures are embedded. The values of society regarding access to services such as water and electricity, as well as safety, efficiency, and privacy, differ according to time and location. Consequently, the content of the services that network infrastructures are supposed to deliver is not absolute, but relative, often having to meet different, even conflicting expectations.

In Section 1.2.2, we discuss the specific features of network infrastructures resulting from the close complementarities of their constituting components. With respect to the technological dimension, network infrastructures consist of nodes (for instance, train stations, gas production plants, traffic lights) and links (railways, pipes, roads). We shall argue that due to the technical complementarities of these nodes and links, adequate coordination is required in order to make the infrastructure deliver the expected services. Such coordination takes place through specific arrangements such as electronic devices in vehicles with driver assistance technologies. In such vehicles, sensors receive signals, for instance, about the distance from other vehicles on the road, which are transmitted to the brakes or accelerator of the vehicle by means of an electronic device. The same applies for the institutional dimension: specific nodes (laws, rules, organizations) and links (driving codes, traffic regulators) should be adequately coordinated through organizations such as the National Highway

Traffic Safety Administration (NHTSA) in the United States.[1] We explain in this chapter the importance of coordination of the components in each dimension (technology and institutions) and stress the central role of coordination arrangements.

In Section 1.3, we discuss the question of alignment in relation to the specific characteristics of network infrastructures. Alignment issues arise because of the interdependence between the technological and institutional dimensions. In this respect, they are closely related to the coordination issues already discussed; the coordination arrangements on both the technological and institutional sides must be matched. The alignment question refers to the compatibility (or incompatibility) between the characteristics of coordination arrangements. In this chapter, we shall more closely delineate the intertwined relations between coordination and alignment, and raise questions about their matching. The following chapters will provide specific insights and possible solutions to these issues.

Last, in Section 1.4, we posit this alignment framework in relation to the contributions of microeconomics, New Institutional Economics, and the approaches of socio-technological systems to the understanding of network infrastructures. We shall conclude that these contributions provide valuable insights into specific characteristics of network infrastructures, but that the core issues of the interdependence between technologies and institutions, and the related questions of coordination and alignment, are underdeveloped. Bridging this gap by developing theoretical concepts appropriate to the analysis of network infrastructure and building a coherent approach to the alignment issue is the main goal of the next chapters. In what follows, we put together the pieces of the puzzle, which are summarized in Section 1.5.

1.2 Features of Network Infrastructures

In this section, we discuss the characteristics of network infrastructures. What makes them so specific from our alignment perspective? What are the elements a theoretical framework should capture when analyzing network infrastructures? As a first distinguishing feature, network infrastructures provide services that are strongly related to societal values. Second, the provision of these services is characterized

---

[1] See Chapter 7 of this book for details.

by strong complementarities and the need for tight coordination among and between nodes and links.

1.2.1 The Value-Loaded Provision of Infrastructure Services

Infrastructures are the backbones of the economy, providing support to the delivery of services expected by citizens in a certain society at a certain point in time. We argue that societal values play a key role in establishing which services are considered essential in a society. For instance, the value of safety rather than speed can be prioritized in relation to the services that road infrastructures are expected to deliver. Furthermore, values and norms also impact the way society wants the technological and institutional components to be coordinated. For example, should the technology be fully coordinated through algorithms,[2] or should human agents also have a role to play? Should the institutional coordination be arranged through contracts and competitive market relations, or should a central government institution be in charge?

Expected Services: The Role of Values
In this section, we first briefly point out the existing variety of concepts used to capture the specific services that network infrastructures deliver. After having discussed some different approaches, we explain why we prefer to use the concept of "expected services" in this book.

Infrastructure services are services of specific interest, i.e., services that public authorities classify as essential for a society and its citizens. Following the liberalization of infrastructures in the European Union and elsewhere, with public transport, roads, energy, telecommunication, water, and the like, increasingly provided by private firms, a distinction has been made between two types of essential service: services of general interest and universal services (Finger and Finon, 2011). In the case of the latter, governments formulate universal service obligations, which are considered to be a form of consumer protection. For each specific service provided by the infrastructure, obligations are defined concerning its affordability (are all citizens able

---

[2] An algorithm is a list of steps to follow in order to solve a problem. Algorithms in computers can perform calculations, data processing, and automated reasoning. This is the case in, for instance, automated vehicles, where the technical components act on the basis of an algorithm (see Chapter 7).

to afford the consumption of a service such as drinkable water or train transport?), the quality of the service (does the provision satisfy standards of safety, security, and punctuality?), and its accessibility (do citizens in the countryside also have access to telecommunication, education, and transportation services?). The monitoring and control of the universal service obligations are mostly put in the hands of sector-specific regulators. In the case of services of general interest, broader public policy objectives are included that go beyond citizen protection, such as general security of the energy supply, road safety, environmental protection, sustainable development, among others.

In our perspective on network infrastructures, universal services and services of general interests become essential when government formally recognizes them as a basic right for its citizens and the failure to deliver such services would result in potential risks to the public, the economy, or society. What is considered in the general interest, a basic need, and what is considered a potential risk depends on the societal values of that specific time and place. This can be illustrated using the services provided by road infrastructure.

As already mentioned, the road network infrastructure is a socio-technological system that performs important functions in society; the function of transport and mobility is considered essential from a social as well as from an economic point of view. The road system includes not only roads, bridges, and tunnels but also vehicles and their drivers. The road network infrastructure provides services to drivers of passenger vehicles, trucks, and buses, and also to cyclists and pedestrians. These services should result in safe, efficient, and convenient transportation from A to B. In that respect, the road network infrastructure is a socio-technological system, in which different components have to be coordinated to deliver the expected service.

How important the transportation function is, how and what technology can be used to fulfill the function, and what room is left for people's own responsibility depends on the societal values in place. Gerxhani and Van Breemen (2019) pointed out that societal values affect people's preferences and attitudes, but also encompass broader issues. Through processes of socialization within families, communities, and working environments, societal values become individual social values to be defined as "people's generalized beliefs regarding the desirability of conducts or end-states" (Gerxhani and van Breemen, 2019: 262). Examples of relevant values that become individual social values are "prosocial" and "proself" values, which reflect concern for others' welfare, or, respectively, for self-interest. The former motivate cooperative behavior, the latter motivate the accumulation of personal wealth. "Values have been shown to be vital in guiding evaluation of alternatives and shaping behavioral choices" (Gerxhani and van Breemen, 2019: 263).

People in society may consider it to be important that individuals who make use of the road network are personally responsible for their own safety and that of others. People in society can attribute high value to the personal freedom of road users to decide for themselves with regard to appropriate speed, acceptable maneuvers to pass other cars, etc. People in society may value differently the role of government in setting rules for the users and suppliers of infrastructure services. Likewise, people may value differently the extent to which technology should automatically control users regarding speed and maneuvers, in which case individual responsibility is absent. Values are relative and change over time.

Enlightening in this respect is a document from the National Highway Traffic Safety Administration (NHTSA) in the United States, which shows how, in the 1950s, the Big Three (Ford, Chrysler, and General Motors) competed with each other not so much on safety features but, first and foremost, with big, shiny impressive automobiles. Safety became more and more of an issue after activists such as Ralph Nader (1965) made public how unsafe the cars were, despite the fact that the technology was available to make important improvements.[3] The situation with regard to European car manufacturers was similar. Between 1950 and 2000, more attention was gradually paid to safety (and also convenience) features such as cruise control, seat belts, and anti-lock brakes. Government regulation no doubt played an important role in this. Later, new features were added such as electronic stability control, blind spot detection, lane departure

---

[3] Ralph Nader became a consultant to the US Department of Labor in 1964, and in 1965 he published Unsafe at Any Speed, which criticized the American auto industry in general for its unsafe products and attacked General Motors' Corvair automobile in particular. The book became a bestseller and led directly to the passage of the 1966 National Traffic and Motor Vehicle Safety Act, which gave the government the power to enact safety standards for all automobiles sold in the United States (www.britannica.com/biography/Ralph-Nader; last accessed May 2, 2019).

warning, and forward collision warning, followed by adaptive cruise control and self-parking assistance. The fully self-driving vehicle is nowadays tested not only in specific designated areas but on public roads as well (see Chapter 7 for details).

Next to safety, values surrounding environmental protection have become increasingly important with regard to the services provided by road network infrastructures. Car manufacturers have focused in recent years on the development of less polluting engines, lighter vehicles, and more efficiency. More sustainability and recyclability have become important elements of marketing strategies. These developments show that values that influence policies and the behavior of private agents change over time. These changes are initiated by technological developments, as well as changing norms and values of citizens and related government policies.[4]

Another interesting development in the values related to road network infrastructure is the valuation people attach to having a privately owned vehicle. The introduction of self-driving vehicles is expected to strongly influence the way people make use of passenger vehicles; it is expected that the transportation market will develop in the future into a market with a differentiated offer of transportation services (Arbib and Seba, 2017). People will value a safe, efficient, and convenient mode of transportation from A to B. Whether that service is provided by a privately owned vehicle or by private or state-owned firms offering transportation services, or whether the service is offered as a scheduled service or as a customized service will increasingly become a matter of consumer choice. This development illustrates how technological developments in passenger vehicles not only impact the technological components of the infrastructure but also influence societal values and the related services society expects the road infrastructure to deliver (see Chapter 7 for details). Clearly, government policies play an important role; new technologies can be stimulated or hindered and changing values can be appreciated or disapproved through different kinds of policy measures.

The lesson to be learned from this is that societal values such as safety, efficiency, privacy, etc. are incorporated into "services of general interest" and "universal services." By means of general policies,

---

[4] The change in energy policy as part of energy transition set out in Chapter 5 also illustrates this point very well.

the former are further specified to provide criteria ("standards of judgment"; Bush, 2009) for evaluating the services provided by the network infrastructures. Likewise, new technologies are evaluated by institutional entities such as parliaments and governmental agencies. These values are also specified, in order to provide universal service obligations for firms that provide infrastructure services to the market.

However, the translation of values into specific "standards of judgment" is not always straightforward. For instance, the evaluation of a specific new technology such as the introduction of self-driving vehicles can be problematic when conflicting values are at stake. In the case of road network infrastructures, values of efficiency (speed) can conflict with safety or environmental protection. To solve such value conflicts, a ranking system needs to be established, implying a judgment about the importance of each value involved. A system of judging and ranking values implies that values are subject to assessment, and that political institutions have to debate and decide about their ranking, and about the positive and negative role they play in society (Bush and Tool, 2003; Correljé et al., 2014). This does not mean that values change only through explicit political action. On the contrary, many of the values change "spontaneously" through anonymous interactions. Although they often happen in an incremental way, revolutionary value changes are also possible, for instance, due to a sudden crisis in the provision of an essential service. If research shows how strongly the air is polluted within a range of one kilometer from a highway, and that people suffer from relatively more serious diseases, or that the accident rate in a specific trajectory is relatively high, then the value of efficiency or speed of the road system can rather abruptly be replaced by environmental values or road safety standards.

In short, we consider that what makes services associated with specific network infrastructures perceived to be "essential" is deeply rooted in societal values. Which values in society are important and which services are essential is largely established or consolidated through political institutions. Because values differ over time and from place to place, the content of essential services is not absolute but relative. That is why in this book we shall mostly refer to "expected services" rather than "essential services," "public services," "utilities," and other terminology intending to capture the type of services that network infrastructures are expected to deliver. Values are subject to assessment, can be conflicting, and are ranked through political institutions. Consequently, the performance of network infrastructures with respect to the provision of expected services ought to be monitored, and when standards or universal obligations are not met intervention is needed.

1.2.2 Complementarities between Constituting Components

In this section, we explore in more detail the "network" character of infrastructures, the components and links making up both the technological and institutional dimensions. Central to a network is the concept of complementarity, which points to the need for tight coordination between complementary nodes and links in the networks, a crucial requirement to be fulfilled if expected services are going to be delivered and critical functions safeguarded. In other words, we substantiate the concept of "network" through the notion of complementarity, so as to better pinpoint the nature of network infrastructures in terms of the need for coordination and alignment.

Indeed, a defining feature of network infrastructures is the complementarity between nodes and links; a good or service provided by a network requires at least two nodes with a link between them (Economides, 1996). A node has no value without the other nodes and links; they are complementary to each other. From our alignment perspective, we first focus on technological complementarity, with specific attention paid to the underlying coordination required among the different technical components. We consider a tight technological coordination to be crucial for the network to perform its critical functions well, which we shall elaborate on further in Section 1.2.3. Second, we analyze the institutional dimension of complementarity and the need to coordinate the institutional components adequately. Third, we introduce the core of our perspective, which is about the alignment between the coordination arrangements along the technological and institutional dimensions of network infrastructures.

Technological Complementarities

In the case of road networks with vehicles using driver assistance technologies, or in the case of controlled entry to highways in situations of congestion, technical components need to be installed both as part of the infrastructure and inside the vehicle. Since the components of the infrastructure are in one way or another connected through a physical network, they cannot be operated independently from each other. The complementary components can adequately fulfill their functions only when they are tightly coordinated. The concept of technological complementarity points to a strong need to coordinate the various complementary functions performed by the technical components. For instance, sensors along highways are implemented to detect the number of vehicles, their speed, and the distance between them. That information has to be combined with other technical components, such as the signaling system at the entry points of the highway, in order to instruct vehicles in areas of congestion regarding whether they are allowed to enter or not. To fulfill these functions, the activities of the different technical components need to be well coordinated through specific arrangements such as electronic devices. This type of configuration of technological devices[5] will be discussed further in Chapter 3.

In short: the technological system consists of complementary components that fulfill specific functions and perform specific activities, which need to be tightly coordinated by technological arrangements.

Institutional Complementarities
The different components in the institutional dimension of the network infrastructure fulfill complementary functions as well. Norms provide rules of behavior, which are not explicitly formulated in laws and regulations, but which reside in people's souls and minds. Laws and regulations are formal institutions that are registered. Organizations are institutions that structure behavior within specific boundaries (for details of the institutional components, see Chapter 2). The concept of institutional complementarity points to a strong need to coordinate the different institutional components within and across the different layers of our framework. In relation to road infrastructure, the norms imposed on drivers about their responsibilities and/or the laws and rules about obeying traffic signs need to be tightly coordinated and strictly implemented; otherwise, none of the institutional components will adequately fulfill its function.

Coordination, Monitoring, and Control
Proper coordination of the complementary components along both the technological and institutional dimensions of the network is therefore

---

[5] We use the terms "components" and "devices" interchangeably in this book.

vital for the provision of the expected services. Coordination is the act of creating and organizing the conditions to get different people or components to work together to achieve required effects or fulfill desired goals in a network. Different activities of the components and links of a network have to be adequately tuned and adjusted, in order to make the complementary components all contribute effectively to the provision of expected services.

Adequate coordination, that is, the level of coordination needed to achieve a specific goal, requires monitoring and control. Control is about configuring the components so that they are in accord with the desired performance of the network. Monitoring of the network can be based on the performance of a network in terms of safety or efficiency. When monitoring signals that the performance does not meet specific standards, resulting for instance in congestion on the road, a technological coordination arrangement could automatically lead to adjustments, for example, traffic lights could start to function at the entry points to the road. However, usually a combination of technological and institutional devices and entities is responsible for the monitoring and control; agents responsible for assessing the situation and organizing the control make use of technological devices requiring tight coordination between both the technological and the institutional dimensions of the transportation system.

Monitoring and control come at a cost. Rigid bureaucratic control mechanisms can incentivize opportunistic behavior, whereas control mechanisms based on shared norms can facilitate less costly cooperative behavior (Gerxhani and van Breemen, 2019). Monitoring and control also become more complex and costly when a variety of technical components and many parties are involved. Furthermore, coordination becomes more complex and costly when the system has to deal with high environmental and behavioral uncertainties. It can be assumed that societies tend to be prepared to pay for high monitoring and control costs when important services are involved which affect highly ranked societal values. It is important to take these issues into consideration when explaining concrete coordination arrangements in different infrastructures in different contexts.

1.3 Network Infrastructures: Alignment at the Core

In this section, we first consider contributions to the analysis of network infrastructures in microeconomics, "New Institutional Economics," and

"Socio-Technical Systems" (STS)[6] approaches. We will conclude that from our alignment perspective important elements are missing in these analyses. We then make suggestions about concepts and relations on which to build an analytical framework capable of dealing with the core issues of coordination and alignment.

1.3.1 Insights from Microeconomics, New Institutional Economics, and STS Approaches

Microeconomics

In the microeconomics literature on infrastructures, a distinction is made between the construction of the infrastructure, the production of its services, and the consumption of the services (Kessides, 2004).

With respect to construction, the generally large capital investments required upfront, the extended construction period, and the high level of sunk investment[7] increase risks and require a long-term horizon. This can discourage private investment and once the investments are made new entries might be dissuaded from joining. More specifically, private investors may then ask for guarantees in the form of long-term contracts, including delivery conditions and price controls, and may try to erect forms of barriers to entry. Alternatively, these risks may explain why very often such investments are made by public authorities, even in the context of so-called public–private partnerships.

With respect to the production of services, the characteristic of increasing returns to scale is prominent, leading to market concentration or even to natural monopoly. This leads to policies of "competition for the market" instead of "competition in the market," or alternatively the decision to transfer the production of services to state monopolies. In the microeconomics literature, the increasing returns to scale are connected to the cost and pricing issue. Helm (2009b: 315) points to the "wide gulf between average and marginal costs" in the delivery of infrastructure services. Once sunk investments

---

[6] In this section, we refer to the literature known as the "Socio-Technical Systems" approach. In the rest of the book, we refer to "socio-technological systems," since technology has a broader meaning and allows for the consideration of values, a key point in our view.

[7] Sunk investments are specific investments that, once undertaken, result in their value in alternative uses being substantially below investment costs (non-redeployability).

have been made, the marginal costs are close to zero, unless congestion is reached. Private firms try to solve the pricing issue by means of long-term contracts, in which they bind customers to buy their services for a long period and pay a price that covers average costs. An alternative solution is to rely on public investments. For instance, for a long time in Europe many countries opted for public ownership and socialized costs through taxes or a combination of taxes and user fees.

With respect to the consumption of infrastructure services, both public good characteristics and externalities play a role. In the case of pure public goods, the consumption of services is non-rivalrous and non-excludable, causing free rider problems. Infrastructures such as road networks often provide so-called impure public goods. In the case of transportation networks, when roads have sufficient capacity in relation to demand, all users of the road consume the service without rivalry. However, beyond a specific number of users the road capacity reaches its limits and congestion occurs. Consumption becomes rivalrous and the marginal cost positive. Infrastructures are typical examples of such impure public goods.[8]

Related to the consumption of infrastructure services are the so-called network effects (Economides, 1996). A network effect exists when the consumer value increases with the number of users. This is clearly the case in telephony and social media. The more users that are connected to these communication networks, and the more services individual users can derive from them, the higher their consumer value. Economides (1996) elaborates on the consequences of complementarity and network effects in terms of strategies of firms, types of markets, and the role of competition authorities.

Other issues raised in microeconomics are mainly related to questions of price and affordability. Because the services of network infrastructures are mostly considered "essential" for the users and therefore should be available to everyone at affordable prices, microeconomics suggests applying price discrimination and price regulation.

With respect to externalities, both positive ones (for instance, the effects of the road infrastructure on economic growth) and negative ones (for instance, the effects of the usage of the roads on air pollution)

---

[8] See also club goods, which are considered to be impure public goods because of the limited access allocated to an exclusive small membership aimed at avoiding congestion.

are present and are not internalized, or very partially so, in the prices of goods and services. According to the rich literature on this subject, either private contracting (Coasean solution) or public intervention through taxes or subsidies (Pigovian solution) are possible. Both solutions are not always completely effective, and if essential services and societal values are endangered, governments can decide to completely eliminate the externality by forbidding the activities. For example, restrictions may be placed on traffic during peak hours generating high pollution. However, all such solutions require institutions to establish and implement the underlying norms and rules, an issue rarely discussed in the standard microeconomic approach to infrastructures besides reference to government monitoring (through taxes, regulation, etc.).

Insights from New Institutional Economics
Institutional economics focuses on issues of governance: the efficiency of different modes of organization is assessed in a comparative way. Transaction cost economics, positive agency theory, and the economics of property rights are prominent theories in New Institutional Economics (Williamson, 2000). With respect to the domain of infrastructures, Williamson (1999) paid explicit attention to the transaction cost minimizing function of "public ordering" through regulation and public bureaucracies. Williamson explained that in cases of natural monopolies and specific transactions which implicate the security of the state (such as in foreign affairs), contracting out poses great difficulties that translate into high transaction costs. Regulation or coordination of the transaction through government entities then become efficient solutions according to a transaction cost minimizing perspective. Principal-agent theory addressed the incentive issues required to align the interests of parties involved in a transaction, whereas the economics of property rights dealt with questions of ownership in infrastructures (Groenewegen, van Spithoven, and van der Berg, 2010).

The concept of transaction costs is further developed and applied in the world of public contracting, particularly when it comes to building, operating, and managing network infrastructures. Savedoff and Spiller (1999: 6) discuss the characteristics of infrastructures, emphasizing how "prevalence of sunk costs, economies of density/or scale, and massive consumption, lead to the politicization of utility pricing." As a consequence, infrastructures are characterized by their tight embeddedness in political choices about governance and pricing. The economies of density refer to the fact that in a given distribution network, an increasing number of household connections to the infrastructure reduces the network's average costs. This drives the market structure toward an ever-decreasing number of suppliers. Savedoff and Spiller argue that the characteristics of sunk costs, density, and massive consumption allow governments to behave opportunistically toward the investing company: "For example, after the investment is sunk, the government may try to lower prices, disallow costs, restrict the operating company's pricing flexibility, require the company to undertake special investments, control purchasing or employment patterns, or try to restrict the movement or composition of capital" (Savedoff and Spiller, 1999: 7).

Next to governmental opportunism, Spiller also points to third party opportunism, which is undertaken by parties that are not directly involved in the contract between, for instance, a governmental agent and a private operator. Third parties such as employers' associations, labor unions, environmentalists, representatives of regional interests, and the like "may have incentives to challenge the 'probity' of the public agent involved in the transaction, even if the transaction is being undertaken in an honest way" (Spiller, 2009). In contrast to the Chicago School of regulation (Stigler, 1971), in which rent seeking is at the core, Spiller and others emphasize the institutional aspects that impact on the nature of regulatory institutions. In doing so, they provide deeper insight into the causes of regulatory risk (governments opportunistically changing the regulation rules) and regulatory capture (private parties decisively influencing a regulation that is not beneficial to them), making an important step in the direction of a more inclusive approach to the institutional dimension involved in the functioning of network infrastructures.[9]

Insights from Socio-Technical Systems Approaches

In microeconomics and New Institutional Economics, technology is most of the time ignored[10] or plays a very limited role. Regulatory issues

---

[9] Spiller pays much attention to different types of opportunism related to issues of "public contracting" in industries such as infrastructures; in that respect, his approach also differs from the incentive approach to regulation, as developed among others by Laffont and Tirole (1993).

[10] There are important exceptions, such as Economides (1996) from a micro-neoclassical point of view, or Shelanski (2007) from a new institutional point of view. See also Chapter 2.

are typically discussed without sufficiently taking into account the specific technological characteristics of different network infrastructures.

In the literature on Socio-Technical Systems (STS), the technical dimension is explicitly taken on board. However, we shall argue that although technology and institutions are clearly central in STS approaches, they do not adequately analyze their interdependence as outlined in our alignment perspective.

Socio-Technical Systems are built up from technical artefacts and institutional artefacts. Technical artefacts are physical artefacts with a technical function given to the artefact with human intentionality (Bauer and Herder, 2009; Kroes et al., 2006). This dual character of technical artefacts, with a physical structure and a technical function, is the first building block of a socio-technological system. In infrastructures, different technical artefacts fulfill different functions, which ought to be well coordinated, as explained in Section 1.2.2.

In STS, the technical characteristics are complemented by social components: values, norms, and laws that structure the behavior of the agents. The key structural features of STS (Bauer and Herder, 2009; Künneke, 2008) are that the technical and social parts are intertwined (for instance, when values about safety change, the technical components of the road need to be adapted, such as the introduction of electronic speed control); that each consists of multiple layers (norms about safety or privacy are formulated at the highest layer of abstraction and need to be translated into concrete laws, regulations, protocols, and standards for the agents at the micro layer); and that each layer refers to a different time scale (changes in the layer of norms take much longer than changes at the layer of protocols). These features and also the layers identified in Williamson (2000: 597) connect well to our own alignment framework, as we shall detail in the following chapters.

Much of the literature on STS relates to the so-called blueprint paradigm: the questions about technical artefacts and their coordination are formulated in terms of "optimization under constraints." An objective is formulated, the environmental constraints (technical, physical, and institutional) are identified, and instruments to deal with them are chosen. This connects well to the world of systems engineering further discussed in Chapter 3 of this book. In that respect, the choice of referring to "technical" rather than to "technological," as we do in our perspective, is significant. Socio-Technical Systems are concerned with the design of the technical elements of a system, with the aim that all the elements in combination and interaction fulfill a specific purpose, a specific function. The design and engineering approach also holds for the social part of the system. Most involved disciplines (engineering, economics, law, public administration, and management science) assume, often tacitly, that effective solutions to the design issues can be found and implemented. In this approach, the network infrastructure is typically perceived as a blueprint: the design of the technical as well as the social part is a matter of engineering, submitted to scientifically established physical and social laws and regularities. In this blueprint paradigm, STS such as electricity, transport, and water systems can and should be comprehensively designed and controlled.

In the literature on STS, the blueprint design paradigm is contrasted with the so-called process paradigm. According to this paradigm, the focus in complex, adaptive systems should be on the evolutionary process, in which the technical and institutional dimensions co-evolve. Murmann (2003), Saviotti (2005), Bijker, Hughes, and Pinch (1987), and Vazquez, Hallack, and Perez (2018) explain, among others, how all artefacts in STS are constituted in an interactive process. Such a process cannot be designed, let alone be controlled and engineered toward a specific ex-ante formulated purpose. In the literature of the STS process paradigm, detailed descriptions of specific cases are analyzed to demonstrate how technology and institutions co-evolve in an incremental, but sometimes also revolutionary way. Based on detailed case studies, path dependencies, sub-optimal solutions, and largely unpredictable developments are claimed to be core characteristics of STS.

In a noteworthy publication, Vazquez, Hallack, and Perez (2018) provide a detailed simulation of the co-evolution of technology and institutions in the electricity sector. They are concerned with the evolution of rules in the regulatory framework: how does such a framework emerge from the complex interaction between rule makers and industry? Based on the work of Dosi (1982), Williamson (1998), Künneke (2008), and Ostrom (2009), among others, these authors develop a framework in which technology and institutions interact at different levels. In that sense, they connect well to the process approach of STS and take the process paradigm of STS discussed in this section a step further into formalizing and simulating the dynamics.

What Is Missing?

From the discussion in this section, we conclude that microeconomics, institutional economics,[11] and the STS approach do provide useful insights into aspects of the nature of network infrastructures. Indeed, insights into the monopolistic tendencies, the regulatory issues, the question about efficient governance, and the design and evolutionary aspects certainly prove to be useful for the understanding and designing of network infrastructures. However, none of them provides a satisfying framework, with related concepts, to deal with the core of our alignment issue: the interdependence between technology and institutions. We are primarily interested in dealing with this issue by adopting a comparative static perspective. We do not intend to analyze the interaction between technology and institutions out of which coordination arrangements and modalities of alignment would emerge. We rather focus on the interdependence between technology and institutions at a certain point in time, and aim to deepen our understanding of the (mis)alignment between their respective coordination arrangements. We hypothesize that such an understanding will support a more effective design of STS, helping to formulate better policy recommendations, and ultimately opening ways to better capture the dynamics of STS (see Chapter 8 of this book).

1.3.2 About Coordination and Alignment

In this section, we further explore the core of our alignment framework: the coordination of the technological components within each layer of the technological dimension on the one hand, the coordination among the institutional components within each layer of the institutional dimension on the other hand, and the alignment between these two sets of coordination arrangements within each layer of our framework. In order to better understand these issues of coordination and alignment, we first discuss in more detail the four critical functions we identified in the opening chapter of this book. The four critical functions of system control, capacity management, interconnection, and

---

[11] In the other school of institutional economics, often called American or original institutionalism with authors like Veblen, Ayres, Galbraith, and Myrdal, technology plays a more prominent role, but the way it is analyzed is more at the general level and not adequate for the type of alignment questions we address in this book. See also Chapter 2 of this book.

interoperability have to be fulfilled; otherwise, the expected services cannot be provided by the infrastructure. We hypothesize that adequate coordination and alignment are needed, in order to fulfill these four critical functions and to enable network infrastructures to deliver expected services.

Once we have clarified what these four critical functions mean and their main characteristics, we dig deeper into the issue of coordination and alignment, which is crucial for the fulfillment of these functions. We explore the arrangements that coordinate the technological components on the one hand and the institutional components on the other hand. Further, we raise questions about these two types of arrangements and the alignment between them: how to analyze their compatibility, how to define alignment, how to create it, and when a misalignment has occurred how to restore it. The answers to these questions are provided in the coming chapters.

Four Critical Functions

As should be clear by now, we are primarily interested in those technological and institutional coordination requirements of network infrastructures that are needed to support the complementary activities between the various nodes and links which allow the provision of expected services to their users. We specify these requirements for the four critical functions briefly mentioned in the opening chapter: system control, capacity management, interconnection, and interoperability (Finger, Groenewegen, and Künneke, 2005; Künneke, Groenewegen, and Ménard, 2010).

System control: network infrastructures constitute systems that deliver a specific good or service of an expected quality. *"System control pertains to the question of how the overall system (e.g., the flow between the various nodes and links) is being monitored and controlled and how the quality of service is safeguarded"* (Finger, Groenewegen, and Künneke, 2005: 241). In the case of the road network infrastructure, providing a service of a specific quality concerns safe, efficient, and convenient transportation. Such a service is delivered by an overall system of roads, traffic lights, vehicles, laws, regulations, drivers, cyclists, pedestrians, etc. All these components contribute to the essential service, of which the quality depends on the quality of the components (such as the quality of traffic authorities, the capability of the drivers, the accurateness of specific sensors) and on the coordination among them. In order to perform adequately, the technological dimension of the network infrastructure should be operated according to certain technical requirements. In the case of road infrastructure, the quality of the pavement, the existence of shoulders along the road, the presence of notice boards informing users about accidents, etc., are examples of technical components that contribute to the provision of safe services. With respect to the institutional dimension, the essential services benefit from clear, consistent rules, and competent institutional entities that test vehicles and drivers' competences.

In other network infrastructures such as telecommunication, electricity, railroad, and bus transport, the liberalization of the last decades of the twentieth century has resulted in the entry of competing private firms into the industry, whereas the road network mostly remains the property of public authorities or regulated enterprises. Under these conditions, agents belonging to these different and partly competing entities have an incentive to pursue their own strategic objectives, which can conflict with the need to maintain the quality of service of the entire infrastructure (Kessides, 2004). With growing fragmentation of the technical system due to unbundling, outsourcing, and the like, there is a growing need from the perspective of system control to monitor and control the activities of all agents involved. In Part II of this book, we shall discuss several examples of how the function of system control can be best safeguarded.

Capacity management: *"networks are scarce resources because the capacity of nodes and links is limited. Capacity management deals with the allocation of this scarce network capacity to certain users or appliances"* (Finger, Groenewegen, and Künneke, 2005: 241). For instance, it has to be determined which agents and vehicles will be allowed to use the road infrastructure and under what conditions. For passenger vehicles and trucks, technical standards are developed on the basis of which car manufacturer can get a license for the vehicle to operate on public roads. In order to reduce congestion, the limited capacity can be reallocated to a limited number of vehicles during rush hours. So the actual access to the roads is facilitated by specific regulations regarding the institutional dimension, which can specify how many vehicles are allowed to enter the network at a certain point in time. Another way to manage the limited capacity and resulting congestion is road pricing: high tariffs are, for instance, charged for using roads in city centers during rush hours (see, for example, the London Congestion Charge[12]).

Interconnection refers to the coordination of activities and services between different segments that perform similar or complementary tasks in an infrastructure network. Segments of networks need to be connected with each other, in order to guarantee the technical functioning and the delivery of expected services. For example, the provision of expected services by the road system may depend on the existence and quality of interconnection between the local, regional, national, and even international road networks. This also holds for the railroad and airline network infrastructures, and the interconnection between the different transportation networks. Other typical examples include the interconnection between different parts of communication networks, such as long distance lines and the last mile to the customer. Interconnection sometimes occurs beyond the boundaries of specific infrastructures. This happened in the transportation sector with the introduction of standardized containers, which allows for very fast and efficient intermodal traffic between road, shipping, or air traffic infrastructures.[13] The energy sector is another example, as electric power can, for instance, be used for transport mobility (electric vehicles), which requires establishing an interconnection between the transportation and electric power network infrastructures.

Interoperability refers to the requirements that components of infrastructure networks must satisfy, in order to support the complementarity between different nodes and links that structure the network. *"Interoperability is realized if mutual interactions between network components are enabled in order to facilitate systems' complementarity"* (Finger, Groenewegen, and Künneke, 2005: 240). For example, in the railroad sector, the specification of the tracks needs to be compatible with the requirements for locomotives and cars. *"In the aviation sector, airlines rely on specific navigation systems that guide planes to their destination without accidents"* (Finger, Groenewegen, and Künneke, 2005: 240). In the road network infrastructure, components such as

---

[12] Details of the London Congestion Charge can be found at https://tfl.gov.uk/ modes/driving/congestion-charge; last accessed November 4, 2019.
[13] According to Levinson (2008), in his book on the emergence of containers and how it revolutionized the world economy, two dimensions of interconnection can be identified: "intra," which is within an infrastructure sector, and "extra," referring to different infrastructures.

the width and height of tunnels, or the carrying capacity of bridges, should be interoperable with the dimensions of the transport trucks. With the growth of automation of vehicles, interoperability between the technical components inside the vehicles and on the infrastructure becomes of crucial importance (see Chapter 7). Interoperability ensures that the elements of the network are compatible; technical norms, standards, and regulatory conditions of access are ways to secure interoperability. In this sense, interoperability is also of strategic importance. It determines the conditions of use as well as the rules for entry into and exit from a specific facility.

About Coordination
As outlined above, the complementary components that form network infrastructures require adequate coordination. In the technological dimension, coordination arrangements are often of a technological nature, but it is also possible that interventions are brought about by human beings who are assisted by technical devices. In the case of road networks, the monitoring of the congestion and the control of traffic lights that allow additional vehicles to enter the highway can be fully automated: monitored cameras provide computers with information which instruct the traffic lights. However, it is also possible that human beings, who at a distance monitor the traffic situation and can manually intervene when appropriate, assure coordination. Finally, the decision to fully automate traffic surveillance and control is largely a matter of cost, although values may also play an important role in this respect. As will be explained in Chapter 7, fully automated or self-driving vehicles can be equipped with technical components and algorithms that allow the vehicle to decide in case of threatening situations; for instance, to avoid a collision with another car and to leave the road and enter the cyclist lane. However, it may very well be that the owners and/or passengers of such vehicles prefer not to have fully automated technical components on board, but to have the opportunity to manually intervene. In other words, selecting the algorithm of the software can raise serious questions relating to societal values: who is responsible for the programming of automated vehicles, and should human beings not always have the technical possibility to intervene when the vehicle seems to take a decision that is unacceptable from a values point of view? These issues are discussed in Chapter 7. For the time being, we only wish to stress that different types of

coordination can be chosen: completely technical and fully automated, or allowing human beings to intervene when they consider it appropriate, or a mix of these solutions, as when intervention by human beings is possible only under specific conditions.

In the coming chapters, we shall discuss in more detail the coordination issues within both technological and institutional dimensions, and along the macro, meso, and micro layers. We shall demonstrate that coordination can be of quite different natures. For example, coordination can be closed in the sense that one unique coordinating structure is allowed and no alternatives are accepted. Or the arrangement chosen might be centralized with no autonomy left for decentralized solutions. The opposite is also possible: from the 1980s onwards, we have seen a movement toward more open and decentralized arrangements in network infrastructures. At this point, what we consider to be of crucial importance is the acknowledgment that coordination in network infrastructures can rely on different types of solutions, along the technological dimension as well as the institutional dimension. However, of crucial importance for the provision of expected services is that the different modalities of coordination within the technological dimension be aligned with those within the institutional dimension.

About Alignment of Technological and Institutional Coordination

Alignment and misalignment refer to the compatibility (and incompatibility, respectively) between the characteristics of the technological and institutional coordination needed to safeguard the critical functions along each layer of our framework. Our concept of alignment finds its inspiration in the work of Oliver Williamson. He puts the concept of alignment at the center of transaction cost economics (TCE): alignment is about "matching," about a "fit" of the types of transaction and the structures of governance.

Transactions, which differ in their attributes, are aligned with governance structures, which differ in their cost and competence, so as to effect a (mainly) transaction cost economizing result. (Williamson, 1998: 37)

For Williamson, the question of alignment matters because it has a direct effect on performance: in the world of TCE, misalignment results in relatively high transaction costs, which can be devastating for organizations operating in a competitive environment. It also means that Williamson restricts his analysis of the question of alignment to the third layer of our framework.

Our understanding of alignment is more general and concerns the compatibility of coordination along the three layers of our framework: between the technological architecture and the macro-institutions, between the technological design and the meso-institutions, and between the operational technology and the micro-institutions. However, consistent with the approach developed by Williamson, we also consider that alignment is central to performance. We actually hypothesize that whatever the layer under consideration, if there is misalignment between technology and institutions, then all or some of the four critical functions will not be fulfilled, causing the network infrastructure under consideration to underperform with respect to expected services.

Whether technological and institutional layers are "aligned" (or misaligned) can therefore be assessed by taking the expected performance of infrastructures into consideration. Signals of a potential misalignment can come from the users, who can show their dissatisfaction through different modalities, from media to public protest. Such signals of dissatisfaction can indicate a lack of coordination within either the technological or institutional dimension, or a misalignment between the coordination solutions along one or more layers. Another way to identify possible misalignments is to compare the performance of the network with the societal values, for example safety, privacy, reliability, or environmental sustainability. For instance, the National Highway Traffic Safety Administration (NHTSA) in the United States could report that the number of accidents on the highway has unacceptably increased and could propose a change in the law regulating the maximum speed, or they could propose a requirement for car owners to have their car checked every year. The responsible meso-institution monitors, investigates, and proposes measures for policy makers or the judiciary to adapt the rules. In line with the importance given in our approach to the role of values, the judgment about alignment is closely related to the societal values that shape expectations about the performance of infrastructures. Because values are time and place specific, there is no absolute degree of alignment or misalignment but only one in relation to these values, which implies that the operationalization of the concept of alignment is always contextual. In other words, what is considered to be (mis) alignment differs over time and from place to place.

1.4 Conclusions

In this chapter, we specified the nature of network infrastructures from our alignment perspective. We first paid attention to the expected services that network infrastructures intend to provide to society: they are the backbones of the economy and they deliver services essential to its citizens. We showed how the infrastructures and the services they are expected to deliver are embedded in societal values, which differ depending on time and place.

We then discussed the two dimensions of network infrastructures, the technological and institutional dimensions, and analyzed the characteristic of complementarity that underlies their components. Nodes and links have no function on their own, but only in complementarity with other nodes and links. Complementarities require tight coordination among the three layers of the technology as well as among the three layers of the institutions. Furthermore, we discussed in this chapter the core of our argument: that the modalities providing technological coordination on the one hand and institutional coordination on the other hand should be well aligned; otherwise, the fulfillment of the critical functions is endangered.

In the opening chapter of this book, we introduced the representation of network infrastructures as socio-technological systems, which are complex layered systems with interdependencies between technologies and institutions within each layer. The outline of our analytical framework was summarized in Figure I.1. In this chapter, we further elaborated on the dimensions, layers, and interdependencies involved in the different aspects of this framework. In doing so, we overviewed the contributions of microeconomics, New Institutional Economics, and the Socio-Technical System approaches to the characterization of network infrastructures. We concluded that they provide useful insights and concepts, but that we need to go further to better understand how network infrastructures operate, and under which conditions they can achieve the expected level of performance. To meet this challenge, we are making the choice to focus on the interdependencies between the technological and the institutional dimensions; on the critical functions as requirements for the system to provide the expected services; and on the necessity to align the coordination arrangements in both dimensions in order to fulfill these critical functions, without which the expected services cannot be delivered.

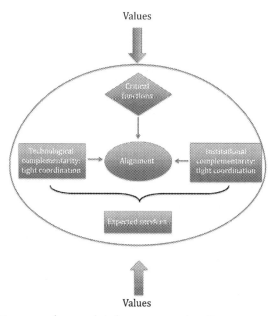

Values

Values

Figure 1.1 Features of network infrastructures: the alignment perspective

Figure 1.1 summarizes the key concepts and relationships of our alignment perspective. First, with respect to the performance of network infrastructure we focus on expected services. Second, with respect to each of the two dimensions, respectively technology and institutions, we focus on the complementarities of the components involved and on the need for their tight coordination. Indeed, the coordination of components within each dimension is crucial for the fulfillment of the critical functions. Third, we stress the importance of alignment between the coordination devices implemented within the two dimensions for the fulfillment of these critical functions. Last, we emphasize that each and all networks are entirely permeated by values in all their components and dimensions: the choice of services to be considered as essential, the choice of the technological components, the choice of the institutional components, the choice of the coordination arrangements, and the choice of the modalities of alignment are all embedded in societal values.

The main lesson to be drawn from this chapter is that infrastructures are very complex socio-technological systems, and that their analysis requires more subtle concepts than those provided by the existing paradigms. To go further in this direction, we suggested that the interdependencies between the technology and institutions can be best analyzed if three analytical layers are differentiated. We also suggested that attention should be focused on the coordination needed within each of the two dimensions of institutions and technology, and that the compatibility of the solutions thus implemented along the three layers we have identified should be explored.

In the following chapters of Part I, we shall further elaborate on the two dimensions of institutions and technology, on why they would be better understood if distinct layers are identified, and on how our concept of alignment can help to figure out the modalities through which network infrastructures become operational. Part II will promote the relevance of this alignment framework through the exploration of relevant characteristics of different network infrastructures, showing the explanatory potential of our framework without ignoring some of its limitations.

2 | *Institutional Embeddedness*
A Conceptual Challenge

2.1 Introduction

Notwithstanding their specificities, different network infrastructures share a fundamental property: they are embedded in and part of general institutional settings. In this chapter, we focus on this institutional dimension. The main point we want to make is that institutions are composed of different layers, and that identifying and characterizing these layers is both challenging and essential for better understanding the alignment issue.[1] It is challenging because representations of institutions tend to aggregate and mix many distinct components such as firms, parliaments, courts, etc. It is essential because it is through different layers that rights are defined, allocated, implemented, and monitored, thereby providing the scaffolding of network infrastructures. Indeed, a central hypothesis of this book is that these infrastructures are socio-technological systems; although subject to physical laws through their technological dimension, their development and usage are framed by human-made rules and rights.

Let us introduce the argument substantiated in this chapter through the case of a specific institutional setting implemented in the airline industry. On May 20, 2009, the Air France-KLM group and Delta Airlines announced that they had formed a specific joint venture to deal with their North Atlantic routes, among the busiest and the most competitive routes in the industry.[2] This venture resulted from a long negotiation between partners who had initiated a strategic agreement

---

[1] The idea of multi-level institutions involved in the development and monitoring of infrastructures is repeatedly mentioned in reports from international organizations (e.g., OECD, 2011; World Bank, 2017). However, the identification of these levels remains purely descriptive; the idea lacks conceptualization, which is what we intend to provide in this chapter.

[2] See https://ir.delta.com/news-and-events/news/news-release-details/2009/The-Air-France-KLM-Group-and-Delta-Air-Lines-Launch-New-Trans-Atlantic-Global-Joint-Venture/default.aspx

ten years before, and who were already members of a broader and looser airline alliance, Sky Team, founded in 2000 and one of the three major alliances[3] that nowadays dominate air transportation, providing over two-thirds of air transport capacities. The move toward giant air alliances followed the partial deregulation of the industry initiated in the 1980s and amplified at the beginning of this century through the so-called Open Skies policy.[4] These alliances developed in order to bypass severe national restrictions on cross-border mergers fed by strategic considerations as well as national pride. They also intended to satisfy the strong demand from users to benefit from seamless services with efficient worldwide interconnections. Building networks also allowed for the achievement of significant economies of scope and density,[5] for example, sharing maintenance services or information technologies and channeling passengers from all over the world.

The innovative venture sealed by Air France-KLM and Delta went much further, with a substantial increase in shared technical, economic, and financial services, shared revenues on the routes concerned, and the implementation of strategic coordination monitored though joint "working committees." It also required agreements from antitrust authorities. Reaching and implementing this agreement was not an easy task and it was confronted with numerous obstacles. First, at the micro level of the firms involved, after the merger between Air France and KLM authorized by the European Union (in 2004) and the acquisition of Northwest Airlines by Delta Air approved by the US Department of Justice (in 2008), the partners had to negotiate a complex allocation of rights specifically for the North Atlantic routes, for which this agreement was mainly established.[6] Two components materialized the arrangement: a contract and a complex set of governing committees. The contract essentially covers the subset of activities related to the North Atlantic traffic of the partners. A dense and short document of 150 pages, it mainly defines the complex financial rules for structuring the

[3] The two others are Star Alliance and One World.
[4] An important step in this respect was the EU-US Open Skies Agreement signed on April 30, 2007.
[5] In the airline industry, economies of scope refer to gains from the supply of a variety of services; economies of density refer to the concentration of passengers that allow lower unit costs. Both favor the concentration of airlines and are behind the development of hubs.
[6] The agreement also concerned other relatively minor routes (between Amsterdam and India and between North America and Tahiti).

agreement, particularly profit and cost sharing rules,[7] and the governing principles for organizing and monitoring the relationship among partners. The contract was complemented by "Codes of Conduct" formally agreed about a year after the formal contract was signed. The piloting of the venture relies on a decision-making process based on consensus to be reached through several "working committees" (covering areas ranging from the daily technical management of the network to control over advertising or consolidation of loyalty) supervised by a steering committee, and ultimately by the CEOs of Air France-KLM and Delta.

Second, in order to implement this agreement, partners had to address remaining regulatory constraints after the adoption of the so-called Open Skies policy in the 1990s, especially those related to competition laws. Two complementary issues particularly matter in that respect. (1) Would the proposed venture substantially reduce competition? (2) Should conditions be imposed on partners (e.g., "carve-out" measures) to cure potential competitive problems? Predicting answers to these questions was quite challenging, with two institutional sets of rules involved: European laws and American laws. To go ahead with the agreement, Air France-KLM and Delta had to obtain "antitrust immunity" from both sides. In the United States, this meant convincing the Department of Transportation (DOT) as well as the Department of Justice (DOJ) that the new venture would benefit consumers without hampering competition on the routes concerned in the agreement. In Europe, it required agreement from the Directorate-General for Competition, under the supervision of the European Commission and, if challenged, ultimately the European Court of Justice.

Third, tensions eventually developed between some of the institutions in charge of implementing the competition rules of the game. For instance, the United States DOJ was much more skeptical than the DOT about the advantages and legitimacy of the arrangement: would it bring public benefits and private gains without threatening competition on the relevant routes? Arguments were exchanged between the two institutions, some going back to the very creation of the airline alliances. Ultimately, an agreement was reached to deliver "antitrust

---

[7] The contract also addresses other important financial issues; besides the profit-cost sharing rules between the European and American partners, it includes provisions for sharing indirect revenues generated due to connections made possible by the agreement, modalities of transfer of benefits/deficits among partners, and the creation of a specific accounting system.

immunity" restricted to the North Atlantic routes of the partners, a decision by the regulating authorities that allowed the venture to go ahead and develop its joint operations. This alliance within an alliance has so far been able to overcome several severe disturbances and disruptions; from the 2008 financial crisis that developed while negotiations were going on, to significant fluctuations in air transportation demand, which in combination with harsh competition affected the profitability of partners.

What this schematized example shows is the challenging intricacy of the institutional layers involved; from firms participating in the agreement, with their changing boundaries and modalities of pilotage, to the general laws and international agreements framing the airline industry and beyond, and in between the role of intermediate institutions in charge of implementing these rules and monitoring participants in the agreement. The institutional setting we have described suggests three distinct layers involved in the definition and implementation of the agreement. At the micro level, there is the role of the firms who took the initiative of creating the venture and had to anticipate its consequences on the organization of transactions, the allocation of their respective rights, and the possible impact on their technologies (e.g., changes required in their information system). Within the macro layer, besides the changes introduced by the Open Skies Agreement, partners were still required to comply with competition laws that partially differed due to the distinct institutional environment in which they were embedded. And last, they also had to deal with meso-institutions, those intermediate arrangements (e.g., competition authorities) in charge of implementing and monitoring the rules established through these laws.

Disentangling more rigorously these institutional layers is the main goal of this chapter. In what follows, we conceptualize and characterize them at both the general and the abstract level, with the assumption – to be substantiated in future chapters – that understanding the differences between these layers allows us to capture the framing of specific network infrastructures, and their capacity (or not) to fulfill their critical functions and to deliver expected services. Figure 2.1 summarizes these different institutional layers and their specific roles, which are developed hereafter.

The next section of this chapter discusses some leading approaches to institutions, so as to better delineate our representation of a concept

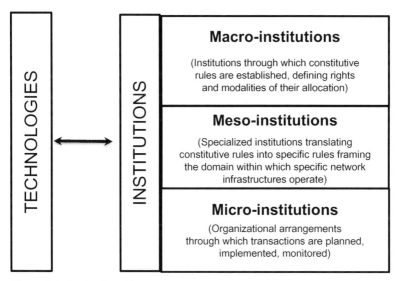

Figure 2.1 Institutional layers

that encapsulates the different, interdependent layers indicated in Figure 2.1. Section 2.3 digs deeper into the characterization of these layers (the macro-, meso-, and micro-institutions), in order to understand their properties, their interdependence, and their role in the fulfillment of the critical functions that condition the efficient running of network infrastructures. Section 2.4 concludes with a look at other key challenges to be explored further in other chapters of this book.

2.2 The Playing Field: Dimensionalizing Institutions

Long relegated to the margins of economic theory, if not totally absent, institutions and their significance for economic activities are now the source of an abundant literature, exemplified by the stimulating contributions of Davis and North (1971), Schotter (1981), North (1990a, 2005), Williamson (2000), Aoki (2001), Ostrom (2005), Greif (2006), Acemoglu and Robinson (2012), and Hodgson (2015b). However, there is no unified view about what institutions are. Beyond the now general acceptance that "institutions matter,"[8] the diversity of

---

[8] For a challenge to this acceptance, see McCloskey (2016).

concepts intending to capture the realm of institutions reflects the complexity of the issues at stake, as well as the fact that different definitions fulfill different goals. More puzzling, from the perspective of this book, is the "benign neglect" by most social scientists of the conditions under which institutions permeate technological choices and their diffusion; and the "benign neglect" by most institutionalists of the key role of technologies in shaping and/or providing support to so many central institutions.[9]

This chapter addresses this "benign neglect." Following what was suggested in the Introduction, it proposes disentangling the broad concept of "institutions" (or "institutional environment," the ambiguous expression introduced by Davis and North, 1971[10]), in order to identify the different layers through which interdependence between institutions and technologies shape network infrastructures. Building our framework requires paying special attention to aspects developed in other chapters, namely: (1) the specificity of network infrastructures, especially the non-redeployable investments needed on the supply side, the strong club effect on the demand side, and the social expectations rooted in values that permeate both sides (Chapter 1); (2) the technological features of these infrastructures and their related critical functions (to be developed in Chapter 3); and (3) the sensitive issue of coordination across institutional layers and their alignment (or misalignment) with the properties of technological systems that provide the backbone to network infrastructures (discussed further in Chapter 4).

---

[9] The centrality of the interactions between institutions and technology in shaping economic activities can be traced back to almost two thousand years BC. The Code of Hammurabi, considered among the oldest written set of laws, covered a wide range of economic rules, from contractual practices (almost half of the code) to the transfer of property rights (e.g., liability issues, inheritance, etc.). The code contributed to the success of the Babylonian empire (and remains a vestige of this success) because contemporary scribes to Hammurabi had access to writing (cuneiform) and to the technology for engraving the code ("gravé dans la pierre," as the French saying goes), making it a reliable reference while alternative technologies (e.g., clay or papyrus) remained much more exposed to alteration or destruction. Another illustration is provided by the stimulating analysis by McNeil (1982) of the interactions between the development of military techniques and the building of state apparatus.

[10] The expression suggests that rules are exogenous to the organization of transactions; we rather consider them as endogenously generated through socio-technological interactions, although we do not explore in this book how institutions are generated.

2.2.1 A Variety of Approaches ... with so Little Room for Technology

As illustrated by the studies referenced in the previous section, which are just a few among many others, the last decades have seen the multiplication of inspiring contributions on the nature and role of institutions in the development and running of market economies.

These contributions provide a kaleidoscopic view of the diversity of approach to "institutions." This chapter does not intend to survey this variety of concepts. We rather pick up building blocks from selected contributions to develop a representation of institutions that allows explicit connection to the technological dimension. This research strategy explains why many substantial contributions are discarded up front. For example, the game-theoretic views on institutions are taken on board only marginally. Notwithstanding the richness of this literature, from Schotter (1981) to Aoki (2001), Hurwicz and Reiter (2008), and many others, the focus on institutions as equilibria emerging from the convergence of strategies developed by rational individuals does not allow us to capture issues central to our analysis. Indeed, there is barely any room in these models for considering the different layers that compose institutions (the legal system, agencies that interpret and implement the rules of the game, a firm) as well as their associated technologies (the architecture of a system, its technological components, its operational modalities).[11]

We therefore restrain ourselves to a handful of concepts of "institutions" supportive to the exploration of the interdependence between the layers characterizing technology and the layers defining institutions. North provides insights through his pioneering study of the "institutional environment" as superseding a set of complex "institutional

---

[11] This statement requires some nuancing. For instance, Schotter (1981), Denzau and North (1994), Hurwicz (1996), and Greif (2006) share the idea that institutions are rooted in information processing, which may open up room for technological considerations. There are also more explicit insights on technology from an institutionalist perspective in Mantzavinos (2001, particularly chapter 11), Ménard and Ghertman (2009), Künneke, Groenewegen, and Auger (2009), among others. Nevertheless, with the exception of Mockyr (e.g., 2016), who substantially contributed to the analysis of technologies from a historical perspective, with an emphasis on the role of values and culture, references to the role of technology in this literature remain relatively vague, with little or no concern for its interdependence with institutions.

arrangements"; Ostrom helps to clarify the nature, role, and layers of rules that give flesh to the otherwise vague concept of "institution"; and Greif and Hodgson, notwithstanding their differences, go further in emphasizing the socio-historical values that characterize institutions and permeate the expectations of agents/citizens, an aspect particularly relevant when it comes to network infrastructures (see Chapter 1).

An Encompassing Concept: The Northian Approach

In a now classical contribution, Davis and North introduced the encompassing notion of "institutional environment," defined as "the set of fundamental political, social, and legal ground rules that establishes the basis for production, exchange and distribution" (Davis and North, 1971: 6). An illustration would include rules "governing elections, property rights, and the right of contract." They then pursued their definitional approach by introducing the sub-concept of "institutional arrangement," understood as "an arrangement between economic units that govern the ways in which these units can cooperate and/or compete" (Davis and North, 1971: 7). An illustration of the links between these two layers would be laws that established corporations as "organizational structures," within which members can cooperate and "individuals (or groups) can legally compete."

This last example suggests interactions between the rules of the game and the way agents operate within these rules. However, the conceptualization remains vague about the exact nature of these institutional arrangements and the way they connect to the general rules.[12] North later substituted "organization" for "institutional arrangement," thus minimizing the institutional dimension at stake. Indeed, he defined "organizations" as the way players jointly develop strategies within the rules of the game (North, 1990a: 5), or, more explicitly, as "specific groups of individuals pursuing a mix of common and individual goals through partially coordinated behavior" (North, Wallis, and Weingast, 2009: 15): political parties, firms, trade unions, cooperatives, clubs, schools provide examples (North, 1990a: 5). This makes the Northian concept of organization closer to its accepted definition in economics and management; however, it loses its richness as an

---

[12] Williamson's emphasis on contracts as sets of rules delineating the domain of transactions and the modalities of their organization helps in going further, although it neglects the institutional character of organizations (see Williamson, 1985: chapters 3 and 15).

institutional variety, something we try to restore through the concept of "micro-institutions" (see Section 2.3).

There is another aspect, almost universally neglected, of the Northian approach developed in later contributions, in which he considers institutions as social constructions combining physical capital and human capital. The former corresponds to "all the material artefacts that humans have accumulated and particularly the tools, techniques, and instruments they possess to control their environment; [while] the human capital is the stock of knowledge humans possessed as embodied in the beliefs they hold and the institutions they create reflecting those beliefs." (North, 2005: 49).[13] In Chapter 1, we have already reflected on this opening to the role of values and norms in shaping expectations among users of network infrastructures. Moreover, the reference to the central presence of artefacts explicitly introduces the role of technology.

However, this is a late statement that North never developed further. Actually, there is an ambiguity in the Northian approach in that respect. On the one hand, he is (legitimately) considered as a founder of economic history, which inspired numerous studies on the role of innovation as the main source of growth. On the other hand, North's emphasis has been on institutions, as opposed to technology, as the key engine for development and growth. His groundbreaking analysis of productivity change in ocean shipping is illustrative of this (North, 1968). Having examined the potential role of technical changes, he ended up discarding this role and concluded "that the decline of piracy and privateering and the development of markets and international trade shared honors as primary factors in the growth of shipping efficiency over this two-and-a-half-century period." (North, 1968: 967). Although remaining aware of the technological dimension of economic activities, North thereafter focused almost exclusively on the role of property rights and the analysis of the legal and political systems supporting them. In that respect, notwithstanding variations in contributions spread over decades,[14] North's framework remains of limited help when it comes to understanding the articulation between institutions and technology.

---

[13] Following North, Mockyr (2014: 153) emphasizes the role of "the set of beliefs, values and preferences, capable of affecting behavior, that are socially (not genetically) transmitted and that are shared by some subset of society."
[14] Some of these variations are pointed out in Hodgson (2015).

Within these limits, we can still capitalize on North with respect to: (1) his overarching concept of institutions – all human activities are embodied in and framed by rules of the game that vary over time and across societies; (2) the implementation of these general rules through specific entities, initially identified as "institutional arrangements," later as "organizations," which suggests the existence of different institutional layers; (3) the prescriptive nature of norms and rules, rooted in beliefs that shape human behavior and social interactions; and (4) the possible misalignment between physical capital ("tools, techniques, and instruments" – the technological dimension) and human capital (embodied in institutions through "mental maps").[15]

The Centrality and Diversity of Rules and Norms: Ostrom

Notwithstanding his repeated emphasis on how deeply human activities are embedded in institutions that are rule-oriented, North remained relatively vague when it comes to characterizing these rules. In continuity with the Northian vision, Ostrom went much further in conceptualizing the respective functions of norms and rules that frame agents' behavior, either through a "configurational" role, imposing a social order, for instance when a law regulates specific activities, or an "adaptive" role, for instance when norms of behavior develop through trial and error (Ostrom, 2005; also 2014a). Norms and rules are therefore understood as institutional artefacts that delineate the domain within which actions are "required, prohibited, or permitted" (Ostrom, 1986: 5; see also 2014b).[16] They play this role through transmission mechanisms that fix status and positions, determine conditions of entrance or exit, delineate actions, and frame outcomes.

In exploring these issues, Ostrom went beyond general references to norms and rules. Two insights deserve particular attention with respect to our analysis of infrastructures.

First, she made a sharp and useful distinction between norms and rules. In her perspective, rules refer to the shared understanding by a group of individuals, "that certain actions in a particular situation must, must not, or may be undertaken and that sanctions will be taken

---

[15] For reflections on these views, see Denzau and North (1994) and North (2005; especially chapter 8, "Sources of order and disorder").

[16] This conception clearly connects the so-called Bloomington School (with Elinor and Vicente Ostrom as leading figures) to the commons and original institutionalism (Groenewegen, 2011).

against those who do not conform" (Ostrom, 1998: 10), while norms refer to the valuation individuals attach to particular types of actions (Ostrom, 1998: 9), a valuation that determines the capacity to build relations and implement actions based on reputation and trust. Summarizing her in-depth investigation of a specific network infrastructure, irrigation in Nepal, Ostrom (2014b; see also 2009, section 6) showed how the benign neglect of pre-existing norms and rules, and of their enforcement mechanism, led to the failed implementation of a new, presumably more "advanced" technology. In that respect, rules and norms play a key role in the alignment (or misalignment) between technologies and institutions. Norms (and their supportive social values) create expectations among users that frame their behaviour, while rules establish allocations of rights (decision rights in the Nepalese case) that are central for incentivizing (or demotivating) agents.

Second, investigating more specifically the functions of rules, Ostrom came to identify different layers of rules. In one of her last contributions (2014b), she emphasized the need to differentiate the operational level at which specific rules are elaborated and through which individuals interact; the policy-making level at which rules framing operational actions are defined; and the constitutional level at which overarching rules are produced that define the domain and mechanisms of choice. This is in line with the three layers identified in our framework.[17]

Notwithstanding these insights and some indications about how norms and rules could link technology (e.g., fishermen's equipment) and institutions (e.g., the governance of common-pool resources), Ostrom's ultimate achievement – her "Institutional Analysis and Development" (IAD) framework – focused on "action situations," understood as human interactions when confronted with social dilemmas (Ostrom, 2005: 13 sq.). It is noticeable how little attention this framework pays to technology.[18] Nevertheless, we draw an important lesson from her contributions, which is the need to consider layers of norms and rules that, respectively, frame the relation of users to technology and the allocation of rights through which technical systems are implemented.

---

[17] Ostrom (2005, 2014b) also stressed the numerous variables that are engines of change in collective choices, an aspect that exceeds the scope of our book.

[18] Technology is not even mentioned in her framework.

Institutions as Value Loaded: The Hodgson–Greif Connection

The focus on norms and rules in Ostrom's approach leads naturally to another aspect when considering the interdependence between institutions and technologies, which is that they are both social constructs. Notwithstanding substantial differences in their key concepts and analytical apparatus, "Old" (or "original") and "New" Institutionalists share this view.[19] In their own way, Hodgson and Greif are representative modern contributors to these two approaches to the role of values.

Revisiting "Old" Institutionalism, Hodgson consistently promoted an overarching concept of *institution*, challenging theoreticians who ignore or sideline the embeddedness of all human actions in their institutional environment. From 1988 (chapter 8) to more recent contributions (Hodgson, 2015a, 2015b), he repeatedly emphasized this inclusiveness and the centrality of institutions, understood as "*integrated systems of rules that structure social interaction.*" Close to many aspects developed by Ostrom, Hodgson views rules as operating through historically determined laws, norms, and conventions that regulate the allocation of rights. They involve "injunction" or "disposition," submitting agents to obligations or prohibition (2015b: 2.2), and they require devices to legitimize and enforce rights (2015b: 4.1). Hodgson thus implicitly concurs with Barzel (2002) and North, Wallis, and Weingast (2009) about the role of state "violence" in delineating and enforcing rights, with most of his attention going to the role of macro-institutions, mainly the legal system.[20] He similarly insisted, particularly in his early contributions, on the embeddedness of technology in social interactions and rules (Hodgson, 1988: 15 sq.), although he did not provide any further development in this direction.

---

[19] Sociologists and philosophers of science and technology often pinpoint the interactions between institutions and technologies as Socio-Technical Systems. With respect to our preference for "socio-technological systems," see Chapter 1, Section 1.3, and Geels (2004).

[20] "Once we consider the problems of enforcement in complex legal systems with many agents, and the motivational reasons why individuals might obey the law, then something like the state is required ultimately to ensure enforcement. Law first emerges in hierarchical and complex societies with large numbers of individuals. The state must establish a legal monopoly of force within a territory, restrain vigilantism and minimize extra-legal violence." (Hodgson, 2015b: chapter 3; also 4.1). For a discussion of Hodgson's view on institutions, see Ménard (2019).

Building on the different intellectual tradition of New Institutional Economics, and notwithstanding a shared acknowledgment of the centrality of the law, Greif differs from Hodgson by way of his in-depth exploration of the variety of enforcement devices and the historical conditions of their emergence and sustainability, particularly when formal institutions are weak or plainly missing. His analysis of reputation as a social construct that allows the development of transactions in such contexts is illustrative. Taking advantage of a combination of game theory and detailed historical research, Greif (1993) investigated how the activities of the Maghribi traders of the eleventh century developed in a context of almost nonexistent or unenforced laws protecting property rights. This case study provides a rich example of contract-enforcing devices "making violence economically productive" when macro-institutions default. The development of "organic" institutions (Greif, 2005: 732–738; also Greif, Milgrom, and Weingast, 1994)[21] would fill the void, relying either on private rules rooted in multilateral reputation devices, as in the case of the Law Merchant (Milgrom, North, and Weingast, 1989), or on private rules implemented in the shadow of the law, as in modern corporations (Williamson, 1985: chapter 11).

What comes out of this emphasis on the role of socially embedded rules by both Old and New Institutionalists is that even in the absence of state "violence" instigated to implement the rule of law and to enforce property rights, intermediate (meso-)institutions can "spontaneously" emerge to make the allocation and enforcement of rights possible, thus securing transactions. In doing so, these approaches come close to identifying the interwoven layers of institutions that can provide scaffolds to the organization of transactions even when one layer is deficient. However, far from the stimulating insights provided long ago by Coase (1947), these narratives pay little attention to the technologies within which rules are embedded, or from which they find support, for example in securing the transfer of rights.

2.2.2 Our Approach to Institutions

We are fully aware that the issues pointed out in the previous section, the questions raised, and the limitations emphasized, are highly

---

[21] This concept is close to the concept of "meso-institutions" defined and discussed in Section 2.3.2.

selective and somehow biased. Indeed, we did not intend to deliver a general discussion of the many concepts of "institutions." We rather focused on identifying, within well-known representations, specific instruments that could allow us to better understand the institutional dimension of network infrastructures.[22]

In taking that perspective, we draw three main lessons from the discussion in the previous section. First, we share the view that institutions are about rules, rule-making, and various entities in charge of defining and implementing these rules. When it comes to network infrastructures, the main concern relates to rules regarding the definition, allocation, implementation, and monitoring of rights, and the capacity for these rules to fulfill the requirements of the critical functions characterizing specific infrastructures. For example, with respect to capacity management and system control, what rules guide the rights of access to airports? How are they defined and by whom? How are they interpreted and implemented, by what authorities? Second, rules vary in scope according to the different institutional layers to which they belong and which they contribute toward shaping. For example, rules defined by a law differ in scope and conditions of application from rules established by a corporate board. Notwithstanding differences in their conceptions, the authors reviewed in Section 2.2.1 converge when it comes to intuitively acknowledging the existence of distinct institutional layers fulfilling different needs. Our analysis intends to go further, explicating key components that allow the identification and characterization of these institutional layers. Third, rules do not embrace the entire domain within which transactions are framed and organized. As emphasized by the authors we have discussed, values and norms also play an important role in providing motivation and incentives with respect to the choice and operationalization of the technology(ies) at stake.[23] In the example introduced at the beginning of this chapter, nationalism clearly plays an important role in the regulation of the airline industry.

A Generic Concept

Taking inspiration from these contributions and keeping in mind our focus, which is to understand the interdependence between institutions

---

[22] The technological dimension is explored in Chapter 3, and the interdependence between technologies and institutions is discussed in detail in Chapter 4.

[23] See Chapter 1; and, for more specific aspects, Part II, particularly Chapter 7.

and technologies supportive to network infrastructures, we define "institutions" as *the intricate combination of norms and rules embedded in entities and devices that provide the foundations to interactions among agents and their connection to the socio-technological systems in which they evolve.* From an economic standpoint, it means that norms and rules provide the social foundation for transactions. They delineate boundaries within which transactions are allowed or prohibited, and they frame how transactions are monitored and organized. And they do so through a variety of institutional/organizational arrangements.

Our emphasis on "layers" refers to the differences in scope and scale of rules, norms, and the values in which they are embedded. In our airline industry example, general laws regarding competition define rules (different in Europe and the United States) that had to be adapted in response to the specific requests of firms wishing to develop their international cooperation. This adaptation was carried out through the specific role of the regulatory authorities that delivered "antitrust immunity" for the venture. In turn, this decision allowed parties to the agreement to implement tight coordination made possible by the development of information and communication technologies. Another illustration is the adoption by the European Union of general rules to restructure the railway sector (e.g., opening railroads to competition). More specific rules and norms had to be defined according to the technological architecture of the system (e.g., fast trains and local trains do not obey the same standards and constraints). This translation of general rules into specific ones, carried out by way of the so-called subsidiarity principle, which delegates adaptation to national authorities and their specific institutions, provides guidelines that shape the strategies of potential suppliers of rail transportation.

2.3 Institutional Layers and Coordination

The next chapters will explore the technological dimension in more depth, and they will examine how the different layers of rules and norms connect to technology. For the time being, we shall focus on the identification, delineation, and characterization of the different institutional layers that compose what North and Davis called the "institutional environment." Indeed, we shall argue, and this will be substantiated through empirical analyses in Part II, that rules and norms, which are embedded and made operational through a variety of organizational "entities," differ according to whether we consider them as encompassing a broad set of activities at the very abstract level (e.g., a law defining and/or prohibiting some rights), at the operational level of entities delivering specific services (e.g., behavioral requirements imposed on employees within a firm), or at the intermediary level linking the definitional and the operational levels (e.g., a commission establishing technical standards for a specific infrastructure). As can be anticipated, the impact of these layers on the architecture and expected performance of different network infrastructures varies substantially.

2.3.1 Macro-Institutions: Configuring Rules and Rights

At the most abstract level, and with respect to network infrastructures, rules and norms and their associated entities and devices primarily encompass formal conditions under which transactions are allowed (or prohibited) and can be organized. Laws establishing the "rules of the game" for an entire sector (e.g., opening the electricity network to competition) or even for multiple sectors (e.g., legal provision to introduce public–private participation) are illustrative of this. We consider such abstract sets of rules and norms as belonging to the macro-institutional layer, understood as *the institutional layer within which "constitutive" rules are established and enacted.* "Constitutive" here refers to the fundamental meaning of the word: "having the power to institute, establish, or enact" (American Heritage Dictionary, 2011). These "constitutive rules"[24] delineate "rights-to-use," establish procedures and entities to support, coordinate, and transfer these rights, and determine conditions of their exercise, thus providing the spinal column for the organization of production, distribution, and exchange. In a market economy, rules and norms regarding how property rights are defined and implemented and by what entities (e.g., a parliament, a court, etc.) are typically "constitutive." Without such rules of the game, there is no game at all!

This is so because a central function of macro-institutional rules is to reduce uncertainty, thus making transactions possible

---

[24] Our approach is very close to what Ostrom identified as "constitutional" rules, while North, focusing almost exclusively on this macro level, used the generic term "rules."

(North, 1990a: 3).[25] At an empirical level, this function is performed through actions of the political-judiciary-administrative setting that frames the domain within which transactions can be initiated (e.g., contract law) and/or that configures devices (e.g., regulation) and entities (e.g., regulators) through which institutions and technologies become interdependent (e.g., defining and imposing technical standards by law or directives). Important examples with respect to network infrastructures are macro-institutions allocating rights between public authorities and private entities (e.g., laws facilitating expropriation to allow the development of infrastructures), or framing the activity of a specific industry (e.g., the US law prohibiting foreign interests to control more than 25% of national airlines). As these examples suggest, macro-institutions deeply interact with "societal values"; they are permeated by social norms and beliefs (e.g., citizens' expectations regarding technical as well as institutional conditions under which drinkable water should be delivered).[26]

Formal and Informal Rules

The centrality of constitutive rules comes from their role in determining not only *what can* be done, but also *what cannot* be done. As such, they delineate the domain and conditions under which economic activities can develop, and they frame the modalities of their coordination. A good example is provided by the discussions and controversies about what rules should accompany the introduction of self-driving vehicles (see Chapter 7).

One difficulty facing the analysis of rules (as well as their operationalization) is that not all of them are formal. Davis and North (1971; see also North, 1981) introduced a now well-known distinction between formal and informal rules. This is an important issue because it may explain why similar rules may entail very different outcomes.[27] *Formal rules* are codified, traceable, and transmissible without direct

---

[25] The macro-institutional layer is also the level at which political transaction costs (North, 1990b) tend to be at their highest, a key issue for understanding the conditions and difficulties of trade-off among alternative institutional settings.

[26] The hot debates in many countries about pricing water illustrate these differences: should water be considered a "gift of Mother Nature," with free and universal access? Or should it be processed as a "normal good," to be priced and its usage regulated?

[27] Alternative explanations have been provided, mainly (1) path dependence; (2) differences in organizations operating within the same rules; (3) differences in

human support (e.g., the engraved Hammurabi code). Constitutions defining political systems, laws regarding property rights, or corporate laws are typical examples. Levy and Spiller (1994) have illustrated well how the intricacy of political, judicial, and administrative rules shaping the privatization of telecoms in several countries had a major impact on the differentiated performance of these reforms. By contrast, *informal rules* are embedded in customs[28] and traditions that depend on human beings for their transmission. Customary rules determining the allocation of water for irrigation and the role and duties of beneficiaries in Nepal is a good illustration of this (Ostrom, 2014b). Informal rules, which largely depend on beliefs and values, can directly influence technological choices. In Denmark, notwithstanding the adoption of formal rules favorable to the development of nuclear power, a bottom-up decision-making process embedded in Danish institutions allowed informal norms and beliefs to prevail, imposing the choice of alternative technologies, particularly wind power. An important criterion that helps to differentiate between the two types of rules is their enforcement mechanism: formal rules are enforceable by state apparatus, while informal rules depend on other means of enforcement, often rooted in the social status of those transmitting the rules.

At the empirical level, there is a fine graduation between strictly formalized rules, for instance, when Common Law is compared with the Civil Code regarding the definition and transfer of property rights (Shleifer et al., 2003), and the much less formalized transfer of rights through "handshake" agreements (Macaulay, 1963), which largely rely on shared values, as illustrated by the medieval Maghrebi traders (Greif, 1993). Although formal rules tend to prevail in the modern organization of infrastructures, informal ones still play an important role. For example, the emerging phase of smart grids in electricity largely relied on interconnections monitored directly by agents, with enforcement embedded in social values since formal rules lagged behind (see Chapter 5). Similarly, the initial development of Wi-Fi relied on decentralized and weakly coordinated norms and standards (Lemstra, Hayes, and Groenewegen, 2011).

---

entities linking general rules to their actual implementation by actors (e.g., regulators with different characteristics).

[28] We understand customs as a usage and/or practice "so long established that it has the force or validity of law" (American Heritage Dictionary, 2011).

Property Rights, Decision Rights, and Rights of Access

Constitutive rules frame what can, must, should be, or cannot be done, thus connecting to values and contributing to the establishment of norms or becoming embedded in them. When it comes to network infrastructures, they determine the broad modalities through which critical functions can or should be met.

A typical example is the establishment of rights of access for providers as well as users of network services. These rights, which in contemporary market economies tend to be determined through laws and/or decrees assigning modalities to allocate them (e.g., the adoption of the Open Skies policy) and/or creating entities to enforce them (e.g. a public bureau, a regulating authority), define structural conditions for securing the four critical functions identified in Chapter 1. Economists inspired by the legal literature define these "rights-to-use" in relation to the capacity of their holders to make a resource fruitful and capture its benefit as residual claimants. There is a propensity to identify these rights as private property rights, which can be misleading, particularly when it comes to network infrastructures. As emphasized by Alchian (1965), "rights-to-use" may well be in the hands of a collectivity, as in common-pool resources; or of government, as when a network is a public multinational company. Moreover, this confusion leads to the mixing of owners' rights and decision makers' rights. The corporatization of public utilities illustrates well how property rights may remain in the hands of public authorities while the actual exercise of these rights is transferred to quite autonomous managers.

This last example leads us to note the important distinction between property rights and decision rights (Alchian and Demsetz, 1972; Baker, Gibbons, and Murphy, 2008). Property rights are about *who* can transfer "rights-to-use" and determine the conditions of such transfers, and, ultimately, *who* the residual claimant is. It has been argued (Long, 2018; Zhang, 2018) that the absence of well-defined property rights in China and the prevalence of informal rules have handicapped the development of reliable infrastructures and innovation.[29] Decision rights are about *how* these rights can be exercised and decisions made, with decision makers most of the time operating by *delegation* for

---

[29] However, this significance of formal property rights in relation to Chinese development has been challenged (see Ho, 2013).

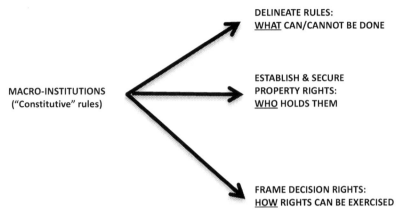

Figure 2.2 Dimensionalizing macro-institutions

holders of property rights.[30] The distinction is central to the analysis of network infrastructures: besides raising the classical principal-agent problem of aligning the preferences of the beneficiaries of these different rights, it also introduces the issue of the impact of this separation of rights on the technological dimension, such as when holders of property rights (e.g., public authorities) are able to impose a technology viewed by the decision makers as misaligned with the existing technologies (or with available resources).

Figure 2.2 summarizes these dimensions of the concept of macro-institutions, with constitutive rules establishing what can or cannot be done, to whom and under what conditions the capacity to use related rights will be allocated, and how decision rights can be exercised in that context.

Embedded in the values and institutional setting proper to a specific society, these constitutive rules and the rights they define might not be

---

[30] Disconnection between property and decision rights is a major feature of modern corporations, following the establishment of their legal status in the nineteenth century. In their famous book on corporate governance, Berle and Means (1932) pointed out malfunctions that this disconnection may produce, which they viewed as a major explanation for the 1929 financial crash and the ensuing crisis. However, corporatization is only one among alternative solutions. By contrast, historians have comprehensively documented the key role played by private owners holding both property rights and decision rights in the development of railroads, electricity, or water and sanitation in the nineteenth century.

appropriate for safeguarding the critical functions that network infrastructures must satisfy: one size does not fit all![31]

2.3.2 Micro-Institutions: Delivering Services through Adequate Organization of Transactions

Although their economic impact remains difficult to assess and is still a source of controversy (Rodrik, 2008; Shirley, 2008; Acemoglu and Robinson, 2012), there is now an abundant literature on macro-institutions. Notwithstanding differences in terminology, the micro-institutional layer has also been well documented, thanks to developments in organization theory following the seminal contributions of Oliver Williamson and many others. Our point of entry to micro-institutions is unambiguously rooted in this tradition. We define the micro-institutional layer as *the institutional layer within which transactions are organized, providing coordination mechanisms required to make technology operational and create value* (see Williamson, 1996: 378; and already Barnard, 1938: 73; and Selznick, 1948). Following Coase (1960, 1998) and Williamson (1985: chapter 3), we understand *transaction* as the transfer of rights to use goods and services across technologically separable activities.

   Whatever the arrangement they choose, operators of network infrastructures must acquire inputs and combine and transform them through the usage of specific technologies in order to deliver expected services. In that respect, network infrastructures do not differ from other economic activities; each step needed for the delivery of services involves the organization of transactions. What makes them distinct is that the resulting transfer of rights (both property rights and decision rights) must satisfy the critical functions: transactions need to be organized in a way that secures the alignment between the micro-institutional arrangement chosen and the operational arrangement of the technology/technologies in use.

The Variety of Micro-Institutional Solutions
This alignment issue faces a problem that modern organization theory has begun to explore: the variety of possible micro-institutional solutions for the usage of similar technologies, which makes the choice of

---

[31] See Chapter 4 and Part II for more on this.

organizational arrangements much more complex than the now classical trade-off between relying on markets versus integrating within a unified firm. The Air France-KLM and Delta venture is illustrative of this. On the one hand, Air France-KLM and Delta remain distinct firms, with their own strategies, financial arrangements, etc. On the other hand, the venture they formed to monitor their North Atlantic routes delineates a coordination arrangement that differs from the arrangement operating within each firm, as well as from that regulating the broader Flying Blue Alliance of which they are central components.

In microeconomics and industrial organization, the attention to network infrastructures, often discussed under the umbrella of "public utilities," has long focused on the choice between delivering expected services through market transactions, leaving it in the hands of competing firms, or through the organization of transactions within an integrated firm. From Marshall (1908; 1919) and beyond to Baumol, Willig, and Panzar (1982), network infrastructures have been viewed as a challenge to market solutions; economies of scale and network effects are considered major drivers pushing toward concentration and integration, ultimately resulting in "natural monopolies." Policy considerations focused on the need to regulate these monopolies, in order to avoid abuse of power and/or to reallocate property rights (e.g., through nationalization).

Coase (1938, 1960, 1972) and Williamson (1985) challenged this view, and the latter went further in providing tools to analyze the trade-off between delivering the so-called public services through market arrangements or producing them in-house. These contributions paralleled the increasing awareness of misalignments between existing micro-institutional solutions and rapidly changing technologies in almost all network infrastructures, as well as a renewed attention to severe flaws in the governance of utilities. The initial transaction costs model (Williamson, 1985: chapters 1 and 3; 1996: chapter 3) provided powerful tools to analyze what was still viewed at the time as the basic trade-off between "markets" and "hierarchies." It established that in a competitive environment, decision makers have strong incentives to align their micro-institutional choice with the attributes of the transaction this arrangement intends to organize. As is now well known, three attributes (or variables) are considered central to that choice: (1) the specificity of investments required to make a transaction possible (e.g., the type of coal needed with respect to a specific technology selected to produce energy[32]); (2) the uncertainty that may challenge the organization of a transaction, regardless of whether this uncertainty is of exogenous (e.g., the emergence of a new technology) or endogenous origin (e.g., a poorly designed licensing agreement); (3) the complexity[33] that may surround the organization of a transaction, regardless of whether it has its roots in technology/technologies (e.g., the co-existence of different signaling systems on a rail network) or in institutions (e.g., the Air France-KLM/Delta venture having to deal with different regulations and regulatory entities).

These analytical tools were later used to explore the existence and characteristics of a variety of alternative arrangements that correspond neither to pure market solutions nor to hierarchical ones and which are identified as "hybrids" in a substantial part of economics and managerial literature. These tools are also used to explore the drivers behind the choice of such "non-standard" arrangements.[34] The resulting trade-off becomes far more complex, with a central prediction that can be summarized as follows: the more specific an investment is, or the more exposed to uncertainty, and/or the more complexity it has to face, the more powerful are the drivers pushing decision makers to move from market solutions to hybrid arrangements, and ultimately to full integration.[35] This enriched model has recently been complemented and revised (in some aspects quite substantially) by considerations regarding the need to take on board the distinction between property rights and decision rights.[36] Indeed, this distinction impacts the way to conceptualize contracts and their role as a major coordination mechanism in alternative organizational

---

[32] Joskow, 1985.

[33] Williamson (1985: chapter 3) initially considered the "frequency" at which a transaction happens as the third variable. However, frequency has ubiquitous effects: making parties familiar with a transaction facilitates market arrangements; allowing the implementation of routines facilitates hierarchical control within integrated firms. Recent contributions instead consider complexity as the third variable (Williamson, 1996: chapter 4; Klein, 2008 [2005]; Ménard, 2008 [2005]; Tadelis and Williamson, 2013).

[34] Williamson (1996: chapter 4); Ménard (2004, 2013).

[35] For surveys of the empirical tests based on these predictions, see Shelanski and Klein (1995); Lafontaine and Slade (2007); Joskow (2008 [2005]); Klein (2008 [2005]); Ménard (2013).

[36] For a presentation and discussion of this extended model (and the status of relational contracts), see Ménard (2013).

arrangements. This impact can be interpreted as coming from the gap between these two sets of rights, which results in the existence of non-contractibilities that can be monitored only through "relational contracts" – contracts leaving room for substantial and unpredictable adjustments by those monitoring the agreement, typically managers (Baker, Gibbons, and Murphy, 2002, 2008; Ménard, 2004, 2013; Gibbons and Henderson, 2012).

What Is the Relevance for Network Infrastructures?

This short discussion of major developments spread over a huge literature has one specific purpose: to point out the existence of a whole range of micro-institutional solutions, going far beyond the archetypical organizational arrangement of "markets" or "hierarchies" (Williamson, 1975, 1985). The theoretical contributions providing the backbone to these developments helps to better identify factors that decision makers must consider when selecting a specific way to organize specific transactions in a given network infrastructure.

Surprisingly, very few contributions have gone in this direction so far, with the exception of elements provided by a handful of analyses (e.g., Levy and Spiller, 1994; Savedoff and Spiller, 1999; Shirley, 2002; Künneke, Groenewegen, and Ménard, 2010: 501 sq.; Ménard, 2017). This paucity may result from the long dominating view of network infrastructures as "natural monopolies," thus excluding de facto consideration for alternative organizational solutions. This situation began to change when the status of "public utilities" was called into question. Indeed, as soon as transactions monitored under "natural monopolies" are considered technologically as well as economically separable, issues of organizational choice become relevant.[37] On the one hand, many transactions needed to deliver network services can be done through market arrangements (e.g., selling airline tickets through competing outlets and websites). On the other hand, some transactions are critical in that they require tight hierarchical coordination to safeguard and secure critical functions (e.g., interoperability of equipment to secure air traffic) because of technical constraints (e.g., allocating slots for landing or taking-off) or socio-economic reasons (e.g., the

---

[37] This was a very strong point made by Williamson (1985: chapter 3; 1996: 379). See also the pioneering paper by Joskow (1985) and numerous examples provided in Ménard and Ghertman (2009).

prohibitive costs of building parallel competing airports).[38] This diversity of factors likely commands a diversity of possible organizational solutions.

However, beyond considerations that fall within the domain of the theories referenced above, there are also aspects arising from what this book identifies as specific to network infrastructures: the necessity to fulfill the critical functions in order to deliver expected services and performance. For instance, to secure interconnections, which are central to network infrastructures, transactions must be implemented and coordinated in specific ways, which require choosing organizational solutions accordingly. In air transportation, implementing and coordinating communication technologies linking air traffic controllers and pilots is illustrative of this. Consequently, the choice and performance of specific micro-institutional arrangements depend on the capacity to *identify, implement,* and *coordinate* the transactions at stake, with the goal of fulfilling the critical functions. This capacity relies on the rules internally implemented by each specific micro-institution, and more precisely the *incentives and guidelines* adopted to frame and coordinate internal transactions and the role of agents involved, so as to make decision rights operational and, hopefully, efficient. Last, if micro-institutions and the technical requirements embedded in the technology/technologies chosen are well aligned, *residual rent* can be expected with rules for their *allocation*. In shaping the mechanisms responsible for dividing benefits between investments, dividends to shareholders, and bonuses to employees, without creating disruption (e.g., pushing workers to go on strike or investors to walk away), holding property rights is of course a key driving force. Figure 2.3 summarizes the characteristics through which micro-institutions operate and which frame their activity.

However, these rights and the exercise of them through guidelines developed within the organization are deeply embedded in their formal status (e.g., whether it is a public or a private corporation), as well as in specific rules established through other institutional layers. On the one hand, they depend on issues decided within the macro layer. Consider the introduction of competition in European railways, which involved switching from "natural monopolies" established at the national level

---

[38] For a definition and discussion of the concept of critical transactions, see Künneke, Groenewegen, and Ménard (2010).

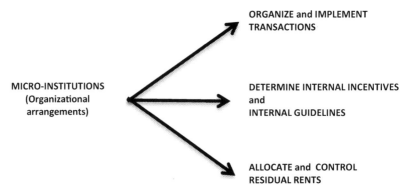

Figure 2.3 Dimensionalizing micro-institutions

to competing oligopolies operating on a European scale. This decision, which involved substantial changes in the definition and allocation of property rights as well as in some technologies in use (e.g., signaling systems), was made by European institutions (the European Council of heads of government, the European Commission, and the European Parliament) with confirmation by national parliaments. Second, the rules thus adopted had to be implemented and monitored through specialized institutional entities, for example, regulatory agencies. This is a missing link in most analyses of institutions.[39]

2.3.3 The Missing Link: Meso-Institutions as Go-Between

As Selznick (1948) once noted, ideal rules would be those fully accepted and internalized by agents so that they would behave accordingly, making implementation and enforcement a non-issue; there would be no gap to bridge between agents' behavior and rules, between the micro layer and the macro layer. Such conditions are never met, of course. Rules defined within the macro-institutional layer require specific enacting entities that can "translate" and adapt them to specific social as well as physical environments, to specific technologies associated with different network infrastructures, and to unpredictable events. For example, the European Union may adopt rules opening infrastructures to competition. However, these rules require

---

[39] But note what has been reported in Section 2.2.1 about Ostrom and the different types of rules.

translation into specific regulations, since norms and beliefs as well as technical requirements differ across member countries as well as among and even within the same infrastructure. Reforming railways is a good illustration: rail transportation does not play the same role in Sweden and France; the expectations of users and labor traditions in Finland and Italy are profoundly different; rail technology differs between Spain and Germany; European Union agreements stipulate that rights of access should be defined and allocated by national institutions (the "principle of subsidiarity"); and so on. Dealing with such complex issues requires going beyond the general rules defined within the macro-institutional layer and far exceeds the jurisdiction of micro-institutions: it requires intermediate arrangements to bridge the gap between constitutive rules and the way organizations and users operate within the architecture thus defined.

Enacting Rules and Rights: Concept and Functions

This is the role of meso-institutions. What motivates the introduction of this concept is the acknowledgment that although their actions are embedded in and framed by constitutive rules, parties to a transaction connect to these rules through specific institutional entities, for example, sector regulators. Symmetrically, constitutive rules require specific institutions to translate and adapt them to the specific temporal and spatial conditions within which different network infrastructures operate. Meso-institutions designate this as the *intermediate institutional layer within which constitutive rules are translated into specific protocols and guidelines that rely on specific entities for their implementation, monitoring and control.* Public bureaus, regulatory agencies, local administrations monitoring private operators of infrastructures, provide examples. These entities differ from micro-institutions in that they are not oriented toward the creation of value; they are rule adaptors, specifying the domain of possible activities for micro-institutions. For instance, the "antitrust immunity" delivered to Air France-KLM and Delta to develop their joint venture on North Atlantic routes was clearly an interpretation by distinct meso-institutions (DOT, DOJ, Directorate-General for Competition, etc.) of the general laws of competition, which are not the same in the United States and the European Union, in order to allow the venture to operate under a derogatory agreement. In doing so, the regulatory authorities operate as an intermediate between the macro and the micro layers.

This is another way of saying that meso-institutions are go-betweens. Because of their role as translators of rules, there are situations in which their responsibilities overlap with those of macro-institutions. And because they operate through entities that can be analyzed as organizations, they also share some characteristics with micro-institutions. In that sense, meso-institutions may be perceived as hybrid institutional arrangements. However, they have characteristics of their own, making them distinct. They differ from micro-institutions in that they do not create value; they delineate the domain within which the creation of value is possible. The Directorate-General for Competition does not deliver air transportation; it establishes rules that allow specific airlines to do so. Meso-institutions also differ from macro-institutions in that their jurisdiction depends ultimately on the rules and norms established within the macro layer. The delivery of "antitrust immunity" required this exception to be compatible with the general law regulating competition. The specificity of meso-institutions therefore comes from their role of intermediation between macro-institutions and operators and/or users.

They do so through complementary functions. First, they *translate* constitutive rules into rules specific to a societal context (e.g., values attached to the quality of drinkable water vary across culture and countries), a sector (e.g., safety requirements for nuclear plants differ from those for coal plants), or a region (e.g., hydrogeology imposes different norms on the building of dams and reservoirs). These specific rules provide essential guidelines to micro-institutions and agents about what they can do or are expected to do, as well as about what is prohibited. Meso-institutional entities also pass upward signals of misalignment transmitted by operators and users, and which may require changes in the allocation of rights. For example, they may have to adapt conditions required to connect to the electrical grid or to get rights to fly. Symmetrically, they may play an active role in indicating to law makers the need to change the rules of the game.

Second, rules established at the macro level need to be *adapted* and *implemented*. For example, if a decision is made to introduce competition among providers of infrastructures, the modalities needed to reach that goal should be defined, (e.g., what type of contract? What conditions must be fulfilled to be allowed to bid?). These tasks can be done directly by a central bureau; delegated to regional authorities; transferred to a sector regulator; left to private meso-institutions

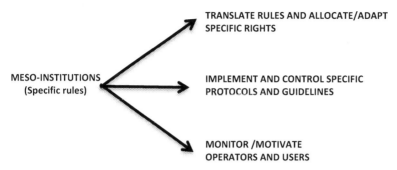

Figure 2.4 Dimensionalizing meso-institutions

relying on participating operators (e.g., the NERC in the American electricity grid), etc. In many situations, meso-institutions are an imbrication of different entities, which raises problems of coherence and is often a source of conflict due to overlapping responsibilities. For instance, numerous ministries, bureaus, and agencies are involved and are often at conflict with each other in the regulation of the water system in Manila (Wu and Malaluan, 2008) or the sanitation sector in Egypt (Wahaab, 2018 [2015]).

Third, there is the need to *monitor* interactions between operators organizing the actual production and delivery of services and the constitutive rules that frame their action. This task may require "translation" into very specific rules; for example, about how intrusive a regulatory agency can be in *controlling* operators' compliance with the law.[40] One way to alleviate monitoring and control is through the adoption of adequate *incentives*, such as when rewards and penalties are introduced to motivate airlines or rail companies to stick to the schedule associated to their "slots." Symmetrically, adequate incentives may facilitate the transmission of information from operators and users, thus easing the implementation of the rules of the game.

In sum, meso-institutions play a key role in organizing the specific domain within which to develop transactions needed for producing and delivering services expected from the relevant network infrastructure. Figure 2.4 summarizes the tasks that give meso-institutions their specific configuration.

---

[40] This is an issue that Coase raised about the role of the Federal Communications Commission (Coase, 1959), and which led to the writing of his famous paper, "The problem of social cost" (Coase, 1960).

Meso-Institutions as a Key Component of Sectors' Governance

This complex set of attributes points out the importance of meso-institutions when it comes to delivering coherent and well-aligned rules with respect to the technology/technologies at stake and securing the critical functions that characterize specific network infrastructures. The entities and devices (protocols and guidelines) through which meso-institutions operate determine different modalities of governance. Governance is a polymorphic term, referring to very heterogeneous problems and serving various purposes (Tropp, 2007). Part of the difficulty comes from its use at different levels of decision-making, from "corporations" to governments. In this book, we systematically refer to governance as the entities, protocols, and procedures through which the interdependence between meso-institutions and context-specific technologies operates, delineating the conditions under which services from a specific network can be delivered.[41]

Thus understood, governance plays a critical role in the alignment (or misalignment) between specific rules and standards and the technological design of specific network infrastructures on the one hand; and in the coordination (or lack of coordination) between meso-institutions and the micro- as well as the macro-institutional layers on the other hand. The New York blackout (see Introduction: Lifting the Veil) illustrates the consequences for critical functions of the combination of a poorly designed regulation, weak entities in charge of implementing rules, and flaws in the technological design of interconnection in a specific electricity network. This example (more cases are provided in Part II of this book) also suggests that there are different modalities of governance (e.g., public bureaus, regulatory agencies, local communities, specialized courts, etc.), which raises the issue of trade-offs among them.[42] For meso-institutions to play their role in fulfilling the critical functions, entities and devices are required that can create (or restore) alignment between technological devices and specific norms and rules; coordinate the way operators and users organize transactions within constitutive rules; shelter dispute resolution devices to solve conflicts and reduce contractual hazards; and be endowed with

---

[41] For a related concept on water governance, see OECD (2015a); also the UNDP Water Governance Facility at SIWI and UNICEF (UNICEF, 2015).

[42] Facing trade-offs among alternative solutions is an issue for all institutional layers (see, e.g., the case of micro-institutions above). However, attributes involved in the trade-offs and conditions of exercise of choice among alternative solutions differ substantially.

capacities to constrain or punish deviant parties to transactions (Chapter 4 and Part II substantiate these issues).

Because of the very nature of network infrastructures, meeting these goals almost always involve public authorities, particularly as enforcers of last resort. It implies costs, making modalities of governance dependent on modalities and efficiency of payment by beneficiaries of networks and/or public authorities (ultimately, taxpayers). The "benign neglect" of this intermediate institutional layer, typically as a result of poor staffing (in quantity and quality) and/or inadequate financial resources, is a significant factor in the failure of so many reforms of network infrastructures (Shirley, 2002; Ménard and Ghertman, 2009; Ménard, Jimenez, and Tropp, 2018).

2.4 Conclusion

This chapter focused on the identification and characterization of the different layers that define the institutional setting within which economic activities develop. More specifically, we argued that the concept of institution needs to be disentangled if we want to understand the modalities through which network infrastructures operate. Our implicit assumption is that these interdependent institutional layers parallel the layers characterizing technologies; this last aspect will be explored in the next chapter. We also assumed and will substantiate in Chapter 4 and Part II that these layers have a differentiated impact on the alignment or misalignment between institutions and technologies, thus raising different problems and challenges with respect to the critical functions that network infrastructures need to perform in order to deliver expected services. In a nutshell, this chapter developed the institutional dimension of our framework, along with the technological dimension, and it argued that this dimension contributes to differentiating the organization of air transportation or railroads from, say, telecoms, internet, water, or sanitation systems!

Besides submitting a clear typology of the layers that configure institutional settings, we went a step further than our predecessors in pinpointing the tasks and roles these layers assume in establishing, through rules and enacting entities, the playing field for network infrastructures and in securing their critical functions.[43] Table 2.1

---

[43] By comparison, Williamson (2000) identifies different layers according to a very different criterion: the time horizon through which theories capture them.

Table 2.1 *A synthetic view of institutional layers (with illustrations from the airline industry)*

	Tasks and responsibilities	
Institutional layers	Main tasks and responsibilities	Responsible entities, with rules and norms generated, and illustrations from the airline industry
Macro-institutions	Delineate rules: *what* can/cannot be done. Establish and secure property rights: *who* holds them. Frame decision rights: *how* they can be exercised	*Congress, parliaments* ... • Adoption of Open Skies policy • US law prohibiting foreign carriers from taking over US airlines • Norms and rules regarding airline certification and rights of access
Meso-institutions	*Translate* rules and allocate/adapt specific rights. *Implement* and control specific protocols and guidelines. *Monitor/motivate* operators and users	*US Department of Justice* • Issue of antitrust rulings *US Department of Transportation* • Guidelines governing airline operation *Airport authorities* • Imposing penalties on flights delayed
Micro-institutions	*Organize* transactions. *Determine* internal incentives and internal guidelines. *Allocate* and control residual rights	*Air France-KLM and Delta venture* • Contract regulating the venture • Internal "working committees" to monitor operations • Internal rules to allocate benefits and deficits

summarizes our findings and proposes illustrations from the case of the airline venture described throughout this chapter.

However, there are still several issues to explore. First, in order to differentiate these layers, we emphasized the tasks and roles that make the macro, meso and micro layers distinct. In the "real world," they often overlap and combine, so that understanding what is going on requires an enrichment of our framework through a detailed analysis of specific cases (see Part II). Indeed, it is precisely such mixes that make different network infrastructures distinct with respect to their institutional setting as well as their technological characteristics over time and space. It is the role of empirical analysis to establish these variations, their significance, and their impact within the fundamental modeling of institutions introduced in this chapter. Second, and of particular significance for our goal, these layers connect differently to the critical functions, determining distinct modalities of alignment/ misalignment between these institutional layers and the layers that typify the technology of various network infrastructures. Third, there is a need to better understand the impact of the interdependence between these different institutional layers and their technological counterparts on the delivery and performance of services expected from these networks. The coming chapters deal with these issues.

3 Technology in Three Dimensions
Economics Meets Systems Engineering

3.1 Introduction

From a technological perspective, network infrastructures typically comprise large-scale systems of complementary physical components and linkages. These man-made material objects provide essential services through human action that are structured by institutions (Kroes et al., 2006: 806). In the previous chapter, we elaborated on the features of institutions needed for safeguarding the critical functions of network infrastructures at three layers of analysis. In this chapter, we proceed in a similar way with respect to the technology of network infrastructures. Comparable with our approach in Chapter 2, we distinguish three layers of analysis for the technology of network infrastructures: architecture, context-specific design, and technical operation.

The case of high-speed rail is used to elucidate our approach. A distinctive feature of high-speed rail is that it is operated at a speed of at least 250 km/h (International Union of Railways, 2015). Like traditional rail systems, the generic complementary physical components include tracks, signaling devices, stations, and rolling stock. However, the components of high-speed rail systems must meet technological requirements in order to be operated at high speeds. For instance, particular tracks are needed, containing a certain quality of steel and concrete ties between the rails. Trains need to meet certain specifications, such as a certain power-to-weight ratio, high voltage power systems, aerodynamics, reliability, and safety constraints. Such general features of the complementary components can be attributed to all high-speed rail systems, independent of where and when they are operated. We denote this as architecture, which stipulates the constitutive technological features necessary for providing the expected services of high-speed rail transport.

Substantiating these abstract features in real-world physical systems is addressed in our second layer of analysis, the context-specific technological design. Typically, different options are available for the actual design of network infrastructures related to their historical path-dependent development and the objectives they serve. Obviously, in different countries, regions, and/or points in time, different choices are made. Among others, performance expectations might differ, for example, with respect to the geographic area that is served by high-speed rail systems. Some countries have developed highly interconnected rail systems extending throughout their territory. Spain has the largest high-speed network in Europe with some 2,665 km, followed by France with some 2,037 km.[1] Other countries focus on dedicated lines between selected metropolitan areas such as the United Kingdom, the United States, or China. For each of these rail systems, dedicated devices are applied that are equipped for the provision of these services, such as rail stations, rail switches, and rail traffic monitoring systems. Again, this example demonstrates the institutional embeddedness of the technological choices made in different countries.

Our third layer of analysis addresses the operation of technical processes required to actually provide the services, given a context-specific design and architecture. Within this layer, the operation of high-speed rail systems and the efficient and safe use of the available capacity is one of the key issues (International Union of Railways, 2015). For safe handling of high-speed trains, certain braking distances need to be taken into consideration. For a maximum speed of 200 km/h the braking distance is 1,900 meters. For 350 km/h this is 6,700 meters. Higher speeds require longer distances between trains, but the travel time is reduced. The operating speed needs to be determined such that safety standards are safeguarded while the use of the available capacity meets the traffic demand. This is an example of the interdependence between institutions and technology in our alignment scheme. From a technological perspective, the operational safety of high-speed trains is, among other things, realized by so-called automated train protection (ATP) systems that intervene in the operation of trains in the case of human error.

---

[1] Wikipedia, "High-speed rail in Europe" (https://en.wikipedia.org; last accessed January 3, 2019).

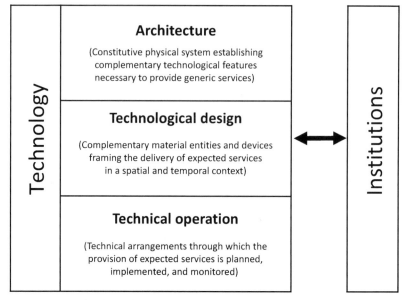

Figure 3.1 Technological layers

The three layers of analysis of the technology of network infrastructures are summarized and illustrated in Figure 3.1.

We argued in the previous chapters that existing economic approaches to technology do not meet the conceptual requirements for an appropriate analysis of the alignment between institutions and technology in network infrastructures. Notwithstanding some useful insights (see Chapter 1), conventional approaches to technology do not provide the conceptual tools needed for the analysis of the technological arrangements that are required for safeguarding critical functions in network infrastructures. As illustrated by the case of high-speed rail systems, our focus is on identifying the technical devices and entities involved in the safeguarding of critical functions at different layers of analysis. We regard this economic approach to technology as innovative.

Indeed, in the economic literature, the issue of the technological coordination of complementary artefacts is not addressed. Rather, technological features of network infrastructures are often related to characteristics of cost functions, network externalities, external effects, and network economics (Chapter 1). Typical characteristics of cost functions of network infrastructures include economies of scale and scope (Rubinfeld, 1998; Cabral, 2000). These economies are related to the high initial sunk investments that are required prior to the actual provision of infrastructure services. Typically, this results in monopolistic or oligopolistic market structures (Joskow, Polinsky, and Shavell, 2007; Helm, 2009b) that are less efficient compared to the ideal competitive market. In this line of reasoning, different market structures can be related to the regulation of liberalized network infrastructures (Jaag and Trinkner, 2011). Network externalities relate the benefits of a single user to the number of other users of networks (Shapiro and Varian, 1999; Liebowitz and Margolis, 2003). This phenomenon is quite common in network infrastructures and reinforces monopolistic markets. External effects arise because the benefits of infrastructure services cannot be appropriated by those who invested in it, causing well-known free-rider problems. The literature on the economics of networks (Economides, 1996) considers topological features of networks, resulting in different market structures. For instance, the topology of star-shaped networks is characterized by a central nodal point that is connected to all other network nodes. From an economic perspective, such a central point provides the possibilities for establishing monopolistic market structures. Some literature addresses the significance of technological changes with respect to the regulation of network infrastructures, specifically with respect to advances in information and communication technology (ICT) (Glachant, 2012; Brandstätt et al., 2014).

However, this body of literature is not conclusive for our purpose. It does not sufficiently specify the complementary technological features that are required to provide expected services. In our framework, we aim to identify how technological devices and entities contribute to the safeguarding of critical functions. In the railway sector, traffic control centers are well-known entities that are essential for maintaining a safe and efficient capacity management of the rail network. They are defined by institutional as well as technological arrangements. From a technological perspective, these entities build on a configuration of different material artefacts required for the monitoring of traffic flows and the physical regulation of access to different parts of the network, including cameras, sensors, rail traffic signals, rail switches, and railway stations.

In what follows, we shall specify features of technology that are relevant for the safeguarding of the critical functions at the three layers

of analysis identified in our framework. Section 3.2 builds on insights
from the field of systems engineering to specify and delineate the technological features and components of network infrastructures. Doing so
allows a better understanding of the issues of coordination among the
complex combination of artefacts that provide the physical foundations of
infrastructures. Section 3.3 pushes the analysis further, identifying and
delineating the three layers through which these artefacts and their coordination operate. These developments are essential to specify the conditions
under which the four critical functions at the core of network infrastructures can be secured, namely, system control, capacity management,
interconnection, and interoperability. Section 3.4 concludes with some
reflections about what we have learned from the systems engineering
approach, but also about how our framework differs in important aspects.

3.2 Technological Features of Network Infrastructures

In Chapter 1, we characterized network infrastructures as socio-
technological systems in which technological and institutional artefacts
are strongly interdependent. In this chapter, we focus on the technological
features of network infrastructures. These technological features can be
described by their constituting physical components and their complementary relationships, required to provide expected services and fulfill the
critical functions. Given a certain state of knowledge and available
resources, the expected services determine the technological building
blocks and their interdependencies, based on well-known physical laws.
This approach is inspired by systems engineering (Faulconbridge and
Ryan, 2014). In general terms, technological systems are complex combinations of technological artefacts (Kroes et al., 2006: 805). These
artefacts are combined to serve certain objectives. To stay with our
example, high-speed rail systems are composed of tracks, rolling stock,
signaling devices, and stations, which in combination provide the system
service of high-speed rail transport. This description of a system is typical
for systems engineering. A technological system is defined as "*a combination of interacting elements organized to achieve one or more stated
purposes*".[2] Hence, systems engineering assumes that the features of

---

[2] This is the ISO/IEC 152888 definition of technological systems (Faulconbridge
and Ryan, 2014: 3). A similar definition is provided by Maier and Rechtin
(2000: 27).

systems can be directly related to their operational purpose. Given a certain purpose, such as the provision of high-speed rail transportation, the relevant entities and devices can be determined and identified. This approach provides a useful starting point for identifying and specifying our three layers of analysis of the technology of network infrastructures: the architecture, the technological design, and the operation.

3.2.1 Artefacts, Components, and the Delineation of Network Infrastructures

To achieve this goal, we need to identify which of the many technological artefacts of network infrastructures are relevant for the provision of expected services in general, and the safeguarding of critical functions specifically. Using the terminology of systems engineers, the boundaries of the system need to be determined. These system boundaries are determined by their constitutional elements, namely, the artefacts required to provide an expected service. In the case of high-speed rail transportation, artefacts such as specific tracks, rolling stock, signaling devices, and stations delineate the boundaries of the rail system, since they are instrumental in providing this service. Relevant artefacts include technological devices that are involved in the coordination of critical functions. For instance, signaling devices are important for the capacity management of high-speed rail systems, as they physically coordinate the access to different parts of the network. In addition, this also serves transportation safety as part of the critical function of system control. In the case of an emergency, affected parts of the trajectory can be closed to all traffic. Hence, the determination of system boundaries is crucial for identifying which devices are relevant for safeguarding the critical functions.

Obviously, the determination of system boundaries depends on the expected services to be provided. Are we interested in the provision of local rail services or international high-speed rail transportation? Consequently, different system boundaries have to be considered. Although both services are similar in the sense that they provide transport services using rail tracks and rolling stock, different components are involved. This requires that critical functions are safeguarded by different devices. High-speed trains typically rely on onboard signaling systems, whereas local trains depend on traditional exterior signaling devices. The critical function of interconnection is different for high-speed rail compared to local rail systems. In the case of high-speed rail systems, the rolling stock is sometimes equipped to be used across different national rail systems. For example, in the case of the French high-speed train Thalys, the locomotive can be operated under different conditions of power supply and signaling systems applied in the different countries and regions that are served. This is typically not an issue for dedicated local rail systems. In terms of systems engineering, the system boundaries of local train services are different from high-speed train services because these systems serve different objectives (long-distance versus local rail transport), require different artefacts (e.g., high-speed rail tracks versus dedicated local tracks), and involve different arrangements for the safeguarding of critical functions (e.g., multifunctional versus dedicated locomotives).

3.2.2 Steps toward Identifying Technological Layers

The systems engineering approach is particularly helpful when it comes to identifying and analyzing the relevant technological system and the different technological layers involved. Both aspects are correlated to the expected services. If we stick to the previous example, the expected service could be analyzed in a generic sense as the provision of rail passenger transport. This is generic in that it is related to the broad architecture of rail passenger transport in general, ranging from local metro systems to long-distance high-speed services. If we were interested in the performance of the Paris Métro system, this would imply focusing on far more specific material requirements for safeguarding the critical functions of this metro system, which must be related to the context-specific components involved. Finally, we can also focus on the actual provision of particular services, such as the seamless high-speed rail transport link between Amsterdam and Paris. The critical function involved in this service is the interoperability of the Thalys locomotive required to cope with different national and regional signaling systems. To provide this transport service, technological devices are necessary on board this train to adapt to these different systems, and the decision rights for traffic management need to be allocated among the network operators of the three countries involved (the Netherlands, Belgium, and France). This again illustrates that technological and institutional arrangements are tightly interwoven. We will come back to these issues in the next chapter.

3.3 Technological Layers and the Coordination Issue

What the considerations of Section 3.2.2 suggest is that different layers of analysis can be identified in relation to the degree to which expected services of network infrastructures are specified. This might be generic, related to a context in space and time, or oriented toward operational provisioning of services. Accordingly, three layers can be distinguished, identified as architecture, technological design, and operation. For each of these layers, the material features and arrangements required to safeguard critical functions can be specified to different degrees.

3.3.1 Architecture

The specification of the expected generic services is the starting point of our analysis for the determination and description of the architecture of network infrastructures and the delineation of the relevant system. Network infrastructures provide distinct generic services. Railway systems are expected to provide rail transport services, power networks deliver electricity, gas systems deliver gasified energy sources, and water networks supply drinking water. Characteristic material components are required for the realization of these generic services.

In the case of passenger rail transport, these include rail tracks, rolling stock, stations, and signaling devices. In the case of electricity, power production facilities, power networks, and power transformers are essential building blocks. Gas supply requires gas fields, transport facilities such as pipes or carriers for liquefied natural gas (LNG), and storages. Likewise, the provision of drinking water includes water pumping stations, water treatment facilities, and water pipelines. These material components are mutually complementary parts, constituting the physical networks that provide the above-mentioned services and define the critical functions to be fulfilled.

Coordination arrangements are required to establish and support this complementarity between the constituting components of network infrastructures. For instance, rail tracks are the transport medium for the rolling stock. A safe operation of rail systems requires arrangements such that trains do not interfere with each other on the rail tracks, possibly causing accidents. Signaling devices can be instrumental in this respect, for instance, by indicating a safe operational speed. And so is the allocation of slots, so that institutional devices are required as well. Another example is automated train protection systems that intervene in the operation of trains in the case of human error. There are also institutional arrangements to safeguard this critical function of system control, for example, timetables.

Since electricity cannot be stored at scale, power systems require close coordination between the production and consumption of power; otherwise, the system breaks down, resulting in a blackout, as illustrated by the New York blackout (see our introductory chapter). There are various arrangements of automated power system protection intended to avoid such disturbances (Hewitson, Brown, and Balakrishnan, 2004). For instance, circuit breakers are devices that monitor the required voltage level in different parts of the networks and automatically disconnect them in case of an overload.

In the case of drinking water provision, the pressure in the pipelines needs to be within a certain range of operating conditions to allow for the continuous availability of water and to protect the hydraulic integrity of the system (National Research Council, 2006: 204). Devices monitor the water pressure and induce necessary interventions if it is outside the expected range, for instance, by turning pumps on or off, or making use of local storage facilities accordingly. Quality is a main issue in water systems, involving both the process of filtering and treatment, as well as the run-through time of water in the system.

One central feature of the architecture of network infrastructures is that it changes only very slowly over time (Maier and Rechtin, 2000; Faulconbridge and Ryan, 2014). Network infrastructures are developed for a certain purpose. The general technological means to provide essential services is quite constant over time. Basically, railway systems still rely on the same architecture as in their early years. The generic service is unchanged (e.g., passenger rail transport) as are its essential material components and basic functions. Rail tracks are the transport devices for the rolling stock, to be operated between different railway stations and coordinated by signaling devices. Hence, even the basic nature of the critical functions remains unchanged.

To summarize, the architecture articulates the constitutive technological features of a network infrastructure needed to provide generic services, the constitutive material components, and the technological arrangements of its mutually complementing parts required to provide generic services and safeguard critical functions. Figure 3.2 assembles these features of the architecture of network infrastructures.

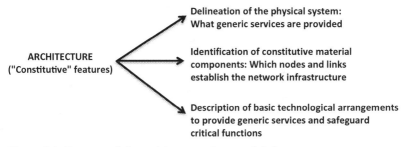

ARCHITECTURE ("Constitutive" features)

Delineation of the physical system: What generic services are provided

Identification of constitutive material components: Which nodes and links establish the network infrastructure

Description of basic technological arrangements to provide generic services and safeguard critical functions

Figure 3.2 Features of the architecture of network infrastructures

3.3.2 Technological Design

Technological design relates to the context-specific arrangement of material components necessary, within a given architecture, to make up a network delivering services specific to a certain time and place. For instance, European high-speed rail systems[3] provide distinct services in terms of operating speed, frequency, geographical accessibility, comfort, reliability, safety, and door-to-door travel time.[4] Figure 3.3 illuminates some of these features. High-speed rail with an operational speed of over 250 km/h is only available in a few countries, including France, Spain, Germany, and Italy. Some countries consider that train connections qualify for a "high-speed" designation even if their operating speed is below 250 km/h. Figure 3.3 also illustrates the geographical accessibility of these networks. Some countries have only a few connections, such as Sweden and Italy, whereas others have developed a denser network, including France and Spain.

According to such service expectations, national high-speed rail systems can be distinguished by typical arrangements of material components, including signaling systems, rail tracks, and engines. The Japanese Shinkansen was one of the first modern high-speed rail systems worldwide. Its constituting components are not compatible with the existing rail system in that country. A dedicated rail track system of 515 km was built between Tokyo Central and Shin Osaka. The Shinkansen locomotives were specifically designed for this service.

---

[3] An interesting overview of European high-speed rail systems is provided by Wikipedia, "High-speed rail in Europe" (https://en.wikipedia.org; last accessed January 3, 2019).

[4] International Union of Railways (2015).

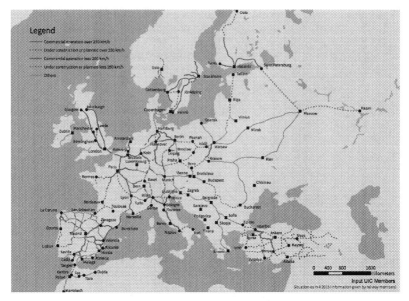

Figure 3.3 European high-speed rail system (Source: International Union of Railways, 2015)

The use of monorail systems is another means of providing high-speed services. Presently, this is only applied for quite short distances, for example, the Shanghai Maglev, which runs between Longway Road station and Pudong International airport, with a journey time of only eight minutes and a maximum speed of more than 400 km/h.[5]

Consequently, safeguarding the critical functions must be adapted to the technological features that characterize the design of specific network infrastructures. In the cases of the Japanese Shinkansen and the Shanghai Maglev, dedicated networks are available that only serve this high-speed service. This has implications for the interconnection of rail services. Under these conditions, locomotives cannot be operated on different rail networks, which for example makes their design different from the French Thalys. In the cases of the Shinkansen or the Maglev systems, the absence of physical connections to the rest of the rail track systems means that interconnection needs to be considered only with respect to the transit to other modes of transportation such as

---

[5] Wikipedia, "Shanghai Maglev train" (https://en.wikipedia.org/wiki/Maglev; last accessed May 23, 2019).

traditional rail services or air transportation. On the contrary, in the case of the French Thalys the interconnection between different national networks is essential to provide its international train services. Thalys locomotives are technically equipped to be operated on rail networks with different power supply and signaling systems. This is an essential precondition for utilizing the Dutch, Belgian, and French rail systems for the international service between Amsterdam and Paris.

The technological design of network infrastructures differs from its architecture: it varies according to the particular regional context and changes over time, typically within decades, as a consequence of technological innovations and the evolution of users' expectations. In rail systems, the early steam engines have been replaced by modern high-speed trains in less than a century. The services of railway systems have improved significantly in terms of travel time, comfort, and available destinations. In Europe, the development of high-speed rail systems started in the 1980s and 1990s as national projects.[6] As a consequence, the critical functions are differently coordinated and implemented, depending on the local technological design. In the early days, the capacity management of the rail tracks was performed by manual signaling devices. Nowadays, information and communication technology (ICT) is very prominent in monitoring and controlling the use of the rail network, such as automated safety systems in trains that intervene in cases of emergency without human action.

To summarize, the technological design of network infrastructures denotes the contextual framing of the generic architecture in terms of particular services, specific material components, and the technological arrangements required to provide services and safeguard the critical functions. Figure 3.4 recapitulates these characteristics.

3.3.3 Technical Operation

This layer of analysis is concerned with the actual processing of network infrastructures. Technical operation refers to the configuration of technical devices such that expected services are provided and critical functions are monitored and controlled, given a context-specific design and architecture. It corresponds with the micro-institutions that organize economic transactions. Both the technical operation and micro-

---

[6] Wikipedia, "High-speed rail in Europe" (https://en.wikipedia.org; last accessed January 3, 2019).

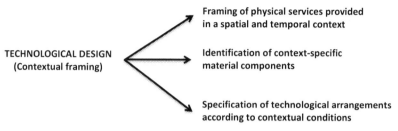

TECHNOLOGICAL DESIGN
(Contextual framing)

Framing of physical services provided
in a spatial and temporal context

Identification of context-specific
material components

Specification of technological arrangements
according to contextual conditions

Figure 3.4 Features of the technological design of network infrastructures

institutions are instrumental in providing expected services (see Chapter 4 for more on this).

Obviously, technical systems can be processed in many different ways depending on the expected services. With reference to our case, metro systems are expected to operate a relatively high number of trains per hour, and achieve a high punctuality of services. High-speed rail systems interconnect major urban agglomerations on long-distance trajectories with a traveling time compatible with air transportation. Regional and national train services are often oriented toward serving many different destinations, providing access to train services to cities and villages throughout the network.

The configuration of the technical devices of rail systems is attuned to these expectations in terms of (Perennes, 2014; International Union of Railways, 2015:18):

- the operating speed of the locomotives;
- the train paths, namely, the railway stations that are served at specific times of the day;
- the number of different types of trains operated on the trajectory (homogeneity of the rolling stock); and
- specificities of the rail network, for instance, single or double tracks, including the possibility of overtaking trains at railway stations using additional tracks.

Accordingly, metro systems are processed with a relatively low operating speed, a high number of trains, homogeneous rolling stock, and dedicated train paths with few intersections. High-speed train systems rely on a high operating speed, a limited number of trains, homogeneous types of trains, and dedicated rail tracks. Traditional national and regional railways are characterized by heterogeneous rolling stock, a variety of rail networks, and different operating speeds. These networks are typically used for multiple purposes, including long-distance and short-distance services for passengers and goods.

The operation of such differing technical systems needs to be monitored and controlled through various arrangements to safeguard critical functions. For instance, in traditional rail systems, capacity management is a challenge, especially if the railway tracks provide little possibilities for overtaking (slower) trains, or if only single tracks are available. This situation can have a negative impact on the regularity of the service, and only allows for a lower number of trains operated per hour. The Thalys, operated between Amsterdam and Paris, with part of the route relying on mixed traffic, provides an example of these operational problems that are ultimately linked to the technological design of the system. The actual processing of technical systems requires making important choices. For example, what is the specific trade-off in the operation of the Thalys between the performance parameters of punctuality, comfort, and safety? Could the safety of passengers be challenged by operating the train at its speed limit in case of unexpected delays? Would it be possible to give the Thalys service priority when it is deviated onto standard networks when there are unexpected delays on its dedicated rails?

This case illustrates that the physical provision of services is not only related to the configuration and processing of material devices, but also to arrangements for safeguarding critical functions. For instance, mission control centers represent technical arrangements to monitor and control the actual status of the network, enabling real-time calculations between planned and actual schedules, automated intrusion detections, and computer-aided conflict resolution (International Union of Railways, 2015: 18). Such technical arrangements typically build on ICT, including sensors, cameras, and computer algorithms. Another example is automated train protection (ATP), which intervenes in the operation of locomotives in the case of human error. Of course, these technical arrangements can only be effective in conjunction with the organizational arrangements that define the micro-institutions (more on this in the next chapter).

To summarize, the third layer of technical operation of network infrastructures is determined by the material processes required for the actual provision of services, related to the configuration and processing of technical devices, and the arrangements required for monitoring and controlling the critical functions (Figure 3.5).

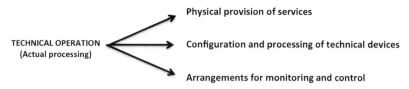

Figure 3.5 Features of the technical operation of network infrastructures

3.4 Conclusion: Some Lessons

In this chapter, we identified technological features of network infrastructures that are relevant for safeguarding their critical functions. Our approach intended to develop further the economic analysis of the technological dimension of network infrastructures by taking on board important lessons from the systems engineering literature. We assumed that the functioning of technological systems can be related to their operational purposes. Different technological layers were identified and characterized, based on the degree to which the purpose of network infrastructures is specified.

In that perspective, architectures are typified by their constitutive features, related to the generic services provided, the constitutive material components, and the basic technological arrangements for safeguarding critical functions. Technological designs articulate the contextual framing of a generic architecture related to the provision of specific services, material components, and technological arrangements. Lastly, the technical operation of network infrastructures is characterized by the actual processing of technological devices and arrangements so that services are physically provided.

The systems engineering approach helped us to characterize the technology of network infrastructures and to identify those components that are relevant for safeguarding the critical functions at the core of these networks. This is a quite common and accepted approach among engineers. However, network infrastructures are typically not designed starting from a green field situation. Rather, they evolve over time, often from a small-scale and experimental setup toward regional, national, and even international systems. The origins of high-speed rail systems can be traced back to 1830 with the construction of the first intercity rail connection between Liverpool and Manchester. The locomotive, built by the British inventor George Stephenson, was called the "Rocket." However, we have to wait until 1964 to experience the first

Table 3.1 *A synthetic view of technological layers (with illustrations from the rail industry, specified for the Paris Métro)*

Technological layers	Technological arrangements and illustrations from the rail industry	
Architecture	*What* generic service is provided?	Provision of local rail transport service
	Which nodes and links establish the network infrastructure?	Tracks, trains, signaling systems, switches, stations
	How are they to be arranged?	Tracks are the transport medium for trains, requiring a standardized rail gauge, a signaling system for traffic allocation, and a control center
Technological design	*Framing* of generic services in a spatial and temporal context	Contemporary provision of metro services in the city of Paris
	Identification of context-specific components	Underground rail tracks and stations, homogeneous types of trains for short-distance passenger transport
	Specification of context-specific arrangements	16 lines with no intersections and double tracks
Operation	*Actual provision* of services	High-frequency operation of Paris Métro trains
	Configuration and processing of technical devices	Short-distance, low speed, high regularity of service that requires tight technical coordination
	Arrangements for monitoring and control	Automated train control system allowing for real time location of trains and traffic control

modern high-speed system in the world built in Japan, the Shinkansen. In 1981, the first European high-speed train was operated in France. In the late 1980s and the beginning of the 1990s, high-speed systems were developed in France, Italy, Spain, Germany, and Belgium. Since the turn of this century, high-speed rail systems have emerged throughout Europe and elsewhere in the world, including China, Taiwan, Korea, and Turkey (International Union of Railways, 2015: 5).

This long-term evolution is typical for network infrastructures. The systems are continuously adapted because of changing societal needs, expectations, and technological innovations. Technological lock-in effects and path dependencies have to be taken into consideration by analyzing the features of such large-scale socio-technological systems. We already mentioned the example of the different European railway signaling systems that are the result of path-dependent developments of national railways. The technological complexity is sometimes even beyond engineering controllability. Rail incidents are not entirely controllable, and some accidents are unpredictable.[7]

Our approach provides an integrated view of the relevant technological features of network infrastructures. Table 3.1 provides a synthetic view of the technological layers, with illustrations from the rail sector and specified for the Paris Métro system.[8]

However, this approach does not address the evolution of network infrastructures, a point we already made in Chapter 1. This is consistent with our alignment framework, which is static by nature. Our approach is also different from systems engineering in the sense that we are not interested in designing a network infrastructure according to certain performance parameters. Rather, we apply this approach for delineating and describing the technological features of these complex socio-technological systems at a specific point in time. This enables us to identify the technological arrangements that are required to provide certain services and that are implemented for safeguarding the critical functions. Relating these technological arrangements to the institutional characteristics of network infrastructures is the core of our alignment framework. This is further specified in the next chapter.

---

[7] Wikipedia provides a classification of railway accidents ("List of rail accidents." Available at https://en.wikipedia.org/wiki/Lists_of_rail_accidents; last accessed May 23, 2019).

[8] Wikipedia, "Paris Métro" (https://en.wikipedia.org; last accessed July 25, 2019).

4 | *Bringing Together Two Worlds Apart*

4.1 Introduction

This chapter brings us to the core of our framework: the assessment of alignment between institutions and technology. This is an ambitious endeavor, since finding a way to evaluate the compatibility of the technological and institutional characteristics of coordination needed to secure the critical functions is not straightforward. In our framework, institutions are related to the modalities of allocation and the monitoring of rules and rights. For instance, coordination of transactions could be provided through markets, hierarchies, or hybrids. On the other hand, the technology dimension needs to consider the devices, procedures, and tools for safeguarding the critical functions. This includes establishing technological routines between different devices to enable activities that are crucial for delivering expected services. The two dimensions of institutions and technology are literally two worlds apart when it comes to coping with coordination processes in network infrastructures. At first sight, they might even appear unrelated.

Take, for instance, the current European gas transmission network (Figure 4.1). From a technological perspective, pipes and compressors are required to pump natural gas from its place of origin (the gas fields) to the final consumers (households and firms). Pipelines are interconnected at so-called hubs, enabling the physical transportation of gas between different geographical locations large distances apart. Storage facilities are essential technological devices, required to balance the production of gas with the fluctuating demand. Compressors are necessary to produce sufficient pressure in the pipelines so as to transport gas at an expected speed. In order to secure the final delivery of gas, all these components need tight coordination.

From an institutional perspective, different features must also be considered. Prior to the liberalization of the European gas sector at

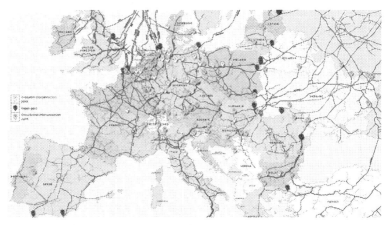

Figure 4.1 The European gas network (2017) (source: ENTSOG Transparency Platform)

the turn of this century, pipelines, storage facilities, and hubs were typically owned and operated by designated national firms. They acted both as operators of the transmission system and as wholesale traders, and were assigned responsibilities for the safeguarding of the critical functions. This included arrangements for capacity management and interconnections between different subsystems, based on bilateral contracts. These firms played the role of coordinating institutions in national and international gas systems (Arentsen and Künneke, 2003).

At first sight, this example provides no evidence as to whether alignment between technology and institutions is realized or not. For instance, for safeguarding the critical function of interconnection, how can the technological coordination of the system, realized by engaging specific sets of compressors and pipelines, be aligned with the institutional coordination through trade arrangements between national transmission and wholesale firms? The same ambiguity holds for capacity management: how can the technological coordination, realized through various physical storage facilities, be aligned with the institutional coordination of the same facilities, implemented by these firms? Based on what considerations can we determine whether alignment is realized or not? And if not, how to create or restore alignment such that expected services are provided? Answering these important questions is not straightforward. The fundamental problem is that we lack the appropriate understanding of the features that make compatible the technological and institutional coordination needed to secure critical functions such as those mentioned above. Features of coordination are addressed in different ways in engineering and institutional economics, and are scarcely related to each other. Our alignment framework takes up the challenge of bringing these two worlds together.

We approach this challenge from three angles. Building on Chapters 2 and 3, we relate alignment to three layers of analysis, designated by "structure," "governance," and "transactions" (Section 4.2). These are the three concepts through which the alignment issue is characterized in our framework. "Structure" is concerned with the interdependence between macro-institutions and technological architecture. For instance, which generic technological features and constitutive rules characterize the European gas transport network, and how do they contribute toward safeguarding the critical functions? "Governance" relates technological design to meso-institutions, framing alignment within the domain in which network infrastructures can operate, for example, gas transport in the Netherlands. Finally, "transactions" deals with the technological arrangements and organizational modalities for implementing expected services, such as the actual balancing of gas demand and supply through contractual agreements so that uninterrupted services are secured.

In Section 4.3, we go a step further and exemplify the characteristics of coordination operating within each dimension, the technological one and the institutional one. These are instrumental for determining the alignment between technological and institutional arrangements, which is needed to safeguard the critical functions. We are aware that alignment is a multifaceted phenomenon that can be specified in many different ways. Our framework focuses on the different coordination arrangements along the three layers just mentioned. We shall illustrate some of these multifaceted features of alignment through the example of the Dutch gas sector before and after its deregulation.

In Section 4.4, we analyze how alignment can be reached or restored. Again, we illustrate using the case of the Dutch gas sector, pointing out possible modalities of alignment or realignment related to the case of the so-called smart gas grids. Section 4.5 summarizes the main contributions of this chapter to our alignment framework.

4.2 Layers of Alignment: Analytical Approach

Chapters 2 and 3 identified three distinct layers, respectively, for the institutional and technological dimensions that are involved in safeguarding the critical functions. These chapters delineated features of network infrastructures along these different layers of analysis. Institutions were specified in terms of macro-, meso-, and micro-institutions. Technology was differentiated into architecture, technological design, and operation. Building on these categories, we now specify the horizontal interrelatedness between these layers. Within the generic layer, "structure" indicates the constitutive features through which the architecture and macro-institutions need to be aligned to fulfill the critical functions. "Governance" is related to the framing of the critical functions in a specific technological context and institutional domain. Finally, "transactions" refer to the organizational and operational modalities through which activities are planned, implemented, and monitored, in order to fulfill the critical functions and deliver expected services.

In the next sections, we elaborate on and illustrate the concepts of structure, governance, and transactions in more detail by addressing the two following issues.

- *The delineation of the horizontal alignment between technology and institutions.* We shall argue that the specification of the services provided by network infrastructures is an important criterion for delineating the three layers. We acknowledge that network infrastructures are purposefully designed to serve distinct objectives (Chapter 1). Hence, at each of these layers the provided services can be specified according to whether they are generic, context-specific, or operational. Accordingly, these different levels of abstraction can be associated with the different technological and institutional features of network infrastructures that characterize each layer, as shown in Chapters 2 and 3.
- *The specification of the critical functions.* Given the aforementioned socio-technological features at the three layers of analysis, we shall identify relevant entities and devices that in both dimensions, institutional and technological, are instrumental for safeguarding the critical functions according to societal expectations. For instance, at the generic layer, the interconnectivity of gas transport systems is

related to expectations about security of supply. Accordingly, institutional entities such as national gas network operators and technological devices such as international pipelines, storage facilities, and compressors and hubs are required to safeguard this critical function attuned to societal values.

By elaborating on these two issues, we shall be able to better specify the modalities of alignment between institutions and technology, so that the critical functions can be safeguarded and societal expectations can be met. Applied to the different layers of analysis, it will allow us to substantiate the three concepts of structure, governance, and transactions.

4.2.1 Structure

Network infrastructures are typically distinguished by the generic services they provide. Natural gas, electric power, rail transport, or drinking water are supplied by distinct socio-technological systems. They are characterized by typical technological architectures, embedded in the physical system and in the constitutive norms and rules that delineate and structure the domain of possible transactions. At this generic layer of analysis, the architecture is largely determined by the characteristics of the physical networks that interconnect complementary nodes and links. The macro-institutions are defined by the norms and rules embedded in entities and devices required to make the technological system operational and to provide the expected generic services.

Delineation of the Horizontal Alignment between Technology and Institutions

Applied to our example, the natural gas infrastructure is intended to provide this energy source to final customers for residential and industrial purposes. This requires a particular physical system and constitutive rules. Technologically, gas is exploited as a natural resource from fields that are only available at certain geographical locations. Considerable distances have to be bridged between the gas fields and the final customers. Long-distance transport is provided through high-pressure transmission pipelines (see Figure 4.1) or by the shipping of liquefied natural gas (LNG) (Glachant and Hallack, 2010). At a regional and local level, low-pressure distribution networks deliver natural gas to the final customers (Correljé, 2013). The institutional layout of the gas sector is largely determined by the rules that establish the rights for the exploration and exploitation of the natural resource, the access to transport and distribution pipelines, and the designation of what firms are allowed to sell and buy gas to whom. Typically, natural gas is perceived as a resource of national interest, generating significant revenues for the public sector as well as for private investors. As with most network infrastructures, the protection of national interests and public values is an important characteristic of the macro-institutions of this sector (Arentsen and Künneke, 2003).

This example illustrates that the identification of generic services, in this case the provision of natural gas, is instrumental for delineating the architecture and macro-institutions of a given network infrastructure. Obviously, generic services can be delimited in various ways, depending on the specificities of given network infrastructures or research interests. The example takes a very broad perspective by focusing on the provision of natural gas in the most general sense.

However, we might also focus on particular network infrastructures for which the provided services can be specified more in detail. For instance, we might be interested in the provision and transport of LNG. Technological devices are required to cool down natural gas to minus 162 degrees Celsius to liquefy it. Specific vessels are necessary for long-distance marine transport. At the place of destination, LNG terminals are needed to unload the vessels, store the LNG, and finally feed the re-gasified natural gas into the transportation and distribution networks. These technological features related to the provision of LNG are associated with specific macro-institutions. Among other things, the rights of ownership and use of these facilities need to be established so that the required technological processes can be economically implemented and safely operated at environmentally acceptable locations.

In a similar way, the provision of expected services can be related to a specific geographical area or country. The Dutch natural gas infrastructure, for instance, derives its specific technological architecture and its macro-institutions from specific historical developments. The Netherlands has a huge gas field in the northern part of the country near the city of Groningen. After its discovery in 1959, Dutch mining law had to be revised. The existing legislation dated back to 1810, a legal heritage from Napoleon who had invaded the country (Correljé,

Van der Linden, and Westerwoudt, 2003). These macro-institutions were not adapted to the mining of natural gas. Specifically, the rights and responsibilities for the exploration and commercial trading of oil and gas needed to be determined, including the allocation of benefits derived from this national natural resource. Also, the physical networks had to be developed, in order to be suitable for the production, transportation, and commercialization of natural gas in the Netherlands and abroad.

Specification of Critical Functions
The critical functions of system control, capacity management, interconnection and interoperability must be related specifically to the technological needs and institutional requirements resulting from the generic features implemented to operate a given network infrastructure according to societal expectations.

The safe provision of natural gas is a good illustration. Natural gas is burned in residential and industrial appliances and in power plants. The safety of such combustion processes largely depends on a constant and well-defined quality of gas. Accordingly, the appliances need to be strictly calibrated to this quality; otherwise, severe safety hazards may occur, including intoxication by carbon monoxide or destructive explosions. Hence, an important technological issue with respect to system control is to secure a constant quality of gas throughout the pipeline system. This also has consequences for interoperability and interconnection. Only pipeline systems with the same gas quality are interoperable and can be interconnected without jeopardizing safety. An important indicator for the gas quality is its calorific value, which indicates the energy that is released in the combustion process. For natural gas in northwestern Europe, there are roughly three different gas qualities: high-calorific gas, low-calorific gas, and the Dutch Groningen gas quality (Van der Wal, 2003). For each of these gas qualities, different gas networks have been established with differently calibrated gas appliances. Accordingly, the macro-institutions need to establish and allocate rights so that these safety hazards can be resolved according to expectations. This includes the assignment of rights to system operators for monitoring and controlling gas quality and the development of industry-wide norms and standards.

To summarize, "structure" refers to the devices and entities involved in the provision of generic services of network infrastructures. It refers to the constitutive features of the architecture and macro-institutions needed to safeguard the critical functions according to certain societal values and expectations.

4.2.2 Governance

At the intermediate layer of analysis, the interrelatedness between institutions and technology is determined by the framing of services in particular technological and institutional contexts. This is the layer within which the generic features of network infrastructures must be translated through entities and devices into specific arrangements necessary for implementing and monitoring the provision of services according to the needs expressed in a certain time and place.

Delineation of the Horizontal Alignment between Technology and Institutions
The Dutch gas system provides once more a nice illustration. Based on the adapted gas mining legislation established in 1962, specific meso-institutions were created to enable the exploitation of this natural resource. The formal concession for the gas field was granted to a private company, NAM (Nederlandse Aardolie Maatschappij), which was responsible for the actual exploitation of the resource. NAM is jointly owned (50:50) by Shell and Exxon (Correljé, Van der Linden, and Westerwoudt, 2003). However, the responsibility for financial exploitation was given to a public–private partnership between the Dutch state, and Shell and Exxon, the so-called *Maatschap Groningen* (Groningen Partnership). The private oil companies each owned 30% of this joint venture, and the Dutch state owned 40%. The responsibilities for the development of the transmission networks and the trade of gas were allocated to the energy network operator Gasunie, which was also constituted as a 50:50 public–private part-nership between the same above-mentioned parties.[1] These arrange-ments are characterized by institutional roles that vertically overlap. They combine the responsibilities of meso-institutions, namely, the regulation of the sector, and micro-institutions that are dedicated to

---

[1] As a consequence of the restructuring of the gas sector, the ownership of Gasunie changed in 2005, when it became the operator of the high-pressure transmission system, completely owned by the Dutch government. The commercial activities of gas trade were unbundled into a different company, GasTerra.

the operation of the gas system.[2] These typical meso-institutions were instrumental for the technological design of the Dutch gas sector. The private companies had the technical know-how for the exploitation of the gas fields and the creation and operation of the high-pressure gas networks. Indeed, the natural gas grid had to be developed by and large from scratch in the Netherlands. Regional city gas distribution systems existed, especially in large cities, and there were some connections between these grids. Nevertheless, city gas had a different physical composition, calorific value, and pressure than the Groningen gas. Hence, these gas systems had to be rebuilt, adapted to the new gas quality, and extended to reach additional users all over the country. Therefore, a new high-pressure transportation network had to be constructed to physically connect various distribution systems to the Groningen field. These requirements resulted in the creation of the unique technological design and set of meso-institutions for the Dutch gas sector, with ultimately some 98% of households connected to the gas grid.

Specification of Critical Functions
Whatever the network infrastructure at stake, safeguarding the critical functions is embedded in and framed by the meso-institutions and the technological design shaping the spatial and temporal context in which the network operates. Specific devices and entities are associated to related tasks, which also depend on context-specific societal expectations.

Historically, interconnection was an important critical function for the development of the Dutch gas transport system as part of the northwestern European gas system (Arentsen and Künneke, 2003). In the 1960s, it was expected that nuclear energy would become the dominant source of energy by the turn of the century, outcompeting fossil fuels such as natural gas. So the Dutch government and the oil companies planned to sell the gas reserves before that time by positioning the Netherlands as a major gas provider in the region, which required developing and interconnecting networks. This characterizes context-specific societal expectations. Gasunie was an important institutional entity for establishing and securing this interconnection. Being

[2] This phenomenon of overlapping institutional roles will be further developed in the case of the Singaporean drinking water system in Chapter 6.

a public–private partnership between the oil companies and the Dutch state, Gasunie was not only responsible for negotiating long-term contracts with neighboring countries, but it also took the lead in planning and building the necessary physical pipeline network. In that respect, Gasunie clearly accumulated the roles and functions usually assigned to meso- as well as micro-institutions.

Gasunie was also assigned to safeguard other critical functions. Monitoring and controlling the specific Groningen gas quality in the Dutch network is part of the critical function "system monitoring." Specific networks needed to be built, dedicated to this gas quality. In addition, blending stations were instrumental in converting high-calorific gas (H-gas) into Groningen gas by injecting nitrogen. These are examples of context-specific features of the technological design and meso-institutions of the Dutch gas sector, and the arrangements required to safeguard all four critical functions.

This example illustrates that "governance" represents an intermediate between the generic structure and the transactions required to provide the actual services. In conformity with what is developed in Chapter 2, this layer is a go-between. This position may partially explain some ambiguities in the status of Gasunie, operating as a meso-institution but also having the functions of a micro-institution.[3] The concept of governance reflects how the generic rules and technological features of network infrastructures are operationalized and translated into a specific technological design and meso-institutions, according to the contextual conditions and expectations. This allows us to specify the critical functions in the particular context illustrated above related to the issues of interconnection and system monitoring.

4.2.3 Transactions

At the operational layer of analysis, the horizontal interrelatedness between technology and institutions is determined by the actual provision of services to final customers. Taking this as our point of reference allows identifying operational arrangements and organizational modalities that are instrumental for implementing and monitoring transactions.

---

[3] Chapter 6 provides another example of a similar overlapping of functions.

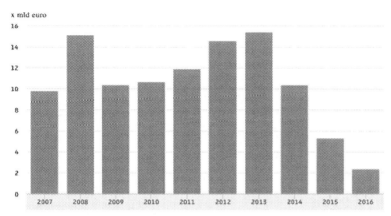

Figure 4.2 Dutch state revenues from the exploitation of natural gas (source: CBS, 2017; mld = billion)

Delineation of the Horizontal Alignment between Technology and Institutions

In the early days of the Dutch natural gas system, the public-private partnerships between the Dutch State, Exxon, and Shell did not only characterize important meso-institutions; they were also deeply involved in establishing necessary transactions to provide expected services. Indeed, *Gasunie* and *Maatschap Groningen* also served as important micro-institutions, facilitating the alignment between technology and institutions. *Gasunie* established and operated the gas transport networks. Incentives for the necessary investments and the operation of the Dutch gas grid were provided by the allocation and control over residual rents to *Maatschap Groningen*. Some 70% of the profits are collected by the Dutch State, leaving the remaining 30% to the private investors. These revenues are considerable. Only considering the Dutch State, it gained some 10–15 billion euros per year (see Figure 4.2). The revenues of the private partners are not publicly available but certainly substantial. *Gasunie* is similarly jointly owned by the same public and private partners, enabling them to articulate their priorities for the development of the gas grid. This has been instrumental for planning and establishing the required investments.

Recently the revenues have been declining. It indicates a significant change vis-à-vis the objectives of the operation of the Dutch gas network infrastructure. The gas exploitation caused considerable earthquakes in the northern part of the country. This raised significant safety and health concerns among the local population, resulting in changing societal values. Accordingly, the expected services are nowadays oriented toward a reduction of natural gas provision in favor of other energy sources, most prominently electricity. The Dutch has decided to shut down the huge Groningen gas field by 2030, indicating substantial change in the macro-institutional environment. The meso-institutions that will be responsible for monitoring the phase out natural gas are still under consideration. The resulting shift in the sources of energy will also requires changes in organizational modalities. Among others, different micro-institutions will be involved, like municipalities or cooperatives, considering different technological possibilities for substituting other energy sources to natural gas, including district heating or electric power.

Specification of Critical Functions

Taking the relation between institutions and technology at this operational level as a point of reference, we can now specify the arrangements that are needed to safeguard the critical functions according to societal expectations. The planning, implementation, and monitoring of transactions required to do so need to be specified with respect to particular technical operations and micro-institutions.

Once more, the Dutch gas sector is illustrative. Besides its functions as a meso-institution, Gasunie also plays the role of an important micro-institution in safeguarding the critical functions at the transactional level. This organizational entity is assigned to operate the high-pressure gas transportation network (Figure 4.3). This includes system control, such as implementing and monitoring the provision of different gas qualities with different calorific values. To technically safeguard this critical function, dedicated networks need to be installed and operated for each different gas quality. As shown in Figure 4.3, there are two major transport networks in the Netherlands, operated for Groningen gas and H-gas. They carry out technical operations at dedicated gas injection stations, storage facilities, and compression and export stations. Gasunie monitors and controls the access to the different networks, the feed-in of appropriate qualities of gas and the conditions of gas transport in the pipeline system.

Safeguarding the critical function of interconnection also imposes transactional requirements. For the conversion of H-gas to Groningen

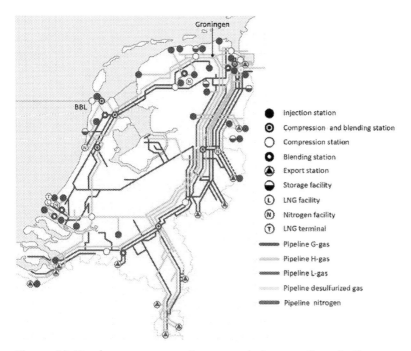

Figure 4.3 Dutch gas transportation network (source: Gasunie Transport Services, 2019)

gas quality, gas blending installations are operated by Gasunie. They make possible the interconnection of the H-gas network to the Groningen gas network at dedicated nodal points. Such blending stations represent a specific technical operation to safeguard the security of supply of Groningen gas quality. From an institutional perspective, this requires contractual arrangements between Gasunie and the suppliers of H-gas, which determine and control the conditions of access to the gas transport network.

Another example is related to the monitoring and control of the pipeline pressure needed to safely transport gas. This critical function of system control is standardized to a bandwidth of around 40 bar units of pressure for long-distance transport, and 8 bar units for local distribution networks. Such standardized pipeline pressure levels are typical of rules defined within the meso-institutional layer but which need to be implemented at the micro layer. The technical operation of specific pipeline pressures to meet these standards and secure this critical function is realized on the one hand by different compressor stations throughout the network, which are operated by Gasunie. On the other hand, the balancing regime requires traders and producers to feed in as much gas as they sell, within a certain period of time (De Bruijne et al., 2011).

The decision made in 2019 to shut down the Groningen gas field raises novel challenges for the technical operation of the Dutch gas system and the safeguarding of critical functions. For instance, a declining availability of Groningen gas needs to be compensated by an increasing import of H-gas. Without going into the details, this is related to all three layers of analysis: the structure and governance of the Dutch gas system as well as the actual transactions. From a technological perspective, this raises the question as to whether the Groningen gas network and all its connected appliances ultimately need to be converted to H-gas quality. Alternatively, the Groningen gas network could be maintained by converting H-gas into Groningen gas. This, however, requires an increased number of gas blending stations. Whatever the solution adopted, which largely depends on macro-institutional choices, the micro-institutions need to adapt to a different operation of the gas system. For instance, a complete conversion to H-gas requires a coordinated transition of all appliances and networks to the new gas quality, with new standards to be defined within the meso layer.

4.2.4 Intermediary Conclusion

In this section we specified the concept of alignment in two ways. First, we delineated each of the three layers of analysis where alignment is an issue. Structure is related to the architecture and macro-institutions that are required to provide the distinct generic services of network infrastructures. Governance represents the specific entities and devices that are necessary for implementing and monitoring the delivery of specific services at a certain time and in a certain place. Finally, transactions are concerned with the operational arrangements and organizational modalities through which the actual provision of services is implemented and monitored. These layers are mutually related to each other, depending on the specification of the provided services and the institutional and technological features needed to meet these goals. Figure 4.4 summarizes these interrelations, which we illustrated through the case of the Dutch gas sector.

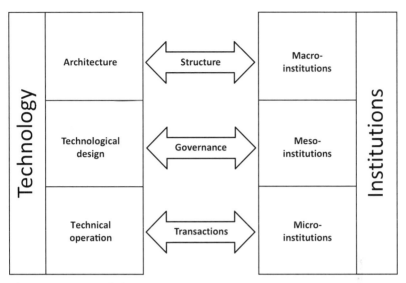

Figure 4.4 Layers of alignment

Second, we characterized the critical functions, also with illustrations from the Dutch natural gas sector, and we introduced considerations on the entities and devices that are required in both dimensions, institutional and technological, to safeguard these functions at each layer of alignment. However, one important question remains to be explored: how can we determine whether institutions and technology are aligned or not? We now turn to this question.

4.3 Multifaceted Features of Alignment: The Role of Vertical Coordination

As suggested in the previous section through the distinction between "structure," "governance," and "transactions," the modalities of alignment vary according to the different layers that characterize both institutions and technology. However, the existence of these strata raises a complementary issue: if we focus on each dimension separately, what are the modalities of coordination among the different components involved, say, the components characterizing operation, design, and architecture on the one hand; and the micro-, meso-, and macro-institutions on the other hand? More precisely, what are the characteristics of coordination on each side that need to be aligned? In this context, coordination refers to the requirements imposed by the complementarities between nodes and links that are at the core of network infrastructures, and that are distinct depending on whether we look at the technological side or the institutional side. Notwithstanding the differences between these two dimensions, the goal is to identify characteristics of coordination that are relevant on each side, and that must be compatible if alignment is to be reached and the critical functions safeguarded. As indicated in the introduction to this chapter, determining which modalities of coordination are relevant for both the technological and institutional dimensions is not straightforward. In what follows, we take advantage of contributions from control systems engineering to make steps in this direction.

4.3.1 A Control Systems Engineering Approach

From an institutional perspective, coordination typically relates to the allocation of rights and responsibilities and their implementation through institutional entities and transactional relations. For instance, with respect to safeguarding the critical functions in gas network infrastructures, the question would be whether the gas quality can be secured by competitive market arrangements, self-regulation, or legally established norms and standards, or various combinations of these solutions. The technological approach is different. Engineers are usually interested in establishing and monitoring relations between technical devices that are needed to safeguard the critical functions. The control systems engineering representation provided by Figure 4.5 is illustrative of this approach.

The point of reference underlying this figure is a technological process that needs to satisfy certain requirements and is influenced by external disturbances. Technological devices and entities are configured in a feedback loop, which attempts to continuously monitor and adapt the technological process. Transport of gas through pipelines is an example of a technical process that needs to meet certain functional, safety, and quality standards, such as the Groningen gas calorific value (reference value). This might be disturbed (external disturbances) by the inflow of gas from different sources, including green (sustainable) gas produced by local farmers, or H-gas that is not properly blended to satisfy the required standard. Hence, a technological device is needed to monitor the actual gas quality (meter). Data need to be compared

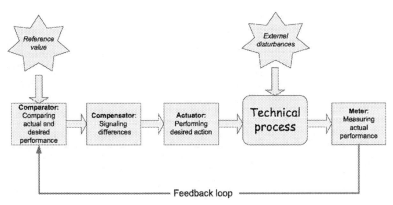

Figure 4.5 Control systems engineering approach to the safeguarding of critical functions (adapted from Dutton, Thompson, and Barraclough, 1997: 3)

with the standardized calorific value (comparator). Possible differences are signaled (compensator), and appropriate actions are taken if necessary (actuator). This includes shutting down entry points which do not meet the required quality or readjustment of gas blending processes. These processes might be fully automated by embedded technological control centers, intervening according to predefined conditions. But ultimately, institutional entities are also involved, such as system operators with assigned rights and responsibilities for safeguarding critical functions using dedicated technological devices.

The challenge is to connect these two different approaches of technological and institutional coordination. How can we identify the relevant characteristics that apply to both domains and are of importance for the safeguarding of the critical functions? Identifying such common denominators can be based on various theoretical and empirical considerations, depending on the specifics of different network infrastructures or research interests! For instance, referring to network theory, the features of social and technical networks could be compared in terms of connectivity or centrality of nodal points (Economides, 1996; Barabasi, 2003). As another example, a typical systems engineering approach applies a top-down approach in which systems are broken down into subsystems, assemblies, and components (Faulconbridge and Ryan, 2014). However, such theories are typically insufficiently equipped to bridge the gap between institutions and technology, an issue already addressed in Chapter 1 (Sections 1.3 and 1.4).

Taking our "framework" as the point of reference, we can identify at least three lines of reasoning along which to explore this issue of compatibility between the modalities of coordination reciprocally characterizing the technological and institutional dimensions, thus determining the conditions of their alignment. First, we have already asserted that network infrastructures are made up of complementary nodes and links (Chapter 1). Hence, in order to assess alignment, we need to look at the modalities of coordination defined differently on each side that can secure this complementarity. Section 4.3.2 elaborates on the trade-off between centralized versus decentralized, and open versus closed modalities of coordination. Second, in Section 4.3.3 we investigate some characteristics and impacts of the spatial aspect of coordination. The argument is that alignment can be realized only if modalities of coordination are compatible with the geographical scope defining and delineating the network infrastructure at stake. Third, in Section 4.3.4 we take into consideration the fact that safeguarding the critical functions also relates to a time dimension, which is based on technological as well as social considerations and imposes specific constraints on the modalities of coordination. In all cases, what is at stake is the possibility of alignment between institutions and technology, and the resulting capacity (or not) to satisfy the critical functions.

4.3.2 Modalities of Coordination: Two Major Trade-Offs

As already mentioned, modalities of coordination are related to the way in which the required complementarity between nodes and links is established. In the following sections, we develop two important trade-offs among modalities of coordination that are instrumental for determining (mis)alignment between institutions and technology.

Centralized Versus Decentralized Coordination

Nowadays, the degree of centralization or decentralization is an important topic in many network infrastructures, including electric power (Beerman and Tews, 2016; Funcke and Bauknecht, 2016). More generally, centralized and decentralized modalities of coordination could be related to the uniqueness of entities and devices needed for safeguarding the critical functions (Hines and Blumsack, 2008). Centralized arrangements refer to a small number or even unique devices and entities delivering the required tasks, whereas decentralized arrangements entail a variety of alternatives that are available and used in different parts or components of network infrastructures to achieve that goal.

In our example of reference, the Dutch gas sector has for a long time relied on centralized modalities of coordination, on both the technological and on the institutional sides. Indeed, Gasunie was the central institutional entity in charge of the development and operation of the Dutch gas system. On the side of technology, significant functionalities are provided at the level of the high-pressure transport network, performed by dedicated devices. This includes the connection to a limited number of production points, gas blending installations, and compressor stations (see Figure 4.3). From the perspective of control systems engineering, the operation of the high-pressure transport network represents the single most relevant production process for safeguarding the critical functions. Hence, significant rights and responsibilities are centralized in a single institutional entity (i.e., Gasunie). A limited number of technological devices are centrally operated at the level of the gas transmission network. This indicates a tight alignment between the centralized technological as well as the institutional modalities of coordination.

However, this alignment has been distorted by the deregulation of the gas sector at the turn of this century. More recently, policies in favor of sustainable energy sources stimulated the provision of green gases, including bio-methane derived from agricultural residuals or landfill sites. As a consequence, the diversity of gas sources increased. Typically, bio-methane is produced in comparatively small quantities, for instance by farmers. They are located close to end-consumers and are directly connected to gas distribution networks. This has significant repercussions for the coordination of complementary components and tasks in the gas sector. Presently, these decentralized facilities can only be operated as long as they do not produce more gas than can be absorbed in the local distribution networks. This is due to the fact that under the present technical conditions, gas can only be provided in a one-way direction from the natural gas fields to the final consumers. In the case of a local surplus of green gas, it would be necessary either to store this gas locally, or feed it into the high-pressure network and deliver it to locations where it is needed. However, the required bi-directional technical functions to do so are presently not available at the interconnection of the transmission and distribution networks. So far, there is no proper assignment of distribution network operations needed to provide these facilities. Gasunie is the only designated entity in charge of safeguarding the critical functions, for instance interconnection or interoperability, and it does so only at the level of high-pressure transport networks. This indicates a growing misalignment between the centralized institutions that have been implemented to safeguard the critical functions, and the development of decentralized technical devices for the provision of gas. We elaborate on this example in more detail in Section 4.3.3.

Open and Closed Coordination

Our second example for assessing the alignment between technological and institutional coordination can be understood as closed versus open modalities of alignment.[4] Closed arrangements completely prescribe the institutional as well as technological entities and devices admissible for safeguarding the critical functions. In terms of the control systems engineering approach, all technological devices and their functions are predetermined; the same holds for the rights and responsibilities of the institutional entities. The Dutch gas sector prior to liberalization illustrates a set of closed arrangements. Critical functions had to be safeguarded by Gasunie, relying on predetermined technological devices, including blending stations and the Groningen gas field. This combination of an institutional arrangement (the role of Gasunie) and the predetermined technical devices provided the required alignment.

Open arrangements differ from closed ones in that they only specify the general conditions under which the critical functions should be safeguarded. There is room for specific arrangements, depending on situational circumstances. The internet is an interesting example in this respect. The critical function of system control essentially relies on general rules, such as the TCP/IP protocol standards. The TCP/IP standards specify how information packages are transmitted and addressed throughout the web. Given these general technological and institutional requirements, network providers can decide how they wish to utilize the capacity of their network. Typically, the allocation of network capacity is based on various institutional arrangements

---

[4] Contrasting open versus closed modalities takes its inspiration from North, Wallis, and Weingast (2009).

such as peer-to-peer contracts that specify the terms and conditions of use. Technological entities for system management include a broad spectrum of different routers that meet the general technological requirements. This indicates how alignment between institutional and technological arrangements operates under conditions of openness.

4.3.3 Spatial Coordination: Geographical Delineation of a Network

Considering the spatial aspect of network infrastructures offers one more possibility for characterizing another facet of technological and institutional coordination as a condition for reaching proper alignment between institutions and technology. Indeed, there is a geographical dimension to the safeguarding of the critical functions (Künneke, Groenewegen, and Ménard, 2010). The example of the European railway system, discussed in Chapter 3, is illustrative in this respect. Throughout Europe, the technological features of rail systems differ with respect to gauge width, safety systems, electrification standards, and signaling systems (European Commission, 2008: 16). As a consequence, the interoperability of trains on long-distance trajectories is restricted by such national or regional technological specificities (see Figure 3.3). However, the EU applies legislation to promote the interoperability in favor of the integration of European rail systems. For this purpose, an institutional entity has been established, the European Railway Agency (ERA). The resulting arrangement reveals geographical misalignment. The technological coordination of rail transport is geographically delineated by different national or regional specificities. However, the institutional coordination is oriented toward an integration of European rail transport systems across different national and regional boundaries.

4.3.4 Time as a Coordination Issue

Finally, there can be a time dimension that imposes constraints and limitations of its own on the modalities of coordination, thus contributing to shape conditions of alignment between institutions and technology. For instance, in drinking water systems, health-threatening bacteria need to be detected and eliminated within a very short time frame; otherwise, their dissemination might have major implications for public health. In the electricity sector, the demand and supply of power needs to be balanced continuously; otherwise, blackouts occur. Alignment is realized if appropriate arrangements on both the technological and institutional sides are able to meet the time constraints and requirements – in these examples short-term ones – needed to safeguard the critical functions.

Temporal requirements might also shape long-term coordination issues. As indicated in Section 4.2.3, the Dutch government plans to close down the Groningen gas field by 2030, which raises novel challenges for the organization and technological operation of the Dutch gas grid. Two issues in particular matter in this context. First, alignment needs to be established within this given time frame. By 2030, the Dutch gas system needs to be either completely converted to H-gas quality, or sufficient blending capacity needs to be available for the conversion of H-gas to Groningen gas quality. Both are characterized by different technological and institutional features. Second, the necessary adaptation of institutional as well as technological coordination has to be closely harmonized. For instance, if the Groningen gas quality is to be maintained in the Netherlands, the construction of additional blending stations needs to be planned so that they are operational when the gas field is closed down. This illustrates the temporal requirements of coordination needed to realize alignment between technology and institutions.

4.3.5 Intermediate Conclusion

The different aspects of coordination developed in Sections 4.3.3 and 4.4.4 illustrate the multifaceted features of alignment. They also suggest that alignment can be reached and/or consolidated in many different ways. There is no single answer to the issue of which characteristics must be satisfied to make technological and institutional coordination compatible, thus allowing alignment between the two dimensions. What our framework and its supportive concepts allow is to identify universal and possibly interrelated factors, for example, time, space, proximity, centralization, that make possible or hamper alignment. Making these different tools operational depends on the specific network infrastructure to be analyzed and/or on what the researcher is looking for! It means that when it comes to empirical studies, the issue of alignment needs to be narrowed down to the specific technological and institutional features associated with a specific network infrastructure and to the specific characteristics of the critical functions to be safeguarded. Part II of this book will do precisely that. However, before developing this empirical exploration through different network infrastructures, there is one more question to be addressed in this chapter: how is alignment reached or reestablished?

4.4 Reaching or Reestablishing Alignment

Ultimately, our interest in exploring the institutional and technological dimensions from the perspective of their alignment is to pinpoint *how* alignment is reached or restored, so as to deliver expected services under the most adequate conditions; that is, conditions securing the critical functions and the performance of the network. Identifying these modalities of alignment builds on insights from the previous sections. Considering different characteristics of coordination on both the technological and institutional sides, as we did in Section 4.3, provides ways to explore *how* alignment can be reached or restored.

4.4.1 How to Establish Alignment

In Section 4.3, we identified different characteristics of coordination that are instrumental for assessing the alignment between the technological and institutional arrangements that condition the safeguarding of the critical functions. To establish alignment, we showed through discussion and different examples that the complementary nature of components of network infrastructures requires compatible technical and institutional modalities of coordination. If, for instance, technological devices were coordinated in a completely different way compared with the corresponding institutional ones, the interrelations between nodes and links would not be supportive of the accomplishment of tasks needed to secure the critical functions and deliver expected services.

The Dutch gas system once more provides a relevant example. As a consequence of deregulation, the geographical scope of coordination is differently delineated for institutions compared with technology. Macro-institutions have made room for decentralized and small-scale provision of green gas, encompassing both high-pressure transport and low-pressure local distribution networks. However, the technological architecture of the Dutch gas system only supports coordination at the level of high-pressure transport networks, serving the needs of large-scale provision of gas. Hence, macro-institutions have to encompass a wider geographical scope of coordination, which includes transportation and distribution networks. As outlined above, the critical functions of interconnection and interconnectivity are not effectively coordinated under these new conditions. The result is that the feeding-in of green gas is currently restricted. Besides the resulting misalignment, this situation challenges the decisions made within the macro-institutional layer.

Such misalignment raises the question of how to possibly reestablish alignment. One solution would be to switch to different technology/technologies better suited to the institutional decentralization promoted by policy makers and simultaneously compatible with the broader geographical scope of the network. However, this requires a fundamentally different technological architecture of the gas system, resulting in novel technical design and operations. Without going too much into the details, we would like to illustrate this issue with the currently much debated case of the development of so-called smart gas grids.

4.4.2 Restoring Alignment: The Case of Smart Gas Grids

Smart grids refer to local low-pressure networks that provide energy from sources situated close to the final consumers and supported by advanced ICT technologies for the data exchange, monitoring, and control of the provision and consumption of energy. Figure 4.6 represents such a technological setting. An important technological feature of smart grids with respect to the architecture of the network is that they allow a bi-directional provision of gas: from high-pressure transmission to low-pressure local grids, and vice versa. At the so-called city gate station, gas can be supplied through the transport grid by reducing the pipeline pressure from 40 bar to 8 bar, which is used at the local level. In return, a possible surplus of locally produced gas can be compressed from 8 bar up to 40 bar and thus injected into the national transport system. This contributes to capacity management at the local level. As stated in Section 4.4.1, in the Netherlands such bi-directional gas flows are technologically not yet facilitated. The coordination of the complementary devices that characterize the Dutch gas system only

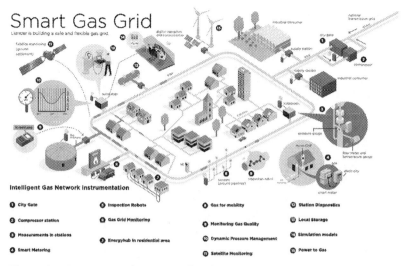

Figure 4.6 Smart gas grid (source: Alliander Network Company, @loekwijts.nl)

allows for one-directional delivery of gas, from the transport network to the distribution grid. Very simply speaking, the existing compressor systems do not support reversibility. Achieving that goal would require investment in reverse flow loops with compressors, as shown in Figure 4.6.

The context-specific technological design of smart grids is related to local conditions, such as the availability of gas production sites and the consumption profiles of households and industry. Figure 4.6 depicts a commercial greenhouse as a possible industrial consumer. Households might be able to interchange the use of gas and electricity as alternatives energy sources, for instance, for heating and cooking. Gas could even be used for mobility, as fuel for cars. Some details of the technical operations of smart grids are illustrated in this figure; for instance, monitoring gas quality, station diagnostics to ensure sufficient pressure in the system, operation of compressor stations, and various other metering and monitoring devices.

How should alignment issues raised by the development of such smart grids be resolved? With respect to the structure's layer, rights and responsibilities would need to be reallocated in order to safeguard the critical functions, not only for the operator of the high-pressure transport network, but also for the various distribution operators in charge of local networks. This suggests that decentralization is required, causing macro-institutions to be realigned with the technological architecture of smart grids.

With respect to governance, meso-institutions must specify guidelines and protocols for the implementation of the rights and responsibilities of distribution network operators vis-à-vis the national grid operator on the one hand, and local consumers and producers on the other hand. Among other aspects, there is a need to clarify who is ultimately responsible for safeguarding the critical functions in local gas grids and the national transport network, and to what degree there is a requirement for mutual assistance. For instance, in the case of regional problems regarding gas quality, is this to be resolved by the distribution network operator only, or should the national grid operator be committed to intervene? Mutual interventions would suggest the adoption of a decentralized governance of smart grids. The entire allocation of responsibilities to the distribution network operators would indicate the transfer of centralized coordination to the local level. The decentralized technological coordination of smart grids might then show a misalignment with the existing centralized institutional coordination arrangements.

Finally, with respect to the layer of transactions, the actual planning and delivery of services is closely related to the technical operation of the local distribution network. For instance, safeguarding gas quality could be technically performed at the different production sites and its responsibility institutionally allocated to the gas producers. However, if monitoring and control of these obligations is centralized in the hands of the company in charge of the network, while securing quality is decentralized, this could result in potential misalignment.

This example of the introduction of smart grids in the gas sector and the changes it would require on both the technological and institutional sides illustrate how our framework can be operationalized, providing tools to identify potential sources of misalignment and to explore modalities for reaching or reestablishing alignment.

4.5 Conclusion

This chapter assessed factors of alignment between institutions and the technology of network infrastructures, and how to reach or restore alignment. It is an ambitious endeavor. At first sight, technology and institutions appear to be two worlds apart, dealing with different aspects of the functioning of these complex socio-technological systems. Institutions are related to the definition and modalities of the allocation of rules and rights. Technology is concerned with devices, procedures, and tools implemented through interrelated nodes and links. We took up this challenge of bringing together these "two worlds apart" in three steps.

First, we specified how technology and institutions are interrelated at the three layers of analysis identified in Chapters 2 and 3. Within the generic layer, "structure" indicates the constitutive features through which the architecture and macro-institutions need to be aligned to provide expected services and fulfill the critical functions. "Governance" relates to the framing of the critical functions in a specific technological context and institutional setting, a framing required for the provision of context-specific services. Finally, the "transactions" layer refers to organizational and operational arrangements through which the critical functions are planned, implemented, and monitored, in order to actually deliver expected services to final customers. By connecting these three layers of analysis with the services to be provided, we were able to identify the conditions to be met within each layer in order for the critical functions to be safeguarded.

Second, we focused on characterizing different problems of coordination that develop either within the technological dimension, or within the institutional dimension. Our underlying argument was that modalities of coordination adopted to solve these problems may partially differ, regardless of whether we are considering the technological side or the institutional side, but that they ultimately need to share compatible characteristics if alignment is to be reached and the critical functions satisfied. From that perspective, we focused on specific characteristics of coordination that we consider as playing a key role, ultimately determining the conditions of alignment. These characteristics relate to modalities of coordination, spatial scope, and time horizon. In order to illustrate, add flesh to the bones of our analysis, and show the relevance and usefulness of our framework, we systematically referred to the Dutch gas sector and the profound changes it is facing. We are aware that focusing on these facets of coordination and, finally, on the alignment issue is highly selective. Other variables involved in

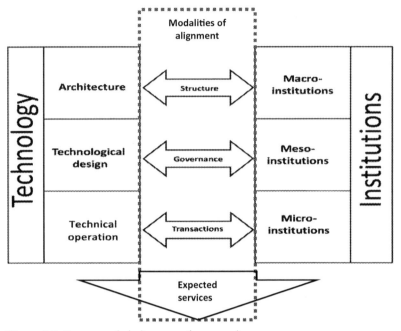

Figure 4.7 Our extended alignment framework

coordination and alignment could also be considered, depending on the specific aspects of a given network infrastructure and/or the focus of interest of a specific research project. In that respect, we followed Ostrom (2005), who considered that a framework can be specified in many different ways. Our goal has been to identify components of coordination and relations among these components that have a sufficient level of generality to provide relevant tools for an in-depth analysis of alignment between institutions and technology for a whole set of network infrastructures.

Third, we went further in using our framework to provide indications as to how alignment can be reached or reestablished at the three layers we have identified when disturbances of different orders challenge the existing arrangements. Again, we referred to the Dutch gas sector to illustrate and dig deeper into this issue.

Figure 4.7 summarizes some of the many aspects that were developed in this chapter and which enrich our initial alignment framework.

In the coming chapters, this framework will be implemented more extensively through a more detailed exploration of empirical cases. The coming chapters thus focus on different network infrastructures and different layers of analysis, raising different issues of alignment in line with what has been discussed here.

PART II

Empirical Explorations

A theory needs validation: its relevance depends on its extension; that is, its capacity to cover the largest possible set of facts it intends to capture; and its comprehensiveness, that is, its capacity to give sense to complex observations without discarding non-fitting facts (Canguilhem, 2019: 505). Validation can take many different forms, from a mathematical demonstration to experiments, econometric tests, etc. Because our framework has not so far reached the level of a formalized model, we rely on a modest approach, based on extensive case studies. However, in order to substantiate its relevance as far as possible, we explored very different cases, commanding partially different approaches. The resulting empirical explorations submitted hereafter intend to show (1) the usefulness and adaptability of our framework when applied to substantially different cases, showing its extension; and (2) its capacity to provide relevant insights into complex and diversified sets of facts, showing its comprehensiveness.

Chapter 5 develops the case of the transition toward sustainable electricity systems. It explores problems of alignment at the most generic layer of our framework, investigating the interdependence between the technological architecture and macro-institutions in the context of the development of sustainable energy sources. Chapter 6 focuses on issues of governance, linking meso-institutions and technological design. Through a detailed analysis of a spectacular example of an urban water and wastewater system, it examines how the implementation of decisions by policy makers led to the introduction of technologies that generated problems of alignment in the existing mode of governance. Chapter 7 deals with the ongoing revolution in passenger transportation systems with the development of automated and self-driving vehicles. It pays particular attention to the challenges it raises, particularly with respect to the organization of transactions in a way that can secure the alignment between micro-institutions and the requirements to make the technology operational.

Chapter 8 summarizes the pieces assembled through the entire book with the aim of answering the core question that has motivated our investigation: what features can align the institutional and technological dimensions of network infrastructures, in order to obtain performance that meets societal expectations? The chapter indicates how the conceptual foundations of our framework and the variety of empirical cases developed also provide guidance for public policy as well as for private sector initiatives.

The rich empirical cases developed in this Part II lead to the conclusion that our alignment framework can encompass many different types of network infrastructures that face substantially different challenges. Besides supporting the empirical relevance and usefulness of the framework when it comes to understanding "real world" situations, our analysis also enriches the theoretical perspective on network infrastructures by refining the concepts and simultaneously pointing out paths for future research.

5 | Structures
Unraveling the Energy Transition

5.1 Introduction

The transition toward sustainable energy systems is one of the major contemporary challenges worldwide. The 2015 Paris Agreement on climate change, negotiated by 196 countries, clearly demonstrates this. The agreement emphasizes the need for CO_2 reductions, in order to deal with global climate change and to keep a further increase in global temperature below an estimated 2 degrees Celsius target. Energy provision needs to be fundamentally revised in order to realize this ambitious objective. Polluting fossil fuels such as coal, natural gas, and oil are to be replaced by sustainable energy sources, including wind, solar, and bioenergy. This requires structural technological and institutional changes in energy systems, often referred to as the energy transition. Currently, the energy transition is most significant in the electricity sector. In the past century, electricity has been typically produced by large-scale fossil fuel power plants. To realize the ambitions of the Paris Agreement, the share of fossil fuel power plants needs to decline significantly in favor of clean power generation technologies based on wind, solar, and other renewables. A scenario of the International Renewable Energy Agency (IRENA, 2018) illustrates the need to increasingly rely on such clean energy sources (Figure 5.1).[1]

The energy transition requires fundamental technological and socio-economic changes in the energy sector that are not widely understood. We illustrate in this chapter how our alignment framework helps to unravel the complex interdependencies between institutions and technologies that are typical for such transition processes. This offers novel perspectives on how to safeguard critical functions of future sustainable energy systems. We focus on the layer of structures, since this provides a vivid illustration of how fundamental changes in network

---

[1] This refers to a report by IRENA's REmap program (IRENA, 2018: 18).

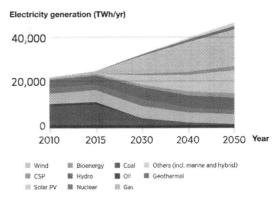

Figure 5.1 Deployment of renewable energy sources required to meet Paris climate objectives (source: IRENA, 2018: 24)

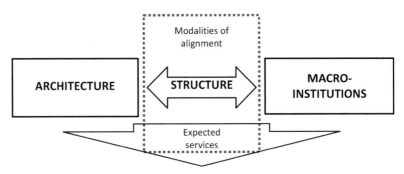

Figure 5.2 Alignment between architecture and macro-institutions: structure (layer 1)

infrastructures, such as the electricity sector, are related to the alignment between macro-institutions and architecture (Figure 5.2).

The following section (Section 5.2) outlines some remarkable socio-economic and technological developments that coincided with the energy transition. This results in the identification of three archetypes of electricity infrastructures – traditional, contemporary, and future power systems – that can be used to characterize the energy transition. Each of these archetypes is delineated through its typical architectures and macro-institutions, and is analyzed from our alignment perspective. In Section 5.3, we argue that traditional energy systems are characterized by the alignment between their architecture and macro-institutions. However, in contemporary power systems (Section 5.4) misalignment occurs, which poses major challenges for safeguarding critical functions and providing expected services. Finally, the structural alignment of future energy systems (Section 5.5) is described and analyzed from a more general perspective, identifying challenges for future alignment research. Section 5.6 draws conclusions and reflects on the lessons learned.

5.2 Energy Transition

The energy transition is taking place in the context of significant socio-economic and technological changes in the power sector. This includes the worldwide trend in the restructuring of electricity sectors, providing opportunities for competition and private sector involvement. In addition, remarkable technological innovations in the fields of digitalization and sustainable power technologies have created novel possibilities for the provision of electricity. These developments are permeated by changing societal values in favor of sustainability. The 1987 report by the World Commission on Environment and Development (WCED, 1987), the Brundtland Commission, and the aforementioned 2015 Paris Agreement on climate change are all important milestones in this respect. Both the restructuring of the electricity sectors and technological innovations provide opportunities for a fundamental reorientation of this sector in favor of sustainability.

5.2.1 Restructuring of Electricity Sectors

Starting in the 1990s, electricity systems are increasingly being restructured on a worldwide scale in favor of competition and private sector initiatives (International Energy Agency, 2017: 16). This is being substantiated in many different ways, depending on local economic, political, and technological circumstances. Without going into the details, two extreme setups can operate at either end of a range of possibilities. At the most basic level, independent power providers are allowed to build and operate power plants and offer their output to a single (national or regional) buyer. This enables competition between large-scale power producers, while other parts of the power sector remain vertically integrated and monopolistic. At the other end of the spectrum, competition is realized through a wide range of commercialized economic services related to the production and trade of power. Under these conditions of so-called retail competition, network services are considered natural monopolies that require regulation, in order to assure non-discriminatory access and reasonable pricing, providing a level playing field for competing commercial services.

Under the conditions of retail competition in particular, this restructuring provides incentives for adjusting the provision of energy according to changing societal expectations and values. Offering sustainable "green" energy in competitive markets increasingly provides advantages vis-à-vis "grey" fossil fuel power generators (Brunekreeft, Buchmann, and Meyer, 2016), since it serves changing societal values. Consumers can even get directly involved in the provision of sustainable energy, for instance as members of energy communities. Such energy communities invest in small-scale sustainable energy production, such as wind turbines, and operate them for the benefit of their local members. European countries such as Germany, Denmark, and the United Kingdom have witnessed the growing importance of local energy communities in the provision of electric power (Yildiz et al., 2015; Bauwens, Gotchev, and Holstenkamp, 2016; Kooij et al., 2018). Even individual households can acquire and operate solar panels, making them "prosumers," that is, combined producers and consumers of electricity (Wolsink, 2018). These developments are supported by fundamental technological innovations.

5.2.2 Technological Innovations

From our alignment perspective, two technological advancements are of special interest. First, advances in the digitalization of the power sector, building on innovations in information and communication technology (ICT). This has been instrumental in integrating technological devices for monitoring and control into energy systems. This opens a broad range of new applications and services in the energy sector, often referred to as "smart" technologies (Royal Academy of Engineering, 2012). For instance, smart energy grids, as illustrated in Chapter 4 (Section 4.4.2) through the case of local gas networks, are good examples in this respect. ICT-based devices are instrumental in monitoring and controlling the provision and retraction of power from the networks. This is especially useful and necessary in systems with an increasing number of small-scale power production devices, operated by energy communities (e.g., wind turbines) or even individual

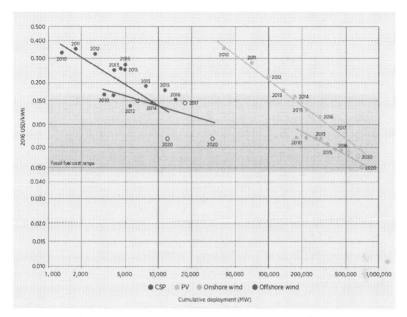

Figure 5.3 Indexed cost reductions in intermittent energy technologies (source: IRENA, 2018: 53)
CSP, concentrated solar power (large-scale); PV, photovoltaic (solar) cells (small-scale); offshore wind (large-scale); onshore wind (small-scale).

households (e.g., solar panels on residential houses). Consequently, these smart technologies facilitate stronger consumer engagement in the provision of sustainable electric power (Xenias et al., 2015) and serve changing societal values. As another example, smart residential power meters offer possibilities for demand response and flexible power pricing. Depending on the temporal availability of sustainable energy, smart meters are instrumental in introducing variable power prices, and hence stimulate consumers to adjust their power consumption according to the variability of intermittent electricity supply.

Second, innovations in sustainable power production technologies have contributed to significant cost reductions in the past decade. Figure 5.3 shows that the levelized costs of energy for wind and solar power, both large and small scale, are becoming more competitive compared with the costs of traditional fossil fuel power plants. This supports the ongoing decentralization of energy provision, with onshore wind and photovoltaic (solar) cells as the most prominent examples. These small-scale devices provide electric power close to the end consumers, typically connected to the low-voltage network. This implies different power flows. In traditional power systems, large-scale power plants are connected to high-voltage networks, delivering energy in a one-way direction to final consumers. However, in decentralized systems, power is provided on both voltage levels, that is, high voltage and low voltage. Hence, electric energy potentially flows in both directions: from high voltage to low voltage and vice versa. This can be enabled using the above-mentioned smart grid technologies. Such technological innovations are required to facilitate the energy transition, which is illustrated by the three archetypes of energy systems.

5.2.3 Three Archetypes of Energy Systems

The distinction made between three archetypes of energy systems is mainly based on the share of sustainable energy sources in the provision of electricity, and its implication for the technical functioning of power systems.[2] Unlike fossil fuel, typical sustainable energy sources such as wind and solar are not continuously available, but fluctuate depending on meteorological and seasonal conditions.[3] In technical terms, they are intermittent or "non-dispatchable;" that is, they cannot be adjusted to fluctuating demand patterns. Whereas traditional power systems are technically balanced by continuously ramping up or down fossil fuel power plants, the use of renewable energy sources requires a fundamentally different approach. Dealing with intermittent power supply, while meeting societal expectations of uninterrupted availability of electricity, is an important challenge for contemporary and future energy systems.

Traditional Energy Systems
Traditional electricity infrastructures rely almost entirely on fossil fuel as their primary energy source. Fossil fuels such as oil, gas, and coal

---

[2] The archetypes build on different phases of the evolution of sustainable energy systems, identified by the International Energy Agency (2018: 17).

[3] Some renewable energy sources are dispatchable, including hydroelectricity, concentrated solar power, biomass, and geothermal power. However, these dispatchable renewable energy sources are only available to a limited degree. In this chapter, we focus on renewable variable energy sources such as wind and power that are not continuously available. They are often referred to as intermittent energy sources.

can easily be stored and hence are continuously available for firing power production plants. Consequently, the technical balancing of traditional power systems is realized by adjusting the power production to the fluctuating demand patterns. Under such circumstances, even a minor share of intermittent renewable energy supply could be absorbed by the existing fossil fuel power plants. This has no major consequences for the features of traditional power systems.

Contemporary Energy Systems

In many contemporary energy systems, the share of renewable energy sources has increased to such an extent that adjustments are required to provide expected services. Intermittency causes significant swings in the provision of electric power. The power system needs to deal with a high degree of uncertainty in balancing power demand and supply. This requires novel types of system flexibility, including the previously mentioned demand response or smart grid technologies. These issues are further amplified when renewable energy sources become the dominant source of energy supply, sometimes covering the entire demand. Under these conditions, system stability is an important challenge. This relates to the abilities of power systems to withstand short-term disturbances, such as the failure of a large generator or the breakdown of a major high-voltage transmission line. Traditional fossil fuel power systems are characterized by strong system inertia,[4] caused by large rotating generators of fossil fuel power plants. This stabilizing effect is absent in systems with a high degree of renewable energy sources (International Energy Agency, 2018: 19).

Future Energy Systems

In future energy systems, renewable energy sources are expected to be massively employed, so that structural surpluses in energy production occur during periods of favorable meteorological conditions. The provision of power might even completely rely on renewable energy sources. This causes structural problems with regard to seasonal

---

[4] "The term inertia refers to the kinetic energy stored in the rotating mass connected to the generators of large thermal power plants. This rotating mass serves as a type of short-term energy storage. If there is a shortfall in power, generators will experience this as force acting against their rotation. The combined inertia of the power plants on the system will act against this, keeping the grid stable." (International Energy Agency, 2018: 19).

imbalances between the supply and demand of electricity. This goes beyond the capabilities of demand response and short-term storage that can be achieved by contemporary energy systems. It requires innovative technologies for long-term storage of electricity, for instance, by converting power into hydrogen or heat.

Thus, the three archetypes are now characterized according to our alignment framework, with a clear focus on the structural layer. In the course of the energy transition, we expect significant differences to emerge between their architectures and macro-institutions, as well as problems of alignment between the institutional and technological coordination arrangements needed to provide expected services and safeguard the critical functions.

5.3 Structural Alignment of Traditional Electricity Systems

In this section, we demonstrate that the structure of traditional electricity systems is characterized by an appropriate alignment between institutions and technology.

5.3.1 Architecture

Architecture is typified by three features: the generic services provided to final consumers, the constitutive material components, and the basic technological arrangements for providing generic services and safeguarding critical functions (Chapter 3, Section 3.3.1). Figure 5.4 illustrates the architecture of traditional power systems, designed to reliably provide electricity to final consumers.[5] Given this generic purpose, the constitutive material components include power generation plants, transmission lines, and distribution grids. The basic technological arrangements of a traditional system are characterized by the fact that electric power is delivered in a one-way direction from large-

---

[5] The specific operationalization and technical specification of the reliability of power supply depends on societal expectations and the technological and economic capabilities of different countries. Hence, the degree of technical reliability of the power supply typically differs among countries. For instance, high reliability requires more investment in system redundancies, in order to prevent the power system from failure in times of stress. This includes investments in the reserve capacity of power plants and/or additional transmission lines that can be utilized in cases of emergency.

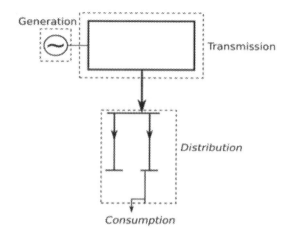

Figure 5.4 Architecture of traditional electricity systems without renewable energy sources[6] (adapted from Verzijlberg et al., 2017: 663)

scale generators to the final point of consumption. Accordingly, arrangements to safeguard critical functions are typically provided at the level of high-voltage transmission networks. Of specific interest are so-called ancillary services, including load balancing, that is, the continuous adjustment of the supply of power to accommodate the varying demand of final consumers. In terms of our alignment framework, this is an articulation of the critical function "capacity management." Frequency control is another example of an ancillary service, which can be related to the critical function of "system control." Electric power is provided by alternate current (AC) technology. The power frequency, typically 50 or 60 Hertz, needs to be identical throughout the entire grid; otherwise, appliances do not function according to expectation. A constant and reliable power frequency is therefore an important characteristic of power quality. These are prominent examples of critical functions in electricity infrastructures.

The addition of a marginal share of renewable energy sources to traditional electricity systems, for example, 2–3% of the electricity demand (International Energy Agency, 2018: 21), does not fundamentally change the architecture of the system (Figure 5.5). Under such conditions, wind and solar power plants are typically connected to

---

[6] For reasons explained in footnote 3, we do not include hydroelectricity, biomass, and geothermal power in "renewable energy sources."

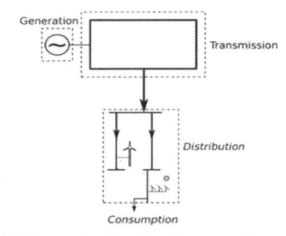

Figure 5.5 Architecture of traditional electricity systems with marginal renewable energy plants (adapted from Verzijlberg et al., 2017: 663)

distribution networks on a very limited scale. Since the installed fossil fuel generation capacity is much bigger, the marginal addition of some renewable energy plants is technically unnoticed. It causes minor system imbalances that are absorbed by the system (International Energy Agency, 2018: 15). Essentially, the provision of renewable energy supply adds to the marginal incidental disturbances that are inherent to energy systems.

5.3.2 Macro-Institutions

Electric power should be reliable and available to all citizens under acceptable economic conditions. Given these objectives, traditional power systems have been perceived as natural monopolies (Joskow, 1996). Under such conditions, electric utilities are typically organized as vertically integrated entities. Property rights are allocated to public entities – including municipalities, regional, or national governmental bodies – or to regulated private firms. Decision rights include the safeguarding of the above-mentioned ancillary services that are important for providing reliable electric power to final consumers. Adding a minor share of renewable energy sources to the energy system does not fundamentally change these institutional arrangements. Integrated utilities remain the most important power suppliers and operators of the electricity grid worldwide.

5.3.3 Structural Alignment

In traditional power systems, the vertical coordination of critical functions is characterized by closed and centralized modalities of alignment. Closed arrangements completely prescribe the institutional as well as technological entities and devices that are admissible for safeguarding the critical functions. Centralized coordination refers to the uniqueness of devices assigned for safeguarding the critical functions (Chapter 4, Section 4.3.2). In traditional power systems, the macro-institutions are characterized by monopolistic entities (so-called public utilities) that are exclusively assigned for safeguarding critical functions and providing expected services. Likewise, the architecture builds on a small number of large-scale power plants to reliably produce electricity and to provide the ancillary services required to safeguard the critical functions. Hence, the technological and institutional characteristics of coordination arrangements are compatible, that is, alignment is realized.

5.4 Structural (Mis)alignment of Contemporary Electricity Systems

In contemporary electricity systems, safeguarding the critical functions is challenged by incompatibilities between the technological and institutional characteristics of the coordination arrangements in the context of emerging new technologies.

5.4.1 Architecture

Indeed, the large-scale integration of renewable energy sources significantly alters the constitutive material components of contemporary power systems, their basic technological arrangements, and the generic services they can provide (Figure 5.6). Accordingly, the architecture becomes characterized by different components and arrangements, including small-scale production units, storage facilities, and different network configurations that partially parallel the traditional system without being fully integrated.

Next to traditional fossil fuel generators, wind and solar power plants hold a significant share of the power generation portfolio. The production capacity of individual renewable power plants is typically

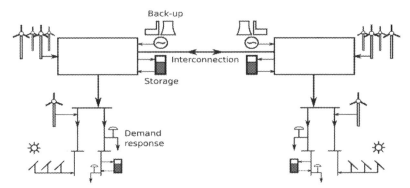

Figure 5.6 Architecture of contemporary electricity systems (source: Verzijlberg et al., 2017: 663)

much smaller than traditional fossil fuel generators (Verzijlberg et al., 2017: 661). Wind and solar power plants are usually distributed throughout the system. Because of the small size of production units, a significant share of renewable electricity is directly fed into low-voltage distribution grids, close to the final consumers. This raises major technological problems for safeguarding the critical functions of capacity management and system control in distribution networks (Siemens, 2016). Low-voltage distribution networks are technically insufficiently equipped for grid balancing when hosting a large number of sustainable power production units. A power overload might occur if the local wind or solar power generation exceeds local demand. Since conventional distribution grids are technically only equipped to receive power, this overload cannot be absorbed or fed into the high-voltage networks.

Dealing with these novel technological challenges requires changing features of the architecture. Innovative components and arrangements are needed. Enabling bi-directional power flows requires technological arrangements for overload control and the installation of smart trans-former devices (De Carne et al., 2017). Various storage technologies can provide temporary back-up, but usually only for quite short time periods of minutes or hours. Typical examples of storage devices include batteries, spinning wheels, or pumped hydro-power resources (Hadjipaschalis, Poullikkas, and Efthimiou, 2009). Such devices are generally not sufficiently equipped for bridging longer periods of low sustainable energy supply of days or weeks (International Energy

Agency, 2014). In addition, stronger interconnections to other electricity systems with different load patterns are an important technological means for providing flexibility to power systems and improving their balancing capacity (International Energy Agency, 2011: 16). Information and communication technologies are instrumental in this respect. They allow an exchange of data between an increasing number of small-scale power generators and consumers with different demand profiles. This provides possibilities for short-term adjustments in both power demand and supply. Such smart grids could serve as technological mediators between variable energy supply and fluctuating demand. Hence, flexibility becomes an additional generic service to be provided by contemporary energy systems, next to the reliable supply of electric power.

However, contemporary electricity systems have not yet succeeded in realizing such fundamental technological innovations and in providing adequate flexibility. Some key technologies are still at an experimental stage, and are not sufficiently advanced for commercial large-scale applications. This includes electricity storage and smart grid technologies, which are perceived as important technological enablers of sustainable electricity systems. Essentially, in contemporary power systems the technological coordination of critical functions still relies on centralized and closed coordination, as in traditional power systems.

5.4.2 Macro-Institutions

In electricity systems, the institutional coordination of critical functions is strongly determined by the rights and responsibilities of system operators. Historically, national or regional system operators are assigned property rights and decision rights for monitoring and controlling the power flows on high-voltage networks, based on the production patterns of large-scale fossil fuel or hydroelectric power plants. This is still the case in contemporary systems.

However, novel institutional arrangements have emerged in the course of the restructuring of this sector, especially under the conditions of retail competition. Competition and private sector initiatives are stimulated by providing third parties with opportunities to own and operate power plants. This has resulted in increasing investments, predominantly in small-scale power plants that are directly connected to low-voltage distribution networks (International Energy Agency, 2018).[7] Rooftop solar panels on residential houses and small-scale wind power are prominent examples in this respect. This raises problems for the quality of electricity provided in terms of ancillary services, namely, power frequency, system inertia, etc. However, current institutional arrangements typically do not entitle transmission system operators to monitor and control small-scale power plants that are directly connected to low-voltage distribution networks. Hence, these plants are operated largely independently of system needs and requirements for safeguarding critical functions. Incorporating these small-scale renewable power plants in the provision of ancillary system services is an eminent technological and institutional challenge (International Energy Agency, 2018: 39). Spain, for instance, established a dedicated control center for renewable energy, which makes it technically possible to collect real-time information on the operation of distributed electric power plants. This control center, a typical example of a meso-institution, calculates the maximum possible contribution of renewable energy sources to the Spanish power system, without endangering its reliability. This institutional coordination accommodates the increasing number of small-scale power producers while safeguarding the system services for the entire electricity system.

At the macro-institutional layer, property rights and decision rights need to be redefined so that system services can be provided even at the local level of individual firms or households. Under the current conditions, the operation of small-scale renewable power plants is mainly oriented toward the needs and requirements of their private owners, rather than meeting the needs of the system to safeguard the critical functions. Accordingly, due to the development of retail competition the institutional coordination of contemporary power systems can be characterized by a combination of centralization and openness.

- *Centralization.* The monitoring and control of critical functions is assigned to single-system operators with respect to the operation of the high-voltage grid. However, in most cases there is no equivalent

---

[7] Another development is the significant investment made in offshore wind energy. Among others, this solution requires the establishment of offshore electricity networks, which raises different institutional and technological challenges that we do not address in this chapter.

for low-voltage networks, the above-mentioned Spanish case being an exception.

- *Openness.* Renewable energy sources are increasingly connected to low-voltage networks that are out of the scope of monitoring and control of the system operator. The operation of these small-scale power plants does not contribute to ancillary system services. This causes serious problems for safeguarding the critical functions.

5.4.3 Reestablishing Structural Alignment

Comparing the technological and institutional coordination needed for safeguarding the critical functions points to the possibility of misalignment. The architecture builds on closed arrangements to achieve this goal, whereas macro-institutions allow for open coordination. More specifically: owners of small-scale power plants are assigned the right to feed in electricity to the grid without having the responsibility of safeguarding the critical functions. In contrast, the architecture of contemporary power systems strongly builds on closed coordination with the predetermined responsibilities of large-scale power producers to provide system services. Under these conditions, securing the operation of low-voltage networks with a high penetration of small-scale power plants increasingly raises problems, illustrating a misalignment between the technological architecture and the existing allocation of rights and responsibilities by macro-institutions. There is a lack of coordination between complementary devices and arrangements with respect to transmission and distribution networks when it comes to monitoring and controlling small-scale power plants (ENTSO-E, 2015; Birk et al., 2017; International Energy Agency, 2018; Villar, Bessa, and Matos, 2018).

This raises the question: how can the macro-institutions and architecture of contemporary electricity systems be adjusted to restore alignment. Among other things, doing so requires a detailed analysis of institutional arrangements that would remain aligned with the current technological architecture while offering possibilities for competition and private sector initiatives. In this respect, some interesting considerations for further analysis are offered by the European Network of Transmission System Operators for Electricity (ENTSO-E, 2015). ENTSO-E emphasizes the need to restructure the responsibilities of transmission system operators (TSOs) and distribution system operators (DSOs) in European electricity networks, and to strengthen their collaboration. Among other things, ENTSO-E recommends the development of a market framework enabling even end-consumers to engage in the provision of system services, including frequency control, storage, or demand response. Price incentives could stimulate those prosumers to adjust their power demand and supply according to the needs of local networks (ENTSO-E, 2015; see also Gerard, Rivero Puente, and Six, 2018). Technically, this can be accommodated by smart grids that could closely monitor the contribution of individual households to the power balance. From an institutional perspective, well-functioning markets would have to be developed for the allocation of local system services. Under these conditions, the modalities of alignment would thereafter rely on open and decentralized coordination.

Another institutional arrangement for involving decentralized power suppliers in the provision of system services are so-called grid codes, another typical example of a meso-institution. These technical standards specify the conditions under which components may be connected to the grid, and how they are operated under normal and exceptional circumstances (International Energy Agency, 2018: 125). For instance, grid codes might require that wind turbines are remotely controllable, so that they can be adapted to the system needs by a system operator. This would be an institutional modality of closed coordination, similar to the current technological architecture. Hence, under these conditions, the modality of alignment can be characterized as closed and decentralized.

An in-depth analysis of such proposed arrangements is beyond the scope of this chapter. But these examples illustrate how the alignment framework is instrumental in analyzing the compatibility (respective incompatibility) between technological and institutional coordination that is necessary for safeguarding critical functions in network infrastructures.

5.5 Challenges for the Alignment of Future Energy Systems

Future energy systems, relying almost entirely on sustainable energy sources, are largely unexplored. This section provides an outline of some basic technological features such systems would have. Based on the alignment framework, we propose an approach for systematically understanding and analyzing the challenges of aligning institutions and technologies in future sustainable energy systems.

5.5.1 Technological Features of Future Energy Systems

Balancing the strongly fluctuating energy supply of renewable energy sources constitutes a major challenge for future sustainable energy systems. Under these conditions, ancillary system services cannot be realized within the traditional technological and institutional boundaries of existing energy sectors (Lund et al., 2017). Rather, system integration is required, encompassing a technological and institutional integration of energy systems across different network infrastructures, including electricity, mobility, heating, and cooling. Traditionally, these sectors are operated and organized largely independently from each other as distinct entities. Heating and cooling networks provide climate control services for industrial and residential purposes. Gas networks are dedicated to the provision of gas. Power networks are designed to provide electricity. Transport networks provide mobility services.

However, in order to cope with the challenges of future energy systems, these distinct network infrastructures need to be operated in a much more integrated way to meet the requirements of sustainability. Essentially, different renewable energy sources and conversion technologies can be used to provide a broad range of energy services. It is often assumed that electricity becomes the most important energy carrier at the expense of gas and heat (Connolly, Lund, and Mathiesen, 2016). Figure 5.7 illustrates such future integrated energy systems. In this scenario, wind, solar, and bioenergy fuels become important primary energy sources.[8] The provision of different energy services – namely, mobility, electricity, cooling, and heating – is intertwined using different conversion technologies, with electricity as the most important energy carrier in all related sectors. Electric cars are

---

[8] Bioenergy fuels derive from biological sources such as wood, straw, manure, and other agricultural byproducts (Wikipedia, "Bioenergy." https://en.wikipedia.org; last accessed July 20, 2019). The physical and chemical characteristics of biofuels resemble those of fossil fuels (Connolly, Lund, and Mathiesen, 2016). Biofuels can be easily stored; hence, variability is not at stake. However, the availability of biofuels remains limited. Accordingly, wind and solar become the most important energy sources, which are by nature variable.

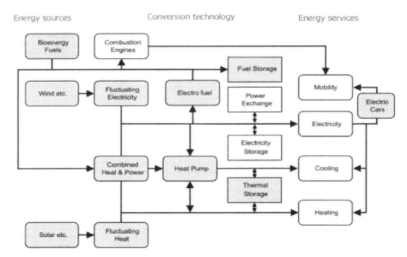

Figure 5.7 Future energy systems, with integrated energy conversion technologies, serving different sectors (adapted from Connolly, Lund, and Mathiesen, 2016)

expected to become dominant means of transportation in the next decades. Heating and cooling are provided by electric heat pumps. Electric power can be converted into storable energy carriers, designated as electro fuels. These include gas or liquid fuels such as hydrogen, biodiesel or butanol, chemicals, and other materials facilitating a temporal storage of electric power.

As a consequence of this integration of different technologies, future energy systems offer the following innovative possibilities for flexibility.

- Interconnected conversion technologies allow for shifting the supply of energy between different services and sectors. For instance, depending on temporary need, wind power can be used for the provision of electric power, heating or cooling, or mobility services.
- Different demand patterns in different sectors allow for temporal shifting of the energy supply. For instance, during night-time when the use of electricity for domestic purposes is low, electric power can be used for charging electric cars.
- Energy can be stored by different technical means. Biofuels can be stored as gas or liquids, electric power in batteries, and heat and cold in thermal underground storage facilities.

5.5.2 Research Challenges

The integration of architectures and macro-institutions across different network infrastructures is a fundamental challenge in the transition toward sustainable energy systems. In the literature, the issue has been addressed only very recently (see Lund et al., 2017). Even the most recent publication of the International Energy Agency addresses future energy systems only in a very rudimentary way, in a single paragraph (International Energy Agency, 2018: 19).[9] Many questions remain open with respect to the characteristics of such future energy systems. What will the features of an integrated architecture and macro-institutions of future energy systems be? Which material components and technological arrangements will be required for integrating mobility, electricity, heating, and cooling systems? Which macro-institutions will provide the support needed by such systems and contribute to make them sustainable? How will new and evolving architectures and macro-institutions be aligned so that the desired transition toward sustainable energy systems can be accomplished?

Our alignment framework provides a systematic approach to explore this eminent field of research. The framework makes it possible to identify and analyze the most suitable technological and institutional arrangements instrumental in meeting various societal expectations and values that will influence the performance of future energy systems. Without going into the details, the following considerations provide starting points for elaborating on answers to the questions raised above, even going beyond their initial scope.

1. *Which societal values can provide guidance for the development of future energy systems?*

An inventory and analysis of societal values that future energy systems should satisfy form an important starting point for considering the architecture and macro-institutions of future energy systems (see Chapter 1). In engineering literature, efficiency and effectiveness are typical values guiding the design of future energy systems (ENTSO-E, 2015). However, future energy systems are expected to serve a broad spectrum of values, including environmental sustainability, citizen involvement, distributional justice, privacy, security, and health

---

[9] The International Energy Agency refers to this as energy systems beyond phase 4.

(Milchram et al., 2018). What important societal values should be embedded in the architecture and macro-institutions of future energy systems? What about the possibility of value conflicts? Can they be resolved? If yes, how can this be done?

According to the concept of value-sensitive design (Friedman, 1996; Albrechtslund, 2007), values are deeply embedded in the technology and institutions of energy systems. For instance, the ownership of data on residential energy consumption could be allocated either to individual households or to energy providers. In the first case, the value of privacy would be safeguarded, since it is up to individual households to determine with whom they will share data. If energy providers were to own the data, the protection of privacy would not be considered as a dominant value. The value of privacy can also be safeguarded by technological means. Smart meters that monitor residential energy consumption could be technically equipped to protect locally stored data. For instance, a physical switch can serve as a gateway for opening or closing data access to third parties (Depuru, Wang, and Devabhaktuni, 2011).[10]

2. *What are the typical building blocks of the architecture and macro-institutions of future energy systems?*

The literature about typical technologies and institutions of future energy systems remains very limited. Connolly, Lund, and Mathieson (2016) provide some basic insights into the architecture of such systems (see Figure 5.7); the view they propose is strongly driven by the need to realize sustainability. The constitutive material components are referred to as energy sources and conversion technologies. Basic devices and entities include storage, power exchange, and power conversion. Generic services concern the provision of electricity, mobility, cooling, and heating. Compared with current energy systems, this represents a much broader and diverse spectrum of components, arrangements, and expected services. From a different perspective, Wolsink (2018) elaborates on a quite detailed overview of how specific sustainable energy technologies contribute to citizens' participation. He also considers the intrusion of sustainable energy technologies into the natural environment, since they occupy much more geographical space than traditional fossil fuel technologies. This contribution is an

---

[10] Adapted from Künneke (2018).

interesting attempt to relate constitutive material components of future energy systems to macro-institutions and societal values. However, more detailed insights are necessary into the constitutive features needed to align the architecture and the macro-institutions, in order to fulfill the critical functions on the one hand, and societal values on the other hand (e.g., protection of landscapes). How can the different institutional and technological arrangements and the expected services be related? Obviously, they do not operate in isolation; their combination jointly contributes toward increasing or hampering the sustainability and reliability of the provision of various energy services. Thus, technologies and institutions need to be aligned across the boundaries of traditional network infrastructures of various sectors, in order to safeguard the shared critical functions of the overall energy system.

3. *How can we specify the relevant critical functions of future energy systems?*

Our framework identified four critical functions that must be achieved to allow network infrastructures to deliver expected services: system control, capacity management, interconnection, and interoperability. In order to appropriately analyze the modalities of alignment, these critical functions must be specified and operationalized with respect to future energy systems. Providing different possibilities for flexibility in the provision and consumption of different energy services constitutes the main difference between present and future energy systems (Lund et al., 2017). However, investigating how more flexibility relates to the safeguarding of critical functions remains an issue. For instance, how can the critical functions of interconnection and interoperability be achieved and monitored between different sectors and energy services such as mobility, electricity, cooling, and heating? As outlined in Section 5.1.1, future energy systems must increasingly integrate these services in order to meet the requirements of sustainability. Renewable energy sources such as wind and solar can provide different services, which means allocating this energy according to societal expectations and values. This requires technological and institutional coordination of energy resources for different services in different sectors. For instance, capacity management of future energy systems will play a central role in monitoring and securing energy storage and conversion. Electricity could be converted into electro-fuel, or temporarily stored in batteries. How can we technically and institutionally monitor and control these different means of capacity management so as to deliver expected services? Can additional, currently unknown, vital technological and institutional arrangements in sustainable energy systems contribute to the safeguarding of critical functions such as capacity management? From this perspective, the provision of flexibility in the demand and supply of power represents a major challenge for innovative energy sources and related institutional arrangements when it comes to dealing with the intermittency of sustainable energy systems.

4. *Which modalities of alignment are feasible and desirable in future energy systems?*

Answering this question requires a detailed analysis of feasible technological and institutional arrangements for safeguarding the four critical functions. Different modalities of alignment might serve different values to different degrees. For instance, some arrangements might favor economic efficiency and free choice by building highly decentralized modalities of alignment. However, realizing sustainability, citizen involvement, and distributive justice might go in the opposite direction, benefiting from centralized modalities of alignment. As already indicated (consideration no. 1), the concept of value-sensitive design might help in solving such dilemmas and guiding choices between different institutional and technological designs of future energy systems (Friedman, 1996; Albrechtslund, 2007).

5.6 Conclusion

The transition toward sustainable energy systems poses a most prominent societal challenge for decades to come. This chapter illustrates the contribution of the alignment framework toward disentangling the complex interrelations between technology and institutions required to provide expected services and safeguard the critical functions at the core of network infrastructures. Since the energy transition requires fundamental changes in the technological architecture and macro-institutions, this chapter focused on this most generic layer of analysis.

To start with, we demonstrated that the structure of traditional power systems relies on a tight alignment between technology and institutions. This alignment builds on the compatibility of centralized and closed coordination, on the side of institutions as well as that of technology. In this environment, safeguarding the critical functions depends on institutions related to transmission system operators (TSOs) and jointly operated large-scale fossil fuel power plants. We then raised questions and provided indications as to the changes in these arrangements that transitions such as those taking place in the energy sector would impose. We illustrated this transition by identifying three archetypes, namely, traditional, contemporary, and future energy systems. This approach enables a comparative static analysis of the (in)compatibility between technological and institutional characteristics of different coordination arrangements when it comes to safeguarding the critical functions throughout the energy transition.

Indeed, reaching this goal in contemporary and future energy systems poses completely new challenges. The supply of sustainable energy sources such as wind and solar is variable and uncertain, depending on natural meteorological conditions. Hence, safeguarding the critical functions can no longer be realized by the traditional supply-side coordination of the power sector alone; it requires novel technological and institutional arrangements. The direct connection of many sustainable power plants to low-voltage networks requires safeguarding the critical functions even in these decentralized parts of the power system. Moreover, in future power systems safeguarding the critical functions will require integrating electricity infrastructures with other sectors such as heating, cooling, and mobility. This new configuration will result in completely different, new integrated energy systems with diverse technologies and institutions that evolve to include formerly unrelated sectors.

The alignment framework provides an innovative approach for understanding and analyzing these complex changes. It allows for systematically comparing technological and institutional features of network infrastructures. For instance, reference to this framework made it possible to demonstrate that current institutional arrangements are only barely aligned with the technological features of contemporary energy systems. The analysis of future energy systems represents an important step in understanding the consequences of the energy transition and the possible evolution of existing energy systems. This is not well understood and has been only recently addressed in the literature. The alignment framework provides a set of rich instruments for exploring this eminent field of research.

6 | Governance

A Tale of a City's Water and Wastewater Network

6.1 Introduction

Water provision and wastewater treatment are crucial for the survival of human beings. Having access to safe drinkable water responds to an essential human need. In 2002, the United Nations Committee on Economic, Social and Cultural Rights stated: "The human right to water entitles everyone to sufficient, safe, acceptable, physically accessible and affordable water for personal and domestic uses."[1] And on July 28, 2010, the United Nations General Assembly formally confirmed access to water and sanitation as a fundamental human right.[2] Although mentioned in this last resolution, sanitation remains the poor relative when it comes to allocating resources to network infrastructures. According to the World Health Organization, 2.1 billion people still lack safe drinking water at home, and more than twice that number lack safe sanitation such as toilets or latrines.[3] The situation is even more dramatic when it comes to wastewater treatment, despite the well-known effect of untreated wastewater on health,[4] agriculture, and the environment, not to mention its contribution to the scarcity of water resources.

---

[1] UN Committee on Economic, Social and Cultural Rights, General Comment No. 15: The Right to Water (Arts. 11 and 12 of the Covenant), January 20, 2003, E/C.12/2002/11.

[2] Resolution 64/292 from the United Nations General Assembly: The Human Right to Water and Sanitation, July 28, 2010.

[3] World Health Organization, July 12, 2017 (www.who.int/news-room/detail/12-07-2017).

[4] According to recent data, 842,000 people in low- and middle-income countries die as a result of inadequate water, sanitation, and related hygiene issues each year (WHO, February 19, 2018; www.who.int/news-room/fact-sheets/detail/sanitation; last accessed December 11, 2018).

6.1.1 Why a Focus on Water and Wastewater?

Beyond pointing out a critical situation, these statements also suggest that water, sanitation, and wastewater treatment are tightly interdependent activities, although with different purposes, commanding different technologies and obeying different norms and rules. Whatever the approach chosen, water production and delivery as well as wastewater treatment require a network, from relatively simple connections to a pipe or a well to the more complex delivery of water or collection of wastewater by tankers, or the even more sophisticated underground network servicing urban needs.

This being said, there is a general perception, particularly among many specialists of other network infrastructures, that water and wastewater networks rely on relatively simple technologies, a basic assemblage of pumps and pipes (Pezon et al., 2011), so that the fundamental issue is about policy-making. As this chapter illustrates, the technological side is far more complex than this restrictive perception suggests. The increasing diversity of technical solutions available and the choices this diversity imposes already create a challenge and are a source of controversies about the most appropriate way to deliver safe water to, and collect wastewater from the booming populations of the megacities of developing and emerging economies.[5]

It is also a challenge for the existing institutional arrangements. For example, if the decision is made to switch from a large integrated water network to small-scale local production, much more than a change in technology is involved. The centrality of water for human beings and the growing scarcity of the resource make such changes in its production and delivery a highly sensitive issue that may require profound institutional realignment. The cultural valuation of water and the simultaneous neglect of the impact of wastewater generate specific constraints that differ according to the solution chosen. For instance, in many societies water is considered a gift of nature, a perception that might feed resistance to pricing the usage of the resource, thus threatening its sustainability. And the practice of open defecation by over one billion people remains a vivid threat to health, to women's

---

[5] An excellent and detailed review of the different dimensions involved is provided in Gabert (2018). See also several illustrations in the special issue on governance produced by Water International (2018); also the OECD (2015a; 2015b).

status, and to the environment in numerous countries, particularly in East Asia and Sub-Saharan Africa. The intricacy of the factors involved motivates public intervention almost everywhere. Simultaneously, it makes water and wastewater provision a politically sensitive issue. Public intervention often translates into overlapping jurisdictions and responsibilities that deliver incoherent and misaligned policies, making the governance of water and wastewater networks particularly challenging.

6.1.2 Why Singapore?

To explore these issues, this chapter focuses on the case of Singapore. One could legitimately ask: why Singapore? Indeed, this city-state, ancient Greece style, now benefits from one of the most developed and sophisticated water and wastewater networks in the world. Moreover, both its size and level of development make it a drop in the ocean of world water needs. Nevertheless, the Singapore water and wastewater network offers a particularly significant field experiment in many aspects. First, it must be remembered that at the time of its independence, in 1965, this island had a level of development only slightly higher than Malaysia, its former home country, with a GDP per capita of just above USD 500, far below developed countries.[6] Second, it had to face a dramatic scarcity of available water resources and an extremely high level of pollution of the existing ones.[7] Third, under the apparent simplicity of its institutional arrangement, embedded in its status as a city-state with highly centralized political power, the governance of the Singaporean water and wastewater network operates through a complex setting, based on a combination of socio-political choices embedded in different institutional layers and a combination of four different technologies.

---

[6] Data adjusted using purchasing power parity. According to the most recent data (2017) from the World Bank, the Singaporean per capita GDP is now higher than that of Switzerland or the United States (https://data.worldbank.org/indicator/ NY.GDP.PCAP.CD).

[7] "At the time of independence, out of a population of 1.6 million, 1.3 million lived as squatters – not to count thousands of others living in slum areas and decrepit buildings" (interview by S. Leyl with Liu Thai Ker, known as Singapore's "master planner" in the 1970s and 1980s, "BBC News," February 28, 2015 (www.bbc .com/news/magazine-31626174).

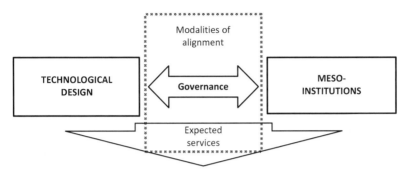

Figure 6.1 Alignment between technological design and meso-institutions: governance (layer 2)

Thus, beyond its current spectacular economic success, Singapore provides a rich example for better understanding the modalities that allowed an initially poor country to align the institutional rules framing the organization of its water and wastewater network with a variety of technological solutions selected to overcome the dramatic scarcity of its resources.

6.1.3 Roadmap for This Chapter

The previous chapter explored the structural conditions needed to secure the alignment between the technological architecture of a network infrastructure and the macro-institutions within which it is implemented. This chapter focuses on the second layer of our analytical framework: it deals with the modalities of governance linking the meso-institutions that translate and adapt the norms and rules defined within the macro layer and the specific technological design resulting from the technological choices that shaped the architecture of the network. In line with Chapters 2 and 4, governance is understood to be the combination of entities (e.g., a regulator) and devices (e.g., protocols) through which context-specific technologies and specific institutional norms and rules are aligned (or misaligned). Figure 6.1 summarizes the core components to be considered.

The next section provides a brief overview of the technological architecture and macro-institutional background of the Singaporean case. Section 6.3 discusses the governance adopted to secure alignment between the technological design of the water and wastewater network and the specific institutions involved in its monitoring. Special attention is paid to the challenges of interconnection and interoperability, and the role of the integrated utility that governs water and wastewater networks in that context. Section 6.4 focuses on the modalities through which this mode of governance deals simultaneously with the overlapping responsibilities of the institutions involved and the redistribution of rights associated with the introduction of new technologies. Beyond high performance, the drawbacks and frailties are pointed out that could derail the so far successful alignment between technological design and institutional ruling. Section 6.5 concludes, drawing some general lessons from the Singaporean case with respect to our framework.

6.2 Framing the Water and Wastewater Network: Architectural and Macro-Institutional Setting

Because it is a unitary, centralized political system, understanding the organization of the water and wastewater network (and all other network infrastructures in that respect) in the city-state of Singapore requires a careful look at the generic structures that frame its technological as well as macro-institutional choices.

6.2.1 Overcoming Water Dependence: Technological Choices Embedded in History

The sensitivity of water systems to political values and interference cannot find a better illustration than the case of Singapore. The following comment from the "founding father" of the Republic about a decisive event at the time the new independent country was formed perfectly summarizes the issue at stake:

A few days after independence, the Prime Minister of Malaysia told the British High Commissioner, "If Singapore doesn't do what I want, I'll switch off the water supply." So I knew that unless I could become less dependent on Malaysia's supplies, I would always be a satellite. So the quest began for water independence." (Lee Kuan Yew, June 25, 2008; quoted in *The Straits Times*, November 24, 2017)

The absence of natural resources has been a continuing challenge shaping the policy of Singapore. When it comes to water, this determined the choice of escaping dependence through the building of an increasingly complex technological water and wastewater network. From the agreements with Malaysia, negotiated in 1961–1962, to the "Four National Taps" strategy adopted in 2001 to make the country independent at the time these agreements would expire, securing the water supply has shaped a strategy based on the development of a complex set of complementary technologies tightly coordinated through a centralized governance. This strategy materializes in the technological architecture of the system, with the constitutive components succinctly described as follows.

Imported Water
Formally established in 1965, independence from Malaysia resulted from deep economic and political differences beween the ruling powers in both countries, with negotiations about strategic issues taking place under the umbrella of British colonial power. Water was part of these negotiations. A 1961 agreement authorized Singapore to draw unrestricted quantities of water from two Malaysian rivers (Tebrau and Scudai) for a period of fifty years. Another agreement, from 1962, gave the city-state exclusive rights to draw 250 million gallons of water per day from the Johor River until 2061. Both agreements were "enshrined" in the Separation Agreement registered under the United Nations umbrella, and which neither Singapore nor Malaysia could change unilaterally. In practice, water catchment was processed at a water treatment plant in Malaysia before being transferred to Singapore through a pipeline. This arrangement defined a closed, centralized network, making Singapore highly dependent on its neighbor. Notwithstanding the mandatory agreements, problems of repeated droughts (in 2016, the reservoir connected to the Johor reached a historically low level, at 20% of its capacity) combined with rapid population growth and economic development pushed Malaysian demand for water up, making this source of water much less reliable.

Local Catchments
To address this problem, a strategy was adopted early on to catch stormwater in the country, which was exposed to substantial tropical rains. In 1972, a water master plan was adopted to dam estuaries and form reservoirs. A network of drains, canals, and rivers was developed

to feed the new reservoirs, and a separate sewerage system was built to avoid pollution of the rainwater thus collected. Another plan was implemented, covering the period 1977–1987, to clean up the Singapore River and Kallang Basin, which were highly polluted, having long served as open sewers and rubbish dumps. At the end of this ten-year plan, much aquatic life had returned. Another step was made in 2008 with the decision to create the huge Marina Reservoir, the fifteenth reservoir to be constructed in addition to the original three that existed in 1960s. Nowadays, it is estimated that two-thirds of rainwater is channeled into the reservoirs. Notwithstanding this success, this resource remains limited because of the limited surface for collection and the effects of climate change, which reduces the amount of rainwater.

NEWater

The first NEWater factory ("Bedok") was established in 2003, with the purpose of purifying treated used water using an advanced membrane technology and an ultraviolet disinfection system. Put simply, used water goes through three steps to purify it: microfiltration through membranes; reverse osmosis using semi-permeable membrane, that is, micro-pores that allow only very small molecules to pass through; and disinfection through ultraviolet rays. Although NEWater is dedicated almost entirely to industrial purposes and to fill the reservoirs in dry months, the reluctance of consumers to drink this water has increasingly been overcome.[8] As of 2017, five NEWater plants provided 40% of water demand, and the target is to reach 55% of total demand in 2060. Recovering used water requires massive investment in what is known as the "Deep Tunnel Sewerage System," an ambitious underground "sewerage superhighway," which is below ground (to save scarce land) and relies on gravity to carry used water to treatment plants ("water reclamation plants"). The first phase of the DTSS was achieved in 2008. The second phase, which covers the west and central parts of Singapore, is now under construction. Over twenty years, Singapore will have spent about SG$ 10 billion on this project.

---

[8] As of the end of 2020, about 95% of NEWater was supplied to industry through a separate network. The remainder is channeled into the reservoirs and some is bottled (mostly as a way to publicize the good quality of this water).

Desalinated Water

One last source of drinkable water for Singaporeans comes from desalination. An initial plant became operational in 2005. As of the end of 2020, four plants were operating, which were intended to provide over 25% of the water supply; and one more plant (Jurong Island) should become operational soon, with the goal of achieving 30% of total water demand by 2060. Desalination, the removal of salt and mineral residues to make water drinkable or available to irrigation, involves complex technological processes, with numerous alternative methods available.[9] A major drawback of all these technologies is that they are intensive energy users, which make them costly, particularly for countries without significant sources of energy. This is of course the situation in Singapore, which has been very proactive in introducing innovative technologies, with two main goals: saving energy and extending the lifespan of the equipment. For instance, the most recent "Tuas desalination plant" combines air flotation with ultrafiltration pre-treatment processes that extend the lifespan of the treatment membrane.[10] To a great extent, desalination has been a main vector in the introduction of public–private partnerships, although one plant (the third desalination plant) is entirely owned and operated by the Public Utilities Board (PUB). One question is whether this exception is related to the dysfunction in earlier desalination plants, generating a possible misalignment in the governance of the network (more on this in Section 6.4).

In sum, the evolution of the water and wastewater treatment network of Singapore can be characterized by an increasingly diversified mix of water provided by substantially different technologies, with NEWater and desalination playing an increasing role, and the remaining supply coming from imported water and local catchment (Figure 6.2).

The resulting technological system is quite complex. First, the political choice of the Singaporean government to integrate four substantially different technologies (and in the case of NEWater or desalination, different plants relying on different technologies) means dealing with a sophisticated global architecture. Second, the option of building a unified and centralized technical network to integrate the output of these different technologies, and to deliver expected services,

---

[9] These range from solar evaporation to vacuum distillation or sophisticated reverse osmosis, which uses filtering membranes, etc.

[10] *PUB Annual Report 2018–2019* (www.pub.gov.sg/annualreports/annualreport2019.pdf; last accessed February 2, 2021).

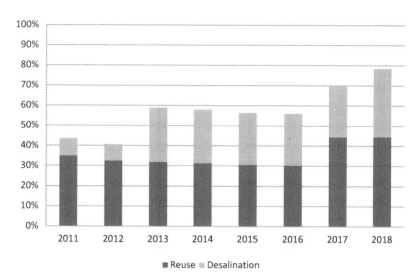

Figure 6.2 Reuse and desalination capacity in Singapore as a proportion of daily sales (compiled by O. Jensen, based on Jensen and Wu, 2018. Data: Singstat and PUB Annual Reports)

requires elaborate and well-designed technical coordination, in order to secure complementarities between the different components of the network. Third, the decision to delegate the implementation and operation of this system to a unique public utility, which also has to manage the provision of part of its resources by private operators, raises specific problems of alignment (to be discussed in Section 6.4). These choices involving the three technological layers of our framework play an essential role: a significant deficiency in any one of them could challenge the delivery of expected services. Figure 6.3 posits these technological layers, with an emphasis on the intermediate one, its interdependence with the institutional dimension being at the core of this chapter.

Before looking at the specificities of this technological design and its consequences on the governance of the system, let us clarify the macro-institutional dimension underlying this arrangement.

6.2.2 Macro-Institutional Context: The Political Regime of Singapore

The decision to target a self-sustainable water and wastewater network and the choice of its organizational modalities as a closed, centrally

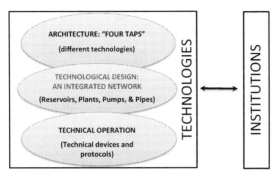

Figure 6.3 Key technological layers of the Singaporean water system

controlled system mirrors the more general nature of the macro-institutions of Singapore, its political regime, and its underlying values. This regime has two main features. On the one hand, it is a Westminster-style system, structured around the legislature (with a unicameral parliament) and the executive (a prime minister and a cabinet). However, for reasons which exceed the scope of this chapter, it is also an authoritarian regime, dominated by the same political party (the People's Action Party) since the island obtained self-government (1959), with considerable power in the hands of the executive, and in particular the prime minister, through which the cabinet operates and judges are appointed.[11]

In this context, it was decided early on to build a centralized water and wastewater network; this was considered as strategic and was tightly controlled by the government. Formally created on May 1, 1963, the Public Utilities Board (PUB), initially under the supervision of the Ministry of Trade and Industry, was in charge of water supply, drainage, sewerage, and wastewater treatment; however, it was also responsible for the organization and provision of gas and electricity. It was only at the beginning of this century that a series of legislative acts were passed which redefined the authority of PUB and limited its jurisdiction to water- and wastewater-related issues.

Nowadays, the allocation, implementation, and monitoring of rights regarding water and wastewater is under the sole responsibility of

---

[11] A revision of the Constitution adopted in 1991 introduced an elected president with very limited power, mostly veto rights on some executive decisions, e.g., the nomination of judges.

PUB, which operates within the context of four main pieces of legislation. (1) The Sewerage and Drainage Act (1999), replacing the former Water Pollution Control and Drainage Act (1975), which played a central role in organizing the depollution of the Singapore River and canals, previously used for sewerage and as dumps. (2) The Environmental Pollution Control Act (1999), which formalized environmental concerns. (3) The key Public Utilities Act (2001),[12] which transferred gas and electricity to another jurisdiction while simultaneously giving considerable power to PUB over water, wastewater, and drainage, under the authority of the Ministry of the Environment and Water Resources (MEWR). (4) The National Environment Agency Act (2002), which created an agency (NEA) responsible for environmental quality, including issues connected to the conditions under which water and wastewater are processed. Within this institutional framework, property rights were and remain in the hands of the public authorities, while decision rights are delegated to the semi-autonomous PUB, acting as leading operator and submitted to a quite complex arrangement that characterizes the governance of the system (see Section 6.3).

6.2.3 *To Sum Up: Issues at Stake*

Singapore has been confronted with the strategic issue of securing its water provision in a geo-strategic context of substantial dependence on resources provided by a foreign and initially hostile country (Malaysia).[13] This is not a unique situation. Many countries having to share this resource so essential for the survival of human beings face similar challenges (e.g., countries with provision of water depending to varying degrees on transboundary rivers, from the Rhine to the Jordan, Nile, Ganges, etc.).

In the case of Singapore, this strategic challenge was and remains exacerbated by its geographical position: a small island surrounded by the ocean, with extremely limited water resources and having initially

---

[12] See https://sso.agc.gov.sg/Act/PUA2001.

[13] It should be remembered that Singapore had a much tormented relationship with Malaysia at the end of the British colonial occupation. Initially part of the Federation of Malaysia (1959–1964), Singapore became independent after the Malaysian parliament voted in August 1965 to expel the then poor island from the Federation to avoid further violence.

to deal with a relatively hostile supplier. Facing a potential "life or death" threat, the Singaporean government gave priority to a value-oriented strategy targeting independence. To reach that goal, it built a macro-structure combining an integrated technological architecture and a centralized institutional arrangement. In the terminology of this book, Singapore opted for a water and wastewater network that is structurally closed, with four technologies tightly interconnected; and centralized under the guidance of the highest level of government, with strict planning and control over the role played by each technology. This structure, determined by a political strategy, has been formalized in the "Four Taps" blueprint from 2001. Once these structural choices were made, the translation, implementation, and monitoring of this strategy relied on the capacity to develop a mode of governance that would align the resulting technological design with the role assigned to PUB.

6.3 Governance: Aligning Meso-Institutions and Technological Design

As already emphasized in Chapter 2 (Section 2.3.3), governance is a polymorphic notion that varies widely according to the purpose at stake and the layers of decision-making involved. In this book, we refer to governance as the set of entities (e.g., a regulator or a basin agency) and devices (e.g., a code of "good practices") designed to address the interdependencies between the context-specific techno-logical arrangement and the context-specific institutional arrangement that shape the properties of a network infrastructure. In other words, governance identifies the modalities through which meso-institutions and technological design interconnect, providing the "modus oper-andi" of a network infrastructure located in time and space.[14]

Because of its key role in the alignment between the technological design that makes a system's architecture technologically viable and the meso-institutions that give a specific content to the general norms and rules underlying the definition and allocation of rights, the gov-ernance of a network is central for safeguarding or restoring the critical functions. Indeed, inappropriate governance, for instance, an

---

[14] This interpretation of "governance" is quite close to that used in several recent empirical analyses (e.g., OECD, 2015a, 2015b, 2015c; Ménard et al., 2018)

incompetent regulator implementing outdated technical standards, introduces disruptions that may derail or even destroy the alignment between the technological design of the network and the specific norms and rules needed to guide agents' choices.

In the case of the Singaporean water and wastewater network, the strategic considerations associated with the production and delivery of water, and the nature of the political regime dealing with this issue, framed the initial choice of the governance implemented, with PUB as the central entity. However, the critical functions to be secured have become increasingly complex with the diversification of technologies on the one hand, the introduction of private partners and the related changes in the allocation of rights on the other hand. This has created the potential for some misalignment in an otherwise well-performing network.

6.3.1 From Architecture to Technological Design

The need to combine and coordinate four substantially different technologies, to interconnect them to the network, to secure their interoperability, and to provide a reliable primary and secondary network to deliver the expected services has been central in the making of the Singaporean water and wastewater system. Figure 6.4 summarizes the different nodes and links that define the technological design through which the selected technologies operate in the water network.

A key feature shown in this figure is the centralized and well-ordered properties of this highly integrated system. On the technological side, water is provided through an interconnection of reservoirs, pumps, and pipes that rely on the integration of a very diverse set of specific components.[15] However, NEWater relies on a partially autonomous network, with specific services mainly oriented toward industrial customers. On the institutional side, the collecting, processing, treatment, and pumping facilities guaranteeing the integration and homogeneity of the input (water) into this unified network fall under the responsibility of PUB, which therefore operates simultaneously as a micro-institution *and* as a regulator (a meso-institution), although only partially so, since PUB does not have full regulatory authority. For

---

[15] This system shows similarities with integrated electricity grids, rail track systems, road mapping, etc.

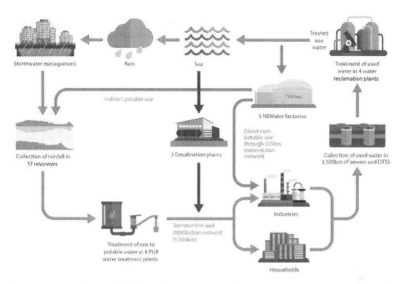

Figure 6.4 Nodes and links characterizing the Singaporean water network (source: PUB, Singapore's National Water Agency)

example, it does not have a say in the agreements with Malaysia for imported water, and it does not have the final word in setting tariffs (more on this in Section 6.4.2). At the end of the day, this interlocking system forms the cornerstone of the operability of the network from production to dispatching water to final users and collecting wastewater.

6.3.2 Interconnection and Interoperability at the Core

Within this technological arrangement, PUB provides key support to the critical functions. Empowered by the macro-institutions to monitor and operate the water and wastewater network, it is this institutional entity and the devices over which it has control that secures (or fails to secure) the alignment between the technological design resulting from the combination of the four technologies, and from the specification of standards and rules PUB establishes in its role as meso-institution. It means that PUB has a dual status, an issue discussed in Section 6.3.3.

The critical functions of capacity management and system control were quite rapidly satisfied. The early establishment (1963) of an integrated public utility coordinating the development of the network has been followed by continuous reinforcement of its jurisdiction and power, most recently through the Public Utilities Act (2001). For instance, PUB has statutory powers to define and control the conditions and modalities of access to the network. At the same time, the political choice of investing massively in education rapidly created an important pool of Singaporean competences, including technicians, engineers, and managers.[16] This environment, with its emphasis on education and the ability to attract foreign experts, gave PUB the opportunity to build a reputable staff base able to secure capacity management. One component of this success, going far beyond the water and wastewater network, has been the combination of powerful incentives (to the point that the high salaries of management have often been criticized) with tough penalties for digressions and a very strong anti-corruption policy.[17] In sum, the alignment between technology and institutions through the building of human capacities to manage complex technologies and operationally control the network was a target reached relatively early on.

In this context, and considering the choices made to build a self-sufficient system using different technologies, a main challenge arises from the need to secure the interconnection and interoperability of the different pieces of the Singaporean network. Meeting conditions to properly satisfy these two functions is not an easy task. First, the network may face exogenous risks, resulting from unexpected events

---

[16] A turning point was the adoption in the mid-1960s of a strategy to diverge from the "warehouse-type" economy of the colonial period to become an export-oriented and service-based economy, thus providing the rationale for a major investment in education. Primary education became freely available, accompanied by an accelerated program to build schools, and was followed by the development of secondary education (with the number of students increasing threefold in the first decade of the young republic). Education already represented about 25% of total public expenditure throughout that period, with some emphasis on technical education. A major reform in the late 1970s addressed the weaknesses of the previous strategy and considerably reinforced the quality of the educational system (for a detailed review, see Chor Boon and Gopinathan, 2008).

[17] This policy ranges from hiring conditions to strict (and low) limits imposed on gifts and entertainment (e.g., the maximum amount for lunch). Non-adherence to these rules is severely punished. For instance, under the Prevention of Corruption Act of Singapore (https://sso.agc.gov.sg/Act/PCA1960) adopted in 1960 and updated in 1993, conviction for a corruption offence is punishable by fines (now up to S$ 100,000) or an imprisonment term of up to seven years or both.

over which agents have no or little control. These risks can affect production (e.g., a drought such as that which happened in 2014; a shortage of electricity paralyzing pumps; a technical defect in one of the technologies in use) as well as distribution (e.g., a tropical storm disrupting interconnections). Second, there are also endogenous risks, partially born out of the combination of different technologies and the complex reallocation of rights related to the introduction of desalination and water reuse. Monitoring the inflow of water and its quality and capturing and recycling wastewater on such a large scale as that targeted in Singapore make interconnection and interoperability as well as system control particularly sensitive to technical disruptions, mismanagement, and/or flaws in maintenance. Third, financing the heavy investments required by the target of self-sufficiency and the recourse to sophisticated technologies created challenges of their own, particularly in a context of political control over tariffs (see Section 6.4.2).[18]

Securing interconnection between highly differentiated technologies and their interoperability so that risks can be faced, for example, through the capacity to switch rapidly from one source of water to another in case of a technical defect in one plant, also raises another problem: how can this complex technological design and the specific entity in charge of its coordination be properly aligned?

6.3.3 The Hybrid Status of PUB

The Public Utilities Board (PUB) is that entity, and is responsible for the alignment between the rules it has to make operational and the specific technological arrangement that characterizes the Singaporean water and wastewater network. This is not without its challenges. On the one hand, PUB is central to the governance of the network, articulating the variety of technologies chosen, and implementing the norms and rules embedded in the institutional environment of this city-state. On the other hand, PUB was also designated from the very moment of its creation (under a different name) on May 1, 1963, as the exclusive micro-institution responsible for producing and delivering drinkable

---

[18] For a general analysis of the diversity of risks in water and wastewater networks, see Ménard (2012).

water, and at the time also gas and electricity, a status later changed to focus solely on water and wastewater.

This dual role, which suggests an overlap between the meso- and micro layers – a not uncommon situation in network infrastructures – is mirrored in the terminology used in connection with this Public Utilities Board; it is also known as Singapore's National Water Agency. This double identity indicates some hybridity with respect to the exact role of PUB. It also raises a question in relation to the second layer of our framework (the meso layer): does this dual status have an impact on the alignment between the technological design and the expected role of meso-institutions?

To explore this issue, one needs to dig deeper into the variety of responsibilities of PUB. According to its legal status, based on the Public Utilities Act of 2001, as a corporate entity, PUB is able to sue and be sued, and to acquire, hold, and dispose of property. PUB benefits from a broad autonomy with direct responsibilities for a host of decisions. In that respect, it shares the characteristics of a private corporation. For instance, it develops strategic planning, implements key investments, and manages relations with all users as well as private contractors operating under standard procurement procedures and/or under public–private partnership conditions. Its internal governance is also similar to a private corporation, with significant autonomy in running the four main divisions in charge of coordinating the technical and human resources of the network. These divisions are respectively responsible for operations (the plants and associated technologies); engineering and technology; policy and development (planning, development, human resources, finance, internal audit); and training (through the Singapore Water Academy). Therefore, although it is not expected to make profit and it receives subsidies in case of losses, PUB operates as a "normal" firm, thus belonging to the category of "micro-institutions."

However, PUB is not only an operator, acting as a firm. It is also in charge of bridging policy-making (by the government, under the leading role of the prime minister) through the operational level at which transactions are defined and implemented. In that respect, part of its status corresponds to key properties of meso-institutions; it is responsible for the allocation and usage of all property rights over the entire water and wastewater network, and holds most strategic decision rights, although under the close monitoring of public authorities.

This is a key point; thanks to clearly defined targets and reporting procedures, ministers can directly monitor the performance of PUB against the political agenda of the government. The modalities of appointment of board members are illustrative of this. The supervisory ministry (nowadays the Ministry of the Environment and Water Resources – MEWR) appoints the deputy chairman of the board. Other members (no fewer than five or more than ten) are also appointed by the ministry. This board selects the chief executive, whose nomination must be approved by the minister and, ultimately, the cabinet and the prime minister. All employees of the board are public servants, and are subject to the general rules regulating this status.

A significant indicator of these overlapping roles is provided in the Annual Report, which PUB must deliver to the minister in charge, then submit to parliament for approval. Besides this chain of command, retaining its activity as a quasi-corporation under the tight control of macro-institutional rules, PUB also acts as the public agency in charge of implementing regulations and monitoring relations with and among stakeholders (private operators, contractors, users). For instance, PUB has full authority to award public–private partnership contracts and monitor them. This dual status has become increasingly complex with this introduction of private partners, who keep control of the rights over specific technologies (desalination or NEWater). It also has an impact on capacity management, with PUB staff having to supervise contracts related to sophisticated and evolving technologies; and on interoperability, with the need to secure contractual rights of access allocated to private partners without disturbing the network.

Figure 6.5 summarizes the hybrid position of PUB as a meso- and a micro-institution.

The Public Utilities Board therefore provides a neat illustration of the overlap among the institutional layers in many network infrastructures. It operates as a micro-institution, producing and delivering expected services through the organization of transactions with external suppliers and final users, and is assessed in this activity by its exclusive stakeholder (the government). And it simultaneously plays the role of a meso-institution, a public agency translating the general rules defined within the macro layer (e.g., the "Four Taps" blueprint from 2001) into more specific rules guiding the activity of its components, as well as monitoring the specific allocation of rights and

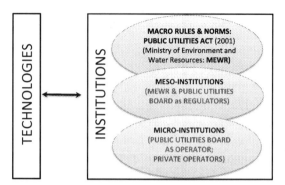

Figure 6.5 The hybrid status of the Singaporean Public Utilities Board

requirements to external participants involved in the technological design of the network. This is quite similar to the well-established and widely used model in network infrastructures, for instance, electricity or railroad networks, with vertically integrated monopolies in charge of delivering specific services and simultaneously acting as regulators responsible for the governance of some subsets of the system.[19]

6.4 Facing Misalignment Issues

This overlapping of roles and layers raises the issue of whether this is a source of misalignment, threatening the capacity of PUB to act simultaneously as the entity in charge of governing the network and the operator in charge of organizing transactions in a way that makes the network efficient. Do this dual status and its potential consequences for alignment challenge the critical functions of the network, particularly its interconnection and interoperability?

6.4.1 Overlapping Responsibilities: Policy Makers in Command

By way of its status as a powerful public monopoly, PUB is the key micro-institution for the Singaporean water and wastewater network,

---

[19] For example, in what was for a long time the highly centralized French electricity system, EDF (Électricité de France) operated simultaneously as a public monopoly (thus, a micro-institution) while implementing regulations and closely monitoring the activity of several independent producers active in some regions, thus fulfilling the role of a meso-institution.

with the leading role in the expansion, planning, technological choices, implementation, and monitoring of the network, and endowed with extensive decision rights as well as control over strategic assets. At the same time, PUB is a central player in the allocation of property and decision rights, coordinating its activities with other relevant agencies (e.g., for solid waste management) under the control of the parliament and the executive. In doing so, PUB not only operates as an autonomous (public) corporation; it also acts as a governing entity, bridging the gap between the macro and micro layers, fulfilling the typical functions of a meso-institution (see Chapter 2).

These overlapping responsibilities create a specific relationship with policy makers. First, the board is tightly controlled by the executive. Notwithstanding an informal principle of "self-restraint," this dependence does not preclude political interference that may challenge the operability of the network, as illustrated by the tariff issue described in Section 6.4.2. Second, PUB shares its regulatory responsibilities with its supervising ministry (MEWR). For instance, the executive and parliament determine broad targets (e.g., reaching full self-sufficiency for the provision of water by 2060) that the MEWR and PUB must jointly translate into intermediate goals and implement through decisions regarding the choice of technologies, investments, etc. However, these entities do not operate on a level playing field. Ultimately, the MEWR remains the prevailing meso-institution.

This institutional arrangement may create tensions between these two entities, both involved in the governance of the network. Four examples illustrate this. One is the tension that developed over the tariff issue, which could have threatened the sustainability of the critical functions. By law, tariffs must meet costs. However, the rejection by policy makers of any tariff adjustments for more than fifteen years (2001–2017) challenged the capacity of PUB to meet the self-sufficiency target assigned by the same policy makers, as its decisions were partially dependent on public subsidies.

A second example is the important decision by the executive to introduce public–private partnerships, with a view to the development of desalination plants, which meant changes in the technological architecture of the system. Although this decision might have been partially motivated by financial constraints due to the frozen tariffs, the need to acquire unfamiliar technologies also played a role. However, in taking this step the policy makers also modified the institutional design. The introduction of private partners required the reallocation of rights, a definition of the modalities of access to the network, and some decentralization in the decision-making process, with the new role of contracts as regulatory tools. It also raised issues regarding the respective responsibilities of PUB and the MEWR in securing the critical functions. Opening up room for some decentralization in the architecture of the network while keeping governance centralized suggests the possible emergence of misalignment between the technological and the institutional arrangements.

A third example comes from the allocation of financial responsibilities with the expansion of the infrastructure. For instance, the development of "water reclamation plants," as wastewater treatment plants are known in Singapore, is managed and financed by PUB through standard procurement contracts with private firms, while contracts related to drainage and the planning, building, and operation of plants using new technologies are financed through the general budget and jointly supervised by PUB and the MEWR. The resulting allocation of decision rights could represent a challenge for the critical functions, particularly system control, since part of it has been switched to private operators.

Last, another potential source of tension and misalignment in governance that deserves a mention relates to incentives. On the one hand, PUB's employees are public servants, although they benefit from rewards closely connected to performance, a factor that permeates the culture at PUB. In that respect, PUB operates as a standard corporation.[20] On the other hand, PUB is also involved in monitoring contracts with private partners for some plants, which rely on different incentive mechanisms. It is not clear and not easy to get information about how this dual approach is managed, potentially creating tensions between PUB employees and the private operators. Does this duality within the same network affect the managerial effectiveness of PUB?

Figure 6.6 captures this overlap of responsibilities within the meso-institutional layer between PUB and the MEWR, making room for possible misalignment in the governance of the network.

---

[20] Considered a central explanation to the success of PUB, the importance of bonuses and career progression has also fed criticisms about possible "excessive" rewards for its staff, particularly high-ranking managers.

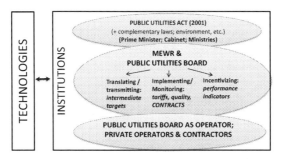

Figure 6.6 Overlapping roles of the MEWR and PUB as meso-institutions

6.4.2 High Performance under Political Supervision: A Paradox?

Notwithstanding these potential sources of misalignment between institutions with overlapping responsibilities and a technological system that interconnects four different technologies and secures their interoperability, the Singaporean water and wastewater network performs exceptionally well. As such, it is considered a success story, a model of its own making.

To properly measure this success, it is necessary to keep in mind that at the time of independence, in the 1960s, Singapore was very poor, with water and sanitation provision typical of underdeveloped countries, decent services being the privilege of the wealthy few, and with almost no wastewater treatment. Nowadays, the city-state legitimately claims to have made water provision as well as sanitation "universal, affordable, efficient and of high quality."[21]

Most of the available data support this view. Universal coverage was achieved in 1989 for water, and in 1990 for sewerage. This is particularly remarkable if one considers the situation at the time of independence. In 1965, one-third of the population was living in slums, half was illiterate, and the GDP per capita was just above USD 500.[22] The sewerage system was almost non-existent, while water was a very scarce resource (at one point in the late 1960s, water was rationed

---

[21] Wikipedia, "Singapore" (https://en.wikipedia.org/wiki/Singapore; last accessed November 26, 2018).

[22] It is now above USD 70,000. See Wikipedia, "Economy of Singapore" (https://en.wikipedia.org/wiki/Economy_of_Singapore#Economic_history; last accessed November 26, 2018).

for ten consecutive months). Not only are water and wastewater services now available to all, but the quality of water is also very high, with over 300 parameters of control, far above the level recommended by international organizations.[23] Non-revenue water, due to leakages, etc., is also very low, in line with the best international practices at 5%, a signal of efficient maintenance.

More specifically, the Singaporean per capita consumption of water for households compares favorably with other developed countries; 165 liters per day in 2003, 148 l/d in 2017, and the target for 2030 is fixed at a low 140 l/d. After having been frozen for a long time, tariffs were finally revised in 2017. However, they remain part of the polit-ical/strategic control of pricing, shaping the governance of the water and wastewater network in Singapore.[24] Tariff policy differentiates three categories of users: domestic (households), non-domestic (busi-ness), and shipping, with prices based on block rates, according to the volume consumed. For households, costs remain low, with expenditure on water, gas, and electricity representing on average less than 1% of the average household income (data for 2017).[25] For non-domestic (business) consumers exceeding the basic block amount (0–40 m^3), prices have undergone an important adjustment, with a 30% increase for standard potable water and slightly more for NEWater, which likely intends to reflect differences in costs of production, although information is scarce on this issue (see Section 6.4.3). Last, potable water delivered to shipping customers, a significant part of consump-tion in Singapore, is priced at a significantly higher tariff, approxi-mately 50% above the inland business price.

Beyond these data, what matters is the quite remarkable achieve-ment of the Singapore network, within fifty years, with respect to the delivery of high-quality water at low cost as well as the recycling of wastewater. This high level of performance has been reached through a centralized mode of governance operating under the tight control of

---

[23] See International Standard Organization (www.iso.org/ics/13.060/x/p/0/u/1/w/0/d/0), and for drinkable water in a subset of countries, see Wikipedia, "Water quality" (https://en.wikipedia.org/wiki/Water_quality#National_specifications_for_ambient_water_and_drinking_water; last accessed November 27, 2018).

[24] Although by law tariffs are expected to cover costs, a controversy developed at the time of this revision about the role of subsidies.

[25] See www.singstat.gov.sg and www.pub.gov.sg/watersupply/waterprice; last accessed December 15, 2018.

public authorities, which has apparently allowed the proper alignment of institutions and technology.[26]

6.4.3 Drawbacks and Frailties: Potential Sources of Misalignment

The organization of the Singaporean water and wastewater network, with PUB as the central entity operating under the tight control of the MEWR and ultimately the executive, seems to be the key to its success. Statutorily, interconnection among the different technologies is monitored and secured by PUB, which keeps a close control over rights of access. Similarly, interoperability is secured through the centralized coordination by PUB, notwithstanding the different sources of water and the different status of plants processing water and wastewater.

However, close scrutiny reveals a more complex picture, with potential sources of misalignment.

First, a changing environment, particularly growth in Malaysia, which threatens its role as supplier, and the multiplication of periodic droughts challenging the collection of rainwater, has reinforced the Singaporean strategy to diversify its sources of water. This move, decided by policy makers within the macro layer, led to the adoption of innovative technologies (desalination and NEWater) different from the existing ones, and about which PUB had limited knowledge. Consequently, external suppliers were involved, the technological design had to be adapted, the modalities of interconnection had to be changed, and governance required the modification of existing rules. There are obviously associated transaction costs and delays in doing all this. For instance, the development of NEWater required the development of a costly separate infrastructure for collecting wastewater and involved the adjustment of interconnections, so that the existing network had to be restructured and PUB had to face pressures on its financial resources.

---

[26] Notwithstanding its specificities, this closed and centralized system resembles water and wastewater networks run by utilities with monopoly power in numerous countries. Insights on different cases can be found in the OECD Studies on Water series, with numerous country studies published since 2011. See also Domanski and Ménard (2011) and Ménard (2017) for leading European countries.

Second, and even more challenging, the intervention of private providers of innovative technologies imposed substantial changes in the allocation of rights. Norms and rules that prevailed under PUB operating as a pure monopoly had to be adapted to secure new conditions of interconnection and interoperability. Contracts had to be signed with partners endowed with their own decision rights and motivations. The choice to rely on design-build-own-operate (DBOO) contracts meant that part of the network would thereafter be monitored through arrangements very close to concessions, with long-term offtake agreements and the transfer of significant decision rights to private parties.[27] These contracts differ substantially from the conventional procurement contracts with private contractors that PUB was used to managing, imposing some decentralization on the governance of the network. Although PUB remains the contracting authority, the introduction of public–private partnerships meant limited control by PUB and the MEWR over the new technologies, and it led to the adoption of new protocols and procedures to face uncertainties. For instance, the technological design of the network had to be altered; the order and conditions of access of plants had to be revised; and new conditions of adjustment had to be implemented in case of discontinuity of production among the new plants. Moreover, PUB had to relax its centralized mode of operation to deal with the logic-guiding decisions of private partners also operating abroad and involved in international competition. In sum, the introduction of private partners represents a challenge to the existing equilibrium of the system.

Third, the diversification of technologies in use also challenges the management capacity of PUB.[28] Dealing simultaneously with a variety of technologies occurs in many other water and wastewater networks, for example, when a unified water network coexists with public fountains, private tankers, and individual vendors.[29] However, the introduction of technologies with unfamiliar technical components and technical modalities of operation may create disruptive asymmetries

---

[27] Two recent desalination plant contracts (Marina East and Jurong Island) awarded in 2017 under DBOO arrangements cover the period 2020–2045.

[28] The allocation of property rights represents less of a problem, since contracts can be relatively specific; for instance, stipulating that assets return to the public domain at the end of the contract.

[29] A similar diversification of technologies can be found in other networks, e.g., electricity (see Chapter 5).

among parties. In the Singaporean model, the implementation of sophisticated and innovative technologies did not only challenge the existing competences of PUB, but it also introduced problems of reliability, safety, and sustainability.

The case of desalination is illustrative. Notwithstanding the scarce information available, desalination plants seem to be far from reaching their expected level of production. It remains unclear as to whether this is due to technical reasons, to unexpected events in the implementation of innovative technologies, to a demand lower than anticipated, to problems of incentives for private operators, or to the misallocation of rights between PUB and its private partners. Recent events have substantiated the existence of dysfunctions. In April 2019, HYFLUX, the parent company in charge of the "Tuaspring" desalination plant, the second desalination plant to be built in Singapore, faced major difficulties and its plant could no longer fulfill its obligations, so PUB had to take it over (on May 18, 2019). PUB and the government remain elusive in their communications about the issues at stake. Responsibilities are discussed behind closed doors, with very limited information and data available beyond the Annual Report, the justification being that this sector is too strategic to Singapore to be publicly discussed! However, these difficulties may well challenge the public policy regarding the modalities of introduction of new technologies. Before the trouble with Tuaspring and its private owner, the government had already decided on the construction of a third desalination plant, Tuas 2, which uses an advanced technology combining dissolved air flotation and an ultrafiltration technique, and is entirely owned and operated by PUB.[30] Moreover, what will happen to two other plants under construction, initially intended to rely on private partners, remains uncertain. One question is whether the building of a public plant signals a policy of benchmarking, allowing tighter control over private partners, or a more radical shift toward "renationalization," in order to restore a better alignment in governance through public ownership and management of the new plants and the private plant that failed.

Last, the hybrid status of PUB can also be a source of misalignment, as already suggested in Section 6.3.3. Besides its central role as a micro-

---

[30] See www.pub.gov.sg/watersupply/fournationaltaps/desalinatedwater; last accessed November 26, 2018.

institution – that is, as an operator buying services from private partners who own and manage high-tech plants – PUB also acts as a meso-
institution, a regulator implementing and controlling rules and norms
established by public authorities (e.g., quality standards), and monitoring the relationships between these private operators and the government. However, the overlapping regulatory responsibilities between
PUB and the MEWR also create tensions, as the issue of tariffs illustrates. Moreover, the secretive approach and the opacity of the
decision-making process that characterizes this joint governance create
suspicion regarding respective responsibilities in relation to the choice
of technological solutions and their management. The absence of
consumer organizations with statutory responsibilities and the very
intermittent public consultations limited to specific topics (e.g., about
flood infrastructure)[31] amplify this lack of transparency in decisions
made behind closed doors, with selected information diffused mainly
through the Annual Report to the ministry and parliament. The lack of
tariff adjustment for over fifteen years illustrates a potential misalignment that may come out of this institutional setting.

6.5 Conclusion: Some General Lessons

The water and wastewater network of the city-state of Singapore
shares a major characteristic with similar networks in many other
countries, relying on a centralized governance under the dual umbrella
of an authoritarian regime and an integrated utility tightly monitoring
its technologies. In Singapore, this combination opened up room for
exceptionally good coordination of different technologies and facilitated tight coordination with other government agencies, for instance,
the Housing and Development Board or the Urban Redevelopment
Authority in charge of spatial planning, a key to the global and well-
controlled approach to the development of the water and wastewater
network (and other networks in that respect). However, besides the
drawbacks already pointed out, this centralized setting exposed PUB in

---

[31] The issue of users' representation is a sensitive one. If the utility is entirely public,
it raises the risk of what Spiller (2009) identified as "third party opportunism,"
with groups of interests interfering with capacity management. If private
operators are involved, it exposes these firms to revealing information that
challenges business rights to confidentiality and may threaten competitive
advantages and innovation.

its role as operator to political interference, such as the freezing of tariffs illustrated. The so-called self-restraint principle that would have limited this interference remains quite opaque, and makes Singapore an exception among many countries with formally similar settings. It also raises the question as to why the "good practices" that Singapore was able to implement were diffused so poorly.[32]

Although it does not provide answers to all these issues, our analytical framework helped to capture key aspects of the success of the Singaporean model. Notwithstanding ambiguities coming out of its dual status as operator and regulator, the role of PUB as an intermediate meso-institution has been crucial in securing the alignment between technologies and institutions. On the one hand, it showed how PUB's role as an operator could be exposed to political interference, but in a limited way thanks to the existence of well-defined institutional rules and a relatively well-established allocation of responsibilities across the institutional layers. On the other hand, the specific setting that frames PUB's regulatory role has allowed efficient coordination within the technological dimension as well as within the institutional one, and has facilitated the monitoring of the proper alignment of these two dimensions.

Figure 6.7 indicates how the specific case of Singapore connects to our general model.

Analyzing the modalities through which general rules and technologies are actually implemented, and identifying the supportive institutions and their characteristics, such as those we observed in Singapore, provide guidelines as to the conditions of alignment that determine the capacity of a network infrastructure to deliver expected services. Pointing out potential sources of misalignment in governance and their possible impact on performance, our framework and its application to the Singaporean case also allowed for a better understanding of the

---

[32] Reviews of urban water networks in Africa (Shirley, 2002; 2008), Asia (Jensen, 2017), Latin America (Savedoff and Spiller, 1999; OECD, 2012), or even Europe (Ménard, 2017) show how the dual status of public utilities routinely feeds distortions and biases. Dozens of reports intend to capture the "best practices" in governance that could prevent this situation (e.g., OECD/G20, 2015; World Bank, 2017). Most of them focus on identifying these practices; very few target what institutional arrangements support or hamper their implementation (exceptions can be found, e.g., OECD, 2012, 2015a).

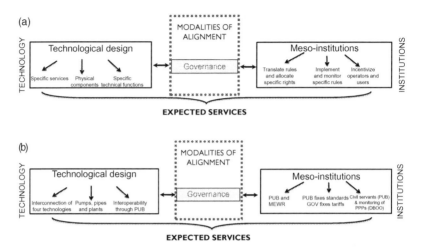

Figure 6.7 (a) Main properties and role of governance and (b) with application to Singapore

importance, complexity, and intricacy of the institutional layers involved.

The city-state has managed the problems of interconnection and interoperability by endorsing the classical solution of a centralized network of plants, pumps, and pipes. In many countries of the developing world, coordinating street vendors, tankers, public fountains, and a partially centralized system raises substantially different problems, requiring different policies. The development of new technologies, for example, desalination in the water sector, smart grids in the electricity sector, could allow more decentralized provision of the expected services. These innovations raise a whole new set of challenges for policy makers. Our analytical framework provides guidance in identifying the technological, economic, and societal components of these different situations and the specific challenges their solutions pose. The next chapter illustrates this through a case of radical innovation in transportation.

7 | Transactions
The Many Challenges Faced by Self-Driving Vehicles

7.1 Introduction

As we enter the second decade of this century, we find ourselves in the middle of fundamental technological as well as institutional changes in our transportation system (Arbib and Seba, 2017; Milakis, van Arem, and van Wee, 2017). As we shall discuss, autonomous and self-driving vehicles will increasingly replace privately owned vehicles driven by humans. These fundamental changes will have large implications for both the technological and the institutional dimension of the transportation system. Not only will the architecture, technological design, and operational technology change, but there will also be a large impact on values, norms, laws, regulations, and property and decision rights.

The transformation is mainly technologically and economically driven. Private firms innovate and commercialize automated and self-driving vehicles for the market, but because important societal values of safety, sustainability, and efficiency are at stake, government will also play an important monitoring and regulating role. In this chapter, we illustrate how our framework helps to identify and analyze some of the fundamental problems that an automated transport sector faces with respect to the safeguarding of critical functions. In the previous two chapters, the focus was on the layers of structures and governance, respectively. In this chapter, we focus on the layer of transactions. Which transactions are critical? How are these transactions coordinated through which micro-institutions? What are the modalities required to align the technical operation and the micro-institutions? According to our approach, such alignment is needed, because otherwise the expected quality of service, such as vehicle safety, is not delivered.

That things can go fatally wrong in a transport system with automated vehicles was illustrated by the case of an accident on March 19, 2018 in a street in Tempe, Arizona. An automated Volvo test car belonging to the cab company Uber, with a back-up driver behind the wheel, struck and killed a pedestrian, who was walking outside of the crosswalk with her bicycle. The US National Transportation Safety Board reported:

According to Uber emergency braking maneuvers are not enabled while the vehicle is under computer control to reduce the potential for erratic vehicle behavior. The vehicle operator is relied on to intervene and take action. The system is not designed to alert the operator. (NTSB, 2018)

Uber engineers had intentionally disabled the emergency braking system of the Volvo car when the vehicle was under computer control (in its automated mode) "to reduce the potential for erratic vehicle behaviour." Such behavior occurs, for instance, when the vehicle's sensors discover "irregularities" on the road and the car stops suddenly. This was considered inconvenient for passengers and dangerous for the other human-driven cars on the road. However, it seems that the Uber engineers did not program the system to alert the human back-up driver to manually intervene when the vehicle detected an "obstacle" on the road while the emergency braking system was disabled. Such an alert system might prove to have been crucial in this case, because first investigations show that the back-up driver was not watching the road carefully at the time of the accident (NTSB, 2018). As will be discussed in more detail below, the Uber engineers seem to have had the possibility, and maybe also the decision rights, to change the technology of the Volvo car. Questions arise as to the decision rights of Uber concerning the technical components of the Volvo car. When, in a transaction between Volvo and Uber, the "right-to-use" is transferred to the buyer, does that imply that the new owner also has the right to adapt the technical components of the car? These questions concern the alignment between the technical operation and the micro-institution, namely, the contract between Volvo and Uber. Using the terminology of our framework, the coordination in the technological dimension was apparently no longer aligned with the coordination of the decision-making rights in the institutional dimension.

From the above example, we conclude that the case of automated vehicles is relevant for testing the explanatory power of our framework. Does the framework provide adequate insights into the complexity of an automated transport system? Does the framework shed light on the accident in Tempe? Does the framework provide solutions to resolve issues of coordination and alignment in the existing experimental stage of the automated transport system?

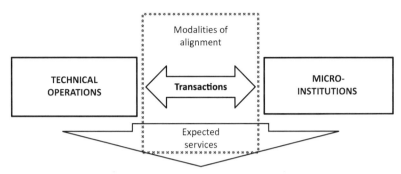

Figure 7.1 Alignment between technical operations and micro-institutions: transactions (layer 3)

In this chapter, we focus on the micro layer. The problems and issues just raised refer to the interdependence between the technical operation and the micro-institutions. This interdependence is encapsulated in Figure 7.1.

This chapter is organized as follows. In Section 7.2, we explore the two upper layers of the system of automated and self-driving vehicles: the macro and meso layer. Section 7.3 discusses the focus of this chapter: transactional alignment. We illustrate with three critical transactions how technological operation and micro-institutions are related. Conclusions and reflection follow in Section 7.4.

7.2 The System of Automated and Self-Driving Vehicles

7.2.1 Introduction and Terminology

In an automated transport system, the transportation of passengers and products takes place through an automated driving system (ADS). In this chapter, we focus on vehicles that transport private passengers. Although the first ADS initiatives were already taken in the 1930s, the development of the technologies stagnated for decades.[1] However, in the 1980s sophisticated sensor and radar technology became available, and ADS developed rapidly, driven by fierce competition between private firms. Nowadays, private firms, such as Uber, test their automated and self-driving vehicles not only in designated areas, but also

---

[1] Wikipedia, "History of self-driving cars" (https://en.wikipedia.org/wiki/history_of_self-driving_cars; last accessed December 27, 2019).

on public roads. The intention is to offer a different type of transport service, known as "Transport-as-a-Service" (TaaS), in the near future.[2]

What Are Automated and Self-Driving Vehicles?
The terminology is sometimes confusing, because several levels of automation can be distinguished, and self-driving would be better separated from automated. The US National Highway Traffic Safety Administration (NHTSA)[3] uses the following classification.

Level 0: no automation. The driver should control the vehicle. Some technological assistance such as parking sensors may be present.

Level 1: specific functional automation such as lane keeping, automatic braking, and adaptive cruise control are available; the car has options for "hands-off driving."

Level 2: combined functional automation such as braking and speed in congested area is available.

Level 3: limited self-driving automation. In specific areas the driver is not expected to constantly monitor the road, but the driver needs to be vigilant in order to take over when necessary (on the highway automated distance and speed control can be used and in cities automated parking is an option); the technical functions allow the driver to ride "eyes-off."

Level 4: full self-driving operation. This marks the change from an automated vehicle to a self-driving vehicle. The driver determines at the beginning of the trip the destination and the car brings the passenger to the destination. At this level the human driver can still intervene and take over the steering wheel. In for instance extreme weather conditions the car will inform the driver it is not able to ride safely and that the human driver should take over. This was the situation in the Tempe case.

Level 5: the self-driving vehicle has no steering wheel and pedals. There is no longer a human driver on board, but only passengers (NHTSA, 2018).

---

[2] It is expected that households and business firms will no longer own cars, but will make use of transportation services provided by specialized companies that own fleets of self-driving vehicles. Transportation will become a service to be delivered on request (Arbib and Seba, 2017). The concept of "Mobility-as-a-Service" (MaaS) is also used.

[3] The National Highway Traffic Safety Administration is an agency of the Executive Branch of the US Government, part of the Department of Transportation.

In the literature, authors use different terminology for the different levels, for example, "connected cars," "autonomous cars," and "self-driving cars." Because legal issues of privacy and liability are involved, we propose to apply a rather strict terminology and suggest calling vehicles in levels 1 to 4 "automated vehicles" and using the term "self-driving vehicle" only for level 5[4] (Holstein, Dodig-Crnkovic, and Pelliccione, 2018). In this chapter, we will refer to automated vehicles as the level 4 type of automation. When we refer to other levels, we will make this explicitly clear.

We will first discuss the technological dimension. What is the architecture of the technology and how is this specifically designed at the second layer? Then we will consider the institutional dimension of the automated transport system. What are the relevant macro-institutions? What values (safety, efficiency, privacy) are at stake, and how do these influence the development and testing of automated and self-driving vehicles? How are values, rules, and laws translated at the meso layer into specific rules and frames to monitor and incentivize operators?

7.2.2 Architecture and Macro-Institutions

Architecture

It appears that in the near future automated as well as self-driving vehicles will be able to make adequate use of the conventional physical infrastructure. The major change in the architecture concerns the role of information and communication technology related to the introduction of the 5G wireless network.[5]

In the conventional transportation system, passenger cars, transportation trucks, and buses use the infrastructure simultaneously. A number of means of communication (such as traffic lights and information panels) are in use to guide drivers of these vehicles, as well as bicyclists and pedestrians. The architecture is interdependent with macro-institutions informed by values such as safety, privacy, and

---

[4] In case of full automation, no driver but only passengers are inside the car. To determine responsibilities, it is important whether a passenger can ultimately intervene and stop the vehicle, or not. With respect to privacy, it is important to analyze the gathering of big data and how this affects the privacy of all road users (for more details, see Section 7.2.2).

[5] Fifth generation wireless systems, abbreviated 5G, are improved wireless network technologies. They were introduced in the Republic of South Korea in 2018, and it is expected that they will be installed in more countries during the 2020s. Tests using the 5G network currently take place in designated areas all over the world.

efficiency. Laws and regulations provide general rules regarding how to behave on the roads (e.g., driving on the right side or giving priority to traffic coming from the right).

In the architecture of the automated transport system of the future, the generic service of the transportation system will still be the safe and efficient movement of persons and goods. The constitutive material components will still be the network of roads (highways, urban roads, and secondary roads in the countryside), connected through crossings, tunnels, and bridges. But on top of that, the architecture of the auto-mated transport system will consist of a new information and communication network: the 5G wireless communication system.

The basic technological function of this new architecture concerns the communication among the vehicles on the road, between the vehicles and the infrastructure, as well as between the vehicles and other road users such as human-driven cars, cyclists, and pedestrians. The 5G network will be able to reduce the time between input and output (so-called latency) to almost zero, meaning that communication takes place in almost real time. That will be of great importance for automated driving systems, because the time between the input of the vehicle's sensors and the reaction of the vehicle will be extremely short. An extremely short reaction time is crucial in order to avoid acccidents. The 5G network will not only be much faster and more reliable than the 4G network, but it will also be able to handle multiple connections simultaneously. In the case of automated driving systems, it means that the network can simultaneously send data from different sensors back and forth between different "machines" (so-called massive machine type communications). Simultaneous communication between vehicles, between vehicles and the infrastructure, and between vehicles and other non-automated road users is crucial for providing safe automated transport services.

Macro-Institutions

Macro-institutions are embedded in the values of society. Our focus in this chapter is on the transport of passengers by private vehicles. Societal values have changed over time with respect to transportation by private cars (NHTSA, 2018). Safety became an important issue from the 1950s onward, resulting in strict regulations and many innovations. From the 1990s on, less pollution and more sustainability also became increasingly important. These changing values are reflected in norms, rules, and laws (see Chapter 1).

Ethical Dilemmas

Alongside the technological developments, fundamental ethical issues emerged in the debates in macro-institutions, such as parliament, when making laws concerning the protocols, standards, guidelines, and directives that frame the decision-making at the micro layer. This can be illustrated using the so-called trolley problem.

The trolley problem in relation to self-driving vehicles is discussed in a number of publications (Holstein, Dodig-Crnkovic, and Pelliccione, 2018). In the setting of the trolley problem, the self-driving vehicle is confronted with an ethical dilemma. The car is driving on the road and is, for instance, unexpectedly confronted with a group of people crossing the road. Due to the high speed, the car cannot stop in time. How should the software of the self-driving vehicle be programmed? Should it brake and hit the group? Should it evade the group and drive onto the lane for cyclists or pedestrians? In the trolley problem, many variants are possible, including the dilemma that the vehicle could evade the group and drive against a wall, probably killing the passengers in the car.

This issue of integrating moral principles into the algorithm of self-driving vehicles raises fundamental questions concerning the rules at the layer of macro-institutions. These rules concerning the programming of the software of self-driving vehicles should be translated through meso-institutions into guidelines and directives for the car manufacturers (e.g., Volvo) and the owners of self-driving vehicles (e.g., Uber).

7.2.3 Technological Design and Meso-Institutions

Technological Design

In the United States, in European countries, and in countries in Asia automated and self-driving vehicles are tested both in designated areas and on public roads. The context in which this takes place differs. Sometimes, the fully automated and self-driving vehicles are tested in isolated controlled areas; sometimes, the context is relatively simple with a few straight streets and no other users of the road; sometimes, there is a human back-up driver on board; and sometimes, the self-driving vehicles only deliver a regular transport service on a predetermined trajectory. Different contexts demand and allow for different specifications of technical components, because they have to perform different functions. For instance, a vehicle that cannot change lanes has different sensors and radars inside the car compared with a vehicle that is equipped to change lanes. The former will have only sensors that measure the speed and distance of vehicles in front, and the computer will instruct the brakes or the accelerator. The latter will also have sensors that measure the distance and speed of other vehicles, and after the computer has made the necessary calculations it will instruct the "steering wheel" to turn to the left or the right. On a fixed trajectory, the vehicle-operating system inside the car communicates with the infrastructure and other vehicles differently than a vehicle that has the option of choosing its own lane.

The quality of the technical components can also differ in different contexts. In very complex situations with different road users, including children, the disabled, and the elderly, the sensors of the vehicles and the speed of the electronic devices making calculations and decisions can be different from vehicles that operate in less complex contexts. Note that a higher quality of components comes at a price, and that producers of components and cars will try to minimize costs.

The presence of a human back-up driver also has implications for the composition of the specific technical components and their coordination. When the technical system, for one reason or another, cannot perform its task adequately, the system will inform the human driver that they have to take over. When no back-up driver is present, the technical components and their coordination would be different. The components would not only monitor and control the system, collect data, and send information to the electronic entity that activates the brakes, steering, or speed, but if the system should fail, then a safe solution would have to be generated automatically to stop and park the car. Passengers should then be informed by the system what to do.

In different contexts, the technical components of the infrastructure or devices attributed to other road users may also be different. For instance, in urban areas with many cyclists and pedestrians, they might have technical devices on their bikes or smartphones that can be detected by the sensors of automated vehicles. In this way, they could be "seen" even when it is dark.

In specifying a technology for a specific context, multiple factors are relevant. The NHTSA uses the concept of the operational design domain (ODD),[6] which describes the specific conditions under which

---

[6] "It is anticipated that vehicles with high and full driving automation will accomplish this through the combination of highly sophisticated detection

an ADS or feature is intended to function. More specifically, it defines where (such as what roadway types and speeds) and when (under what conditions, such as day/night, weather limits, etc.) an ADS is designed to operate.

Many Combinations Possible

How complicated is the specific situation for the technology on board the vehicle? How costly is the higher quality of components? How important is the value that is fulfilled by the expensive high-quality electronics for the consumer and society? Different consumers and different communities will answer these questions differently. Very good sensors that can identify objects many meters ahead in bad weather conditions are much more costly than sensors that are able to detect objects only nearby or only by daylight. But are these high-quality technical components always required or wanted? Can automated vehicles operating in calm suburban areas deliver a lower quality service than vehicles that operate in crowded city centers? Different solutions might be considered acceptable as long as the monitoring and control around the limited operational domain is well organized. Moreover, it is possible that passengers or owners of automated vehicles might accept a lower quality of technical components in the car under the condition that they themselves are always in the position to intervene. So when, for instance, the vehicle is not able to "see" well in bad weather conditions, or the situation is so complex that the electronic devices are not able to cope with it, the passenger might be informed to take over immediately,[7] or the vehicle will stop and will not operate anymore.

systems, systems for digital interpretation of detected objects, data retention and processing, communication protocols, and highly sophisticated decision-making software. Together, this combination of functions is intended to replace and improve upon the ability of human drivers to detect, interpret, communicate and react to vehicle operational needs and conditions. Some vehicles with high driving automation will require an additional design consideration to address human-machine interface when operating outside of their Operational Design Domain. Specifically, given the reliance of those vehicles on vehicle, and not human, systems, the design of those vehicles should account for both the vehicle and human elements of any transition from one type of driver (human or vehicle) to another type of driver (vehicle or human)." (NHTSA, 2018: 23).

[7] "For example, if a vehicle is capable of safely operating automatically only at speeds below 30 mph, NHTSA might consider whether it would be appropriate to require that the vehicle be designed so that it cannot operate automatically at speeds of 30 mph or more unless and until it acquires the capability (e.g., through

At the layer of technological design, different qualities of components and coordination arrangements can therefore be attributed to the self-driving vehicles and the road system, depending on the specific context.

Meso-Institutions

The translation of the structural components determined within the macro layer into specificities for the micro layer takes place through meso-institutions, such as the Singapore Land Transport Authority (LTA),[8] the American National Highway Traffic Safety Administration (NHTSA),[9] and the EU High-Level Meetings on Connected and Automated Driving.[10]

Meso-institutions translate rules defined within the macro-institutional layer into more specific rules, allocate specific rights,

software updates) of safely operating automatically above that speed. Similarly, if a vehicle would become incapable of operating safely if one or more of its sensors became non-functional, NHTSA might consider whether it would be appropriate to require that the vehicle be designed so that it cannot operate automatically in those circumstances." (NHTSA, 2018: 26).

[8] The Land Transport Authority takes many initiatives to provide testing facilities and facilitates innovation. For example, the Singapore Autonomous Vehicle Initiative (SAVI) is a joint partnership between LTA and several research institutes (e.g., A*STAR) to provide a technical platform for industry partners and stakeholders to conduct research and development and testbedding of automated driving technology, applications, and solutions.

[9] NHTSA, an operating administration within the US Department of Transportation, was established as a successor to the National Highway Safety Bureau by the Highway Safety Act of 1970 to carry out safety programs under the National Traffic and Motor Vehicle Safety Act of 1966 and the Highway Safety Act of 1966.

[10] The Declaration of Amsterdam was adopted during the Dutch presidency of the EU in the spring of 2016 in Amsterdam, with the goal of more coordinated EU efforts concerning connected and automated vehicles. This goal is to be achieved through close cooperation between member states, the European Commission, and the industry to promote development in the area of connected and automated driving. Follow-up meetings have been held in Frankfurt, Germany and a third one took place in Gothenburg, Sweden on June 18–19, 2018. For details, see the "Outcome of the first High Level Meeting" (Dutch Ministry of Infrastructure and the Environment, 2017). On the initiative of the Dutch EU presidency, all EU member states endorsed the Declaration of Amsterdam. Jointly with the European automotive industry, the European Union aimed to clear the way for connected and automated driving in 2019. The European Commission has launched a strategy on Cooperative Intelligent Transport Systems, and the automotive industry and automotive suppliers have set up the European Automotive and Telecoms Alliance (EATA).

implement and control rules and rights, and monitor and incentivize the operators in the system. For instance, the safety of the passengers of automated and self-driving vehicles as well as the safety of the users of the road can be considered the core value at the macro layer. But how this can be best specified, implemented, and monitored with such vehicles riding on public roads is still under discussion.

"Learning-by-Doing" and "Proven-in-Use"
What might be the conditions under which a car manufacturer gets a license for automated and self-driving vehicles to be sold for usage on public roads? Would an extension of the present safety standards for road vehicles be sufficient? Would a license be related to testing a car for, say, one million kilometers without any accident? It seems that authorities lean toward applying the approaches of "learning-by-doing" and "proven-in-use" (Dutch Ministry of Infrastructure and the Environment, 2017; Holstein, Dodig-Crnkovic, and Pelliccione, 2018; NHTSA, 2018).

Learning-by-doing refers to the development of regulations and safety standards during the test period in consultation with different stakeholders. In the United States, the National Highway Traffic Safety Administration applies the Federal Motor Vehicle Safety Standards (FMVSS), with which car manufacturers must comply for certification. Depending on changes in values and technologies, the standards will be adapted over time, or exemptions will be applied for specific new vehicles, for instance, without a steering wheel or pedals. New technologies will be first tested in designated areas, and depending on the lessons learned, new technical components and coordination arrangements will be applied in automated vehicles on public roads. Based on this process of learning-by-doing, meso-institutions will establish new mechanisms, new protocols, rules, and standards.

"Proven-in-use" refers to the approach according to which public authorities do not specify how the new standards should be fulfilled. It is left to the car manufacturers and the users of the vehicles to implement the new standards using the technology they consider most adequate. The "how" is left to the producers, and the meso-institution will "only" apply monitoring and control to ensure that the rules are followed and the standards are met. The principle of proven-in-use implies that different car manufacturers can apply different technologies to make a vehicle perform according to specified norms and standards.[11] Among other things, safety conditions will imply that different technologies are interoperable between vehicles and the road network infrastructure. Hence, the critical functions of interoperability and interconnection are crucial for the safe operation of automated vehicles.

Consultation of stakeholders is a crucial element in the approach just outlined, which can be illustrated by the recent Advanced Notice of Proposed Rulemaking (ANPRM)[12] of the NHTSA. The NHTSA (also referred to in the documents as the Agency) is seeking "public comment on matters related to the near-term and long-term challenges of Automated Driving Systems (ADS) testing, development and eventual deployment" (NHTSA, 2018: 2). The Agency plans to launch a Pilot Program for Collaborative Research on Motor Vehicles with High or Full Driving Automation.[13] All kinds of stakeholders (from car manufacturers or local authorities to individual pedestrians) are invited to comment and advise on what such a pilot should look like, in order to provide optimal conditions for the Agency to "learn from the testing and development of the emerging advanced vehicle safety technologies and to assure the safety of those activities" (NHTSA, 2018: 3). In the ANPRM, the Agency lists a number of topics accompanied by questions it is interested in. It is explicitly stated in the document that safety is the first priority, but that it is attempting to make new rules and regulations "while preserving the freedom to innovate" (NHTSA, 2018: 3).[14] The Agency is specifically interested in the

[11] The approach of "learning-by-doing" and "proven-in-use" is a common approach also applied in the past: "As technology has evolved, NHTSA has responded to Congressional mandates to use its authority to specify how and when the hardware components of electronic systems such as air bags, anti-lock braking systems and electronic stability control systems must activate and perform. This approach gives manufacturers freedom to develop the software components needed to control the performance of each system's hardware components" (NHTSA, 2018: 11).

[12] In this notice, the NHTSA announces that it is contemplating creating an ADS vehicle pilot research program for the testing of vehicles and associated equipment and gathering of data from such testing, including in real-world scenarios, which the Agency would consider as setting the terms of the exemptions (NHTSA, 2018: 18).

[13] "The purpose of a pilot program is to allow for safe on-road testing and on-road learning in order to provide feedback for further safe development" (NHTSA, 2018: 27).

[14] In a separate notice published in January 2018 (83 Fed. Reg. 2607, January 18, 2018), the Agency took the next step by publishing a request for public

question as to what kind of exemptions are needed in the existing Federal Motor Vehicle Safety Standards (FMVSS) with regard to the testing, compliance certification, and compliance verification of automated motor vehicles. Moreover, the Agency stresses that the testing should include not only the testing of predictable events (such as changing lanes with other vehicles being around), but also unpredictable events (such as the unexpected crossing of a street by a pedestrian[15]).

Security, Privacy, and Human Intervention
Next to safety, the value of security is also an important issue at the meso layer. How can the software of a self-driving vehicle be protected against cybercrime? In a world full of the dangers of terrorist attacks, the manipulation of cars from outside should be ruled out. But again, in the decision-making process about the necessary technical devices, different stakeholders are involved who have different interests when it comes to decisions about costs and the quality of technical components. In order to safeguard a minimum level of security, our framework suggests that meso-institutions should also specify in this case the rules of the game.

Furthermore, the societal value of privacy is of utmost importance in the world of automated and self-driving vehicles. Even the presence of one sensor in a car which, for instance, registers the behavior of a

comments to identify any regulatory barriers in the existing Federal Motor Vehicle Safety Standards (FMVSS) to the testing, compliance certification, and compliance verification of automated motor vehicles. In that notice, the NHTSA focused primarily, but not exclusively, on vehicles with certain unconventional interior designs, such as those that lack controls for a human driver; e.g., steering wheel, brake pedal, or accelerator pedal. The absence of manual driving controls, and thus of a human driver, poses potential barriers to testing, compliance certification, and compliance verification.

[15] "Similarly, although existing FMVSS generally address specific predictable events (e.g., stopping and turning safely on low friction surfaces, specific types of crashes), it may be desirable, even necessary, to meet the need for safety, for future FMVSS focused on ADS technologies to also address the common, yet unpredictable, events that occur in real-world driving, e.g., the one person among crowds of people standing on two or more corners of an intersection who suddenly decides to cross the street, the approaching vehicle that suddenly turns left, the parked vehicle that suddenly leaves its parking place, and the vehicle that suddenly emerges from a blind alley or other obscured location. Test procedures could replicate those events, including their unpredictability." (NHTSA, 2018: 15)

pedestrian, raises questions about privacy. As soon as data are recorded and distributed without the consent of the individual, the value of privacy is at stake. Our framework suggests that directives and guidelines have to be developed by the meso-institutions about which data it is necessary to collect, who has access to the data, and how long the data should be stored.

The issue of human intervention refers to the need for meso-institutions to specify the rights of individuals to intervene in the automated processing of vehicles. In level 5 vehicles, passengers cannot intervene by means of pedals or a steering wheel. If a passenger feels that the vehicle is not operating according to the correct standard, should they be able to intervene and how? What if a self-driving vehicle violates traffic rules? Could a policeman stop it? What if a policeman wants to stop a self-driving vehicle in order to inspect its passengers? Our framework suggests that the answers to these kinds of questions should be specified by meso-institutions with regard to rules, rights, guidelines, directives, and incentives for agents operating within the micro layer.

7.2.4 Technical Operation and Micro-Institutions

In Section 7.2.2 above, we outlined the technological and institutional dimensions at the macro and meso layers. We will now take a closer look at the third layer of our framework. We assume that the architecture and technological design are given and in place.

In this section, we first discuss the technical operation and illustrate the difficulties engineers experience in building automated and self-driving vehicles that are able to react as human drivers would. Next, we turn to the micro-institutions that coordinate the critical transactions.

Complex Operational Technology

On broad, straight roads in cities like Phoenix (Arizona), or on designated highways in California, or in test areas like One-North in Singapore, the operational technology of automated vehicles is nowadays adequate for transporting passengers safely. Basically, sensors, radar, and cameras provide information to the operating technology of the vehicle about the type of road, obstacles, the distance from other vehicles and their speed, as well as the weather conditions. All the data

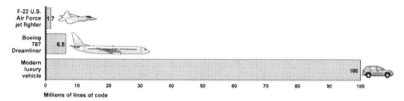

Figure 7.2 Aircraft and automobile software codes compared (grades of automation, GAO, 2016b)

are gathered and presented in a three-dimensional representation of 360 degrees of the operating area, in which the vehicle can find its way. Fifth generation communication networks are important enablers for such technologies. Automated vehicles are able to perform well in places such as Phoenix, due to favorable conditions such as straight roads and stable weather conditions, and due to sufficiently well-coordinated intelligent technological components in and outside the vehicle. However, the complexity of the vehicle operating technology increases massively with the number and type of heterogeneous road users such as non-automated vehicles, cyclists, and pedestrians. The degree of complexity is illustrated in Figure 7.2, which shows that even existing vehicles already have more sophisticated operational technology than aircrafts, due to complex roadway interactions (Holstein, Dodig-Crnkovic, and Pelliccione, 2018).

Mastering the actual complexities of traffic situations proves to be a very difficult final step in the operational technology of the fully automated and self-driving vehicle. In traffic situations with unexpected movements, for instance, by pedestrians or children, technical devices are not (yet) able to recognize a pattern of human behavior and correctly interpret the situation. Level 4 and 5 automated vehicles are presently not sufficiently technically equipped to take the appropriate course of action in novel situations. This is because the operating algorithms are based on the recognition of patterns, which are retrieved from big data, based on traffic configurations known from the past. Such recognizable situations can be anticipated very quickly by the vehicle operational technology, but that is not the case in completely unexpected and novel circumstances.

Automated driving systems are not only very fast in recognizing standard situations and taking appropriate decisions, but they also have the advantage of being able to make use of collective experience.

Data from millions of cars in numerous situations add up to a much greater knowledge base than a human driver can ever build up in an entire lifetime. However, experienced human drivers are mostly superior at recognizing and predicting the behavior of other road users. Moreover, human drivers are able to take decisions in situations that are new to them. Such decisions can be based on intuition, or knowledge of the intentions of others. For human drivers, the body language or small gestures made by other road users are a source of useful information. The interpretation of body language turns out to be difficult to embed into the algorithms of self-driving vehicles. Based on big data, scientists are working on the building of "motion models." Sensors could determine the position of the torso of a human body and interpret facial gestures to signal the need for technical intervention, for instance, to brake immediately. This is the world of "deep learning technology," which is still in its infancy, although important progress has already been made (Braun et al., 2019). Even more big data are needed to monitor and control the processing of highly automated and self-driving vehicles. This is necessary, in order to differentiate and classify complex traffic configurations, and to initiate sometimes rare and strange technical configurations. Sometimes, there may be a necessity for the vehicle to increase its speed above the legal limit in order to avoid an accident, or to drive the car off the road to avoid a collision.

The interpretation of body language also depends on local culture and habits. For instance, shaking your head in Sri Lanka means "yes," whereas in many Western countries this is interpreted as "no." Consequently, general behavioral algorithms have to be adequately adapted at the layer of technical design, and should be further specified with respect to technical operation. They need to be context-specific, including the type of road and vehicle, the region or country, the time of the day, the season of the year, and the weather conditions. At the operational layer, automated and self-driving vehicles have to be equipped with such context-specific operational technology.

Ethical Dilemmas

Another significant operational issue concerns the programming of the algorithms for self-driving vehicles. We have already discussed the ethical issues related to the decision-making of machines. Artificial intelligence builds on guidelines and directives established at the other layers of our framework. In most cases, no dilemmas are expected to occur, and the actual processing of automated vehicles is concerned with smoothly turning the "wheel," braking, accelerating, or stopping to load and unload passengers. But when confronted with situations in which collisions with another vehicles, cyclists, or pedestrians might occur, guidelines and directives are indispensable with regard to potential ways of technically resolving such configurations. This ultimately depends on societal values.[16]

Micro-Institutions

We have outlined how macro-institutions are translated through meso-institutions into protocols, guidelines, directives, and standards for the micro-institutions. Agents at the micro layer transact: car manufacturers buy technical equipment, consumers purchase self-driving vehicles, providers of transport services such as Uber utilize automated vehicles for their purposes, etc. These transactions are coordinated through micro-institutions such as contracts, alliances, vertically integrated firms, and public–private partnerships (see Chapter 2). In the next section, we elaborate on the concept of transactional alignment, and how a misalignment could be identified and restored, with a focus on such micro-institutions.

7.3 Critical Transactions

Transactions are about the transfer of "right-to-use" goods or services across technologically separable interfaces (see Chapter 2). Critical transactions are about those transfers of rights that are essential to secure the critical functions. In the discussions on automated and self-driving vehicles, safety is an important requirement of expected transport services, as the example of the accident in Tempe clearly shows. Consequently, we focus in this section on safety as part of the critical function of system control.

---

[16] Also interesting in this respect are the proposals of Goodman and Flaxman (2016) regarding the right of users of "machines" to know the algorithms applied by the manufacturer. If these are known and the algorithms differ, then buyers of self-driving vehicles would be able to choose to buy a car with the – for them – adequate moral principles.

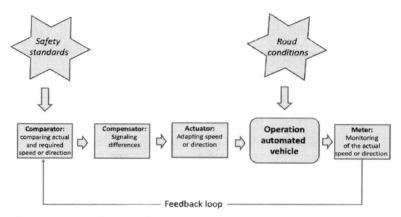

Figure 7.3 Control system for automated vehicles

7.3.1 Illustration with Three Critical Transactions

Three critical transactions are discussed, relating to:

- the operation of automated vehicles,
- the provision of navigation services, and
- the provision of transport as a service.

We have selected these transactions because they are illustrative for the Tempe case, as we shall substantiate in what follows.

Operation of Automated Vehicles

The automated and self-driving vehicle can be conceptualized as a socio-technological system that provides a transport service related to the broader transport system and its infrastructure (see Chapters 1 and 3). From a safety point of view, the components in the technological dimension of the vehicle need to be configured, monitored, and controlled such that expected transport services are delivered. This is related to the "control systems engineering approach" (Chapter 4). Accordingly, Figure 7.3 illustrates the configuration of technical devices and entities involved in the safe operation of automated vehicles.

The relevant technical process is the operation of a type 4 automated vehicle on a road. Driving between two points A and B is influenced by the conditions on the road, such as parked cars, other road users, and the physical state of the road. In addition, traffic rules need to be obeyed, some of which are indicated by traffic signs. Hence, technical arrangements for monitoring and control of the operational environment are required, which are substantiated by the configuration of technical devices shown in Figure 7.3. Metering devices provide relevant information, for instance, about the relative speed and distance from other road users and the operational environment (e.g., approaching a curve, a signal from a traffic light). A "comparator" with inbuilt safety standards – for instance, related to speed, the distance from other vehicles, and the weather conditions – compares these data. A "compensator" signals differences between the actual operation and the desired safe operation of the automated vehicle. If differences are detected, the "actuator" adapts the speed or direction of the vehicle such that the safety standards are fulfilled. This is an ongoing process, shown by the feedback loop in Figure 7.3.

The operation of automated and self-driving vehicles also has an institutional dimension. Traffic rules and safety standards are an integral part of the control systems engineering approach. However, engineers and control systems only take into account a limited part of the institutional dimension, namely, that concerning traffic rules. But there is more to be considered. In particular, the allocation and monitoring of the decision rights is of major importance. The Tempe case clearly illustrates that the organizational modalities for the operation of automated vehicles are closely related to the implementation and monitoring of the technical process. In this case, the Uber engineers disabled the intervention of the "actuator" technical device under certain circumstances, in order to prevent the vehicle from erratically adjusting its speed or direction. They disrupted the feedback loop. Apparently, they had the decision rights to do so without any monitoring and control of its impact on the safe operation of the car. An appropriate allocation of such decision rights should probably be carried out through specific micro-institutions, such as a vertically integrated firm or a contract.

The transaction of delivering the vehicle within the firm (for instance, within Uber) from the engineering department to the service-providing department is coordinated inside the vertically integrated firm. The engineers of the firm should deliver a car that can technically provide safe transportation services. The internal transaction is critical, because safety – as part of the critical function "system control" – is at stake. In the Tempe case, the transaction was not well coordinated internally, causing an unsafe situation on the road.[17]

However, the contractual arrangement between the car manufacturer and the service provider owning a fleet of self-driving vehicles is of a different nature. As the Tempe accident shows, there are conflicting interests and the (ab)use of decision rights can make the vehicle unsafe. In the case of Tempe, Uber wished to deliver transport services with a vehicle that did not show "erratic" behavior (see the preliminary report of the NTSB[18]). However, Volvo had installed the technological components and arranged the coordination between them, so that they would warn a human back-up driver if the car was confronted with an unknown situation.[19] Details of the technical investigation show that the technical components of the car and their coordination were functioning well.[20] So the problem apparently came from the disruption in the feedback loop due to Uber's intervention. The final report from the NTSB (NTSB, 2019a) confirmed the preliminary conclusions and added that a sufficient safety culture within Uber was completely missing. The NTSB report presented to the US Senate (NTSB, 2019b) was very clear in that respect.[21]

[17] The organization of these transactions within the firm is of course one solution among other possible arrangements; for example, the firm could contract out its engineering activities, etc.

[18] The preliminary report from the National Transportation Safety Board (NTSB, 2018) provides preliminary conclusions about the causes of the accident.

[19] The Uber's self-driving car system detected the pedestrian about six seconds before the vehicle hit the woman. But the system never took action to prevent the incident, according to the preliminary results of a National Transportation Safety Board investigation. If the emergency braking system had been activated, it would have been triggered 1.3 seconds before the car hit the pedestrian.

[20] "The vehicle was factory equipped with several advanced driver assistance functions by the original manufacturer, Volvo Cars, including a collision avoidance function with automatic emergency braking as well as functions for detecting driver alertness and road sign information. The Volvo functions are disabled only when the test vehicle is operated in computer control mode (. . .).

According to Uber emergency braking maneuvers are not enabled while the vehicle is under computer control to reduce the potential for erratic vehicle behavior. The vehicle operator is relied on to intervene and take action. The system is not designed to alert the operator." (NTSB, 2018).

[21] "We determined that the probable cause of the crash was the failure of the vehicle operator to monitor the driving environment and the operation of the ADS because she was visually distracted throughout the trip by her personal cell phone. Contributing to the crash were the Uber ATG's (1) inadequate safety risk assessment procedures, (2) ineffective oversight of the vehicle operator, and (3) lack of adequate mechanisms for addressing the operator's automation complacency – all a consequence of inadequate safety culture. Further factors

Provision of Navigation Services

Navigation services are indispensable for the safe operation of electric vehicles. Current navigation systems are often built on GPS technology for the transmission of data through the internet. However, this does not meet the safety requirements of self-driving cars. Among other things, the navigation data are not sufficiently precise. Better high-definition maps are being developed by TomTom (a navigation map specialist), Waymo (a spin-off of MIT and the successor of the "Google car"), and Here (the former map division of Nokia).

The company Here has developed a navigation system with an innovative additional feature. The system not only provides precise information about the current location of the vehicle and the actual traffic situation; it also offers data about past situations. The navigation system recollects traffic configurations at the same location and how they were resolved in the past. Moreover, the navigation system not only builds on data collected by a single user, but it can also relate to the database of all other vehicles using the same technology. Together with the capability of fast machine learning from data provided by other machines, it is expected that vehicles using such navigation services would in principle drive at least as safely as a human driver under known circumstances. The weakness of such services is related to dealing with unexpected situations. A pedestrian or cyclist might suddenly cross the road in a way that is not stored in the database of the navigation system, and consequently no conclusive guidelines or standards are available on how to adjust the operation of the automated vehicle. Under such conditions, one possibility is that a back-up driver could be alerted about these unknown situations so as to take over the operation of the vehicle. Another option is that the vehicle stops in all cases of unknown traffic conditions. Operators would then have more time to consider actions to be taken.

contributing to the crash were (1) the impaired pedestrian's crossing of North Mill Avenue outside a crosswalk, and (2) the Arizona Department of Transportation's insufficient oversight of AV testing.

At the time of the crash, Uber ATG had an inadequate safety culture, exhibited by inadequate safety risk-management procedures and safety policies, lack of oversight of vehicle operators, and lack of personnel with backgrounds in safety management systems. For example, we concluded that Uber ATG's deactivation of the Volvo forward collision warning and automatic emergency braking systems without replacing their full capacities removed a layer of safety redundancy and increased the risks associated with testing ADSs on public roads." (NTSB, 2019b: 2).

This example illustrates the critical transaction between the provider of sophisticated navigation services and the operators of automated vehicles. Micro-institutions need to clearly allocate decision rights on how navigation systems are implemented, monitored, and controlled in the operation of automated vehicles. Sophisticated navigation technology and machine learning can only be safely applied in conjunction with well-specified institutional arrangements.

Provision of Transport as a Service
It is envisaged that in the future specialized firms with fleets of self-driving vehicles will offer transport services to the market. Competing providers will differentiate their services, and customers will be able to choose from several options such as a monthly subscription for a fixed trajectory, or an incidental demand for a specific route. It is expected that providers will first offer services on dedicated roads with fixed schedules. Gradually, customers will become more familiar with automated and self-driving vehicles, and will be more aware of the efficiency and convenience of this new way of private transport.[22] The transactional conditions (uncertainty, asset specificity, frequency, complexity) for buying and selling transport services are similar to those in the mobile phone market. Accordingly, the transactions could be coordinated through a classical type of contract within a regulated market. From this perspective, regulation could be restricted to safeguarding competition and formulating and applying the safety standards for issuing licenses to transport service providers.

The technological arrangements for providing transport services are closely related to those described for the operation of automated vehicles and the provision of navigation services. If transport services are provided by the market, the technological operation of these services still needs to be carefully monitored and controlled, as we have demonstrated in previous examples.

7.3.2 Transactional (Mis)alignment

In this section, we explore the alignment or misalignment between technological and institutional characteristics of the coordination

---

[22] Milakis, van Arem, and van Wee (2017) provide a review of the literature on the private and social costs and benefits of automated driving, both in the short and long term.

arrangements at the layer of transactions. This layer is about the alignment of the technological arrangements that coordinate technical components and the institutional arrangements that coordinate institutional components. We explore their compatibility or incompatibility in terms of open or closed and centralized or decentralized arrangements (see Chapter 4). We discuss modalities of alignment which include entities and devices that designate, respectively, "who" is proceeding to the alignment and "how" the alignment is reached or restored.

Different Qualities of Services
In the case of automated and self-driving vehicles, different qualities of service are possible. The technical operation can be based on different design choices with respect to the quality and technological capabilities of devices and entities. Also, meso- and macro-institutions are important in this respect, since they provide guidelines and standards for the operational safety of transport services. Even consumer preferences (price, quality) have to be taken into consideration.

It is expected that in the future, automated and self-driving vehicles will be operated according to different technological designs depending on the transport service they provide. In the case of homogenous transport services on a fixed trajectory, a designated road, and a specific schedule, the technological design can be relatively simple. However, if the services are provided in a crowded city center with other road users (not self-driving vehicles, cyclists, and pedestrians), or in regions with extremely rapid changes in weather conditions, the technological design needs to rely on more sophisticated material components and material arrangements. Accordingly, the technological operation might include the application of advanced navigation systems and control systems engineering approaches.

Under such conditions, licenses might be issued for vehicles that are permitted to be operated in only a specific "operational design domain" (see Section 7.2.2). That is to say, licensed vehicles can only operate in specific designated domains such as "fixed trajectories," "urban roads," or "city centers." Different qualities of service correspond to different technological designs and processing of transport services, including different technical and institutional coordination arrangements. Among other things, the access to these restricted areas should be well monitored, and technical operation of the vehicles should be well protected against malicious intrusion from hackers.

With respect to the characterization of the technical coordination, the above implies that the technical operation depends on a control systems engineering approach (Figure 7.3). The safety of transport services might then be guaranteed under all circumstances. According to Chapter 4, such a technical coordination can be characterized as centralized and closed.

Likewise, the micro-institutions should very precisely specify the organizational modalities through which different qualities of service can be offered. Given the need for a tight coordination of the technological devices, the coordination of the institutional devices should also be of a closed and centralized nature. This should be the case for different qualities of service: for each quality a specific alignment of the technical and institutional coordination arrangements would be needed.

This also has implications for the issuing of licenses. Only when the technical operation of automated vehicles in test areas performs according to certain standards will the operator get a license for the provision of transport services. Correspondingly, the responsible meso-institution should be assured that the decision rights with respect to the technical standards are adequately allocated. Note also that the license should be restricted to a specific domain of use, technological design, and operation.

Modalities of Transactional Alignment

In our perspective, transactions are modalities of transfer of rights to use goods and services across technologically separable activities, in order to align technical operations with micro-institutions, which is needed to fulfill the critical functions of the network infrastructure at stake. Transactional alignment implies that the required adaptations are made through the micro-institutions when a misalignment is identified in the system. In order to restore alignment, adaptations can be made in either the operational technology and/or the micro-institution. For instance, if the technical coordination arrangement needs to be of a closed, centralized nature, whereas the institutional arrangement allows for decentralized decision-making, then alignment could be restored by centralizing the institutional coordination arrangement. However, if the fulfillment of the critical functions and the corresponding required quality of service allows, alignment could also be restored by decentralizing the technological coordination arrangement (see the illustration in Section 7.4 for the Tempe case).

Furthermore, it is also possible that changes in the wider transport system are needed in order to restore alignment. For instance, this might concern the values embedded in the macro-institutions. The quality of service in terms of safety, privacy, efficiency, and costs can change, and can be changed, over time. It is possible that over time the quality of the transport service in terms of safety changes, and that passengers accept a certain risk (likewise, in the case of services delivered by trains, boats, and planes), which allows for more decentralized coordination arrangements both along the technological and institutional dimensions. Because of the strict safety requirements, alignment in the Tempe case should probably be realized through a change in the micro-institutional arrangement.

As discussed in Chapter 2, institutional economics can provide useful insights in that respect. In his "simple contracting scheme" Williamson (1979) demonstrated which type of micro-institutions private agents would choose, in order to safeguard their interests while minimizing transaction costs. In his scheme, "private ordering" (different modalities of micro-institutional arrangements, e.g., spot markets, relational contracts, firms as vertically integrated organizations) is complemented by "public ordering." Public ordering is needed when the performance of private ordering fails and specific societal objectives (such as a safe transport service) are not met. Then we enter the world of regulation and public bureaus such as government agencies and state-owned enterprises. Previously (and in Chapter 2), we showed how rules and norms established at the macro-institutional level are translated by meso-institutions into guidelines, specific rules, protocols, and standards to guide and direct micro-institutions. In specifying the institutional dimension from macro to micro, while taking the technological specification from architecture to technical operation into account, the concepts of private and public ordering have to be made context-specific at a detailed level of analysis. For instance, this has already been illustrated by the way in which the National Highway Traffic Safety Administration develops its policy with respect to the testing and implementation of self-driving vehicles.

With respect to the Tempe case, the implication is that transactional alignment can be restored by adapting the frame of protocols, rules, guidelines, directives, and standards, within which agents coordinate their transactions through adequately selected and implemented micro-institutions. For a socio-technological frame to be well-adapted, specific micro-institutions such as the firm Uber and the contractual arrangement providers and operators of services will have to be constrained in such a way that the critical function of safety is guaranteed.

7.4 Conclusions and Reflection

From the study of this case of automated and self-driving vehicles, we can draw some conclusions about the application of our framework and about its relevance. There is also another advantage of this application, as well as for the others considered in this part of our book, which is that it provides food for thought about the more general potential of our framework, but also about some of its limitations.

The Relevance of Our Framework
In analyzing the existing and future transportation system in general, and the testing and deployment of automated and self-driving vehicles, we showed that the application of our framework provides a good understanding of the interdependencies between the technological and institutional dimensions at stake. An analysis of both the vertical coordination between the layers along these two dimensions, respectively, and the horizontal alignment between them offers very useful insights into the complexity of the transportation network and the conditions to be met if the expected services are to be delivered.

The changes in the technological architecture, with the introduction of technological designs and the operation of automated vehicles, and their interdependence with macro-institutional values – particularly safety but also security, privacy, and efficiency – offer a rich opportunity to analyze the structural complexities at stake. The technological design of automated and self-driving vehicles depends on the expected services and the spatial and temporal context. It has also become clear how important meso-institutions are in translating macro-institutional rules and norms, and shaping their implementation at the micro layer. Indeed, throughout our empirical analysis of the case of automated and self-driving vehicles, meso-institutions play a crucial role in each phase of the development of these vehicles in monitoring, controlling, and incentivizing the micro-institutions. In doing so, meso-institutions established a mode of governance through which technological design and the allocation and usage of rights are interconnected.

Although the main focus of this chapter has been the exploration of the layer of transactions, we first needed to position this layer within a context. Indeed, the role of values in organizing the new industry and the role of meso-institutions such as the NHTSA proved to be especially important. In that respect, it was of great interest to discern that this meso-institution actually operates as an intermediate between the general rules established – or to be established – within the macro layer and the micro-institutions embedded in these rules. The rounds of consultation of all stakeholders, resulting in a well-prepared pilot experiment before any licenses are issued, seem an original way to deal with changing socio-technological systems that depend on tight inter-dependencies between technology and institutions. Similarly, the "learning-by-doing" and the "proven-in-use" approaches provide rich indications about alternative modalities to deal with the complexities at hand.

Hence, the way the NHTSA works is a good illustration that fits well and appropriately substantiates the theoretical role we identified as characterizing meso-institutions in Chapter 2. Not only are the translating, monitoring, and control procedures in place, but the case of NHTSA also substantiates well the function of meso-institutions to "pass upward signals of misalignment that are transmitted by operators and users and that might require changes in the allocation of rights" (Chapter 2, Section 2.3.3).

Some Challenges
However, what seems to be missing in the positioning of NHTSA with respect to its role regarding the micro-layer is the awareness that some transactions might be more important than other transactions, such that a specification of the critical transactions would be necessary. Our theoretical framework suggests that in order for institutions and technology to be aligned, meso-institutions such as the NHTSA should be aware of the critical functions and the corresponding critical structures, governance, and transactions. For instance, in the case of automated and self-driving vehicles, this would require an institution such as the NHTSA to focus more specifically during the consultation process on the functions that are critical for the values at stake.[23] It

---

[23] The questions that are now raised in the documents on the website of the NHTSA are of a mixed character. Some are of a rather general nature and some

is through consideration of these critical functions that meso-institutions such as the NHTSA could become more precise in identifying the critical transactions and the agents that should be addressed, guided, monitored, and controlled, making coordination and alignment more likely to be reached in an effective way. Take the example of the Tempe case. A more systematic analysis of the two dimensions of the socio-technological system of the automated vehicle, the institutional dimension and the technological dimension, and of the resulting problems of coordination and alignment would have resulted in a better-defined picture of the complexities at the different layers involved. Such a picture could have resulted in the identification of those core stakeholders who are central to the alignment of the two dimensions. It would also help to get a more extensive view of the complexities of changes required in the underlying network infrastructure, and to better identify the core agents and the crucial micro-institutions that support the critical transactions. Who will implement these critical transactions and how will they be coordinated by means of private ordering? What are the expected results in terms of safety and how could public ordering be an effective complement, facilitating this alignment and smoothing the passage to the new technology and its associated network infrastructure?

This last consideration introduces another issue that points out the limitation of our framework. As discussed in the introductory chapter and in Chapter 1 (Section 1.3.1), our framework is essentially a static one. Our first and main goal has been to get a grip on the static interdependencies between technology and institutions. In applying our framework to the case of self-driving vehicles, we stuck to this static approach, without digging into the dynamic interaction within each layer or across the different layers. In that respect, at this point our framework remains more suitable for analyzing comparative static issues than for analyzing a dynamic process. However, the analysis provided throughout the chapter clearly suggests that the introduction of self-driving vehicles is part of a process in which a variety of agents and different institutional layers interact. For instance, during that process the NHTSA purposefully initiated a consultation with the stakeholders, in order to better monitor emergent technologies, explore

are about details, whereas a focus on the identification of the core issues is missing.

how these technologies will be applied, and tentatively anticipate their consequences for societal objectives. In doing so, the NHTSA feeds its findings back into the macro and meso-institutions in order to correct, if necessary, the micro-institutions. Clearly, our framework faces strong limitations in understanding this dynamic process.

We come back to these issues and more in the next chapter.

8 | *Taking Stock, Looking Ahead*

8.1 Introduction

This book addressed the interdependence between institutions and technologies in network infrastructures. This is an important issue, since many network infrastructures are on the brink of fundamental technological and institutional changes. The implications are not well understood, either from a conceptual or from an empirical perspective. Examples include the evolution of "smart technologies" allowing for novel services such as transportation by self-driving vehicles or the provision of energy by smart grids. Traditionally, network infrastructures provided homogenous services to realize economies of scale. As a consequence of technological and institutional innovations, services are increasingly attuned to the needs and expectations of final consumers. Self-driving vehicles can be operated on different trajectories, offering tailor-made transportation services. Smart energy grids provide novel possibilities for engaging households and firms in the provision of energy according to their individual capabilities and preferences. Such developments are accompanied by an evolution toward decentralized modes of coordination, whereas traditional infrastructures typically rely on centralized arrangements. We also argue that the expected services of network infrastructures are less dominated by economic profitability, as in the past, but increasingly support the realization of various societal values. Our alignment framework provides novel concepts to understand and analyze such developments from an institutional economic perspective.

Against this background, we evaluate our framework and reflect on the core question we elaborated on in the introductory chapter:

What features can align the institutional and technological dimensions of network infrastructures, in order to obtain performance that meets societal expectations?

More specifically, we posed four hypotheses as to how alignment can be substantiated with respect to three different layers of analysis (structure, governance, transactions) and the delivery of expected services:

H1: *The structural alignment (or misalignment) between the technological architecture and the general institutional set of rules and norms in which network infrastructures are embedded conditions their existence and frames their properties.*

H2: *General norms and rules must be translated and embedded into context-specific ones linking specific protocols and guidelines with context-specific technological features through modalities of governance.*

H3: *Ultimately, rules and norms and their technological counterparts must be implemented through the organization of transactions that interconnect specific institutional arrangements and specific technical requirements, allowing a network to operate.*

H4: *The alignment (resp. misalignment) along the three interdependent layers of structure, governance, and transactions determines the capacity (resp. failure) of a network infrastructure to deliver expected services.*

Keeping in mind the core question and hypotheses, this chapter returns to the developments submitted in Part I and II from three perspectives. To start with, we summarize the main conceptual contributions of our framework and its ability to specify and operationalize the interdependence between institutions and technologies, and the implications for the provision of expected services (Section 8.2). Second, we reflect on the empirical cases detailed in the second part of the book, in order to draw some conclusions about what we gained from our framework when dealing with "real-world" situations and consider possible improvements (Section 8.3). Finally, we consider how our approach can provide guidance for public policy and private sector initiatives against the background of the ongoing transitions in network infrastructures (Section 8.4). To conclude, we summarize our answer to the core question and the hypotheses in Section 8.5.

8.2 Conceptual Contribution

In this book, we considered network infrastructures as socio-technological systems characterized by the interdependence and complementarity of their two dimensions: institutions and technology. Relying on a combination of nodes and links, infrastructures require coordination along both dimensions in order to fulfill and safeguard critical functions. These critical functions determine the capacity of a network to deliver expected services in line with societal values. The key argument underlying our analysis is that alignment between institutions and technology is central to the fulfillment of the performance expected from these networks. Misalignment can generate discrepancies or gaps challenging the integrity of a network and its capacity to meet its goal. Throughout the book, we elaborated on a framework that specifies the concepts to be taken into consideration for understanding and analyzing alignment. Our framework consists of three interrelated building blocks: critical functions, the interdependent dimensions of institutions and technology, and the modalities of their alignment.

8.2.1 Critical Functions

The concept of "critical functions" designates technological and/or institutional conditions that must be fulfilled in order for network infrastructures to provide expected services. Otherwise, networks will fail to deliver expected performance, or in the worst case might even break down (Finger, Groenewegen, and Künneke, 2005; Künneke, Groenewegen, and Ménard, 2010). We specified four critical functions: system control, capacity management, interconnection, and interoperability.

System control addresses the monitoring and control of the overall system related to the flows between nodes and links and the safeguarding of the quality of service. For instance, a safe provision of natural gas requires that the calorific value and the chemical composition of the gas meet certain quality standards. Fulfilling these requirements is necessary to avoid typical hazards in the operation of gas systems, including intoxication, uncontrolled gas burning processes, or explosions. Institutional and technological arrangements are required to address this critical function. Typically, a system operator is designated to monitor and control gas quality, making use of various technological devices such as sensors and meters. This example also illustrates the interdependence and complementarity of institutions and technology.

Capacity management is concerned with the allocation of the scarce network capacity vis-à-vis different users and appliances. Physical limitations of the nodes and links need to be respected for the provision of services. Hence, technological and institutional arrangements are required for allocating these scarce resources such that societal expectations are satisfied. For instance, the limited physical capacity of railroad systems requires a rigorous allocation of slots to meet the mobility expectations of citizens. Timetables are typical institutional arrangements in this respect.

Interconnection refers to the coordination of activities and services between different segments that perform similar or complementary tasks in an infrastructure network. Segments of networks need to be connected with each other, in order to guarantee the technical functioning and the delivery of expected services. For instance, in the electricity sector the reliability of power provision increases if networks are interconnected with neighboring systems. Interconnection contributes to the back-up capacity required to compensate unexpected failures. Typical entities and devices include technological arrangements such as interconnecting cables, and institutions for monitoring and controlling the power flows between the different subsystems. The European Network of Transmission System Operators for Electricity (ENTSO-E) illustrates such an institution, monitoring power flows between some forty-three transmission systems in thirty-six countries.

Finally, interoperability addresses the capacity of the nodes and links to support the mutual interactions that enable the system's complementarity. For example, in the railroad sector, the specification of the tracks needs to be compatible with the requirements of locomotives and cars. Norms and standards are typical institutional arrangements in support of interoperability.

By focusing on the fulfillment and safeguarding of the aforementioned critical functions, we dedicated our approach to very essential technological and institutional conditions that network infrastructures need to fulfill for achieving their purpose.

8.2.2 Disentangling Institutions and Technology

Obviously, safeguarding these critical functions clearly demonstrates that "technology and institutions matter." However, we were not satisfied with this very general conclusion and we went several steps further. Ultimately, our approach aimed at pinpointing specific arrangements that play a crucial role in the capacity of network infrastructures to deliver expected services. This ambition was clearly articulated through our main research question and the four related hypotheses. As part of that process, we started with the identification of research gaps in the literature, an exercise that provided insights and helped in developing concepts to capture the technological and institutional features that needed to be considered for the fulfillment and safeguarding of critical functions (Chapter 1). This knowledge gap was illustrated by various empirical examples throughout the book. The case of the New York blackout, mentioned in the introductory chapter, is famous in this respect. The blackout was caused by inappropriate technological and institutional arrangements to safeguard and restore the required power balance, resulting in cascading system failures.

Obviously, resolving such issues requires a deeper understanding of the technological and institutional arrangements involved. For this purpose, we disentangled technology and institutions. We specified three layers of analysis and provided concepts to capture the essence of both dimensions. These layers indicate different degrees of specification of institutional and technological features of network infrastructures.

On the side of institutions, we differentiated macro-, meso-, and micro-institutions (Chapter 2). Macro-institutions indicate the most generic layer within which constitutive norms and rules are established that delineate and structure the domain of possible transactions necessary to provide the services expected from the network infrastructure at stake. More precisely, this involves delineating rules (what can/cannot be done?), establishing and securing property rights (who holds them?), and framing decision rights (how can they be exercised?). The airline industry illustrates this: it is dependent on the delineation of rules established by congress and parliaments, for instance, the adoption of an Open Skies policy, the definition of norms and rules regarding airline certification, and the establishment of rights of access to national markets. Meso-institutions indicate the institutional layer within which constitutive norms and rules are translated by specific entities into guidelines and protocols regarding the allocation of rights, and the implementation and monitoring of their usage. The US Department of Transportation is a typical example of a meso-institution for the airline industry: this department provides guidelines for airline operation based on the constitutive generic rules determined by the macro-institutions, in this case primarily the US Congress. Finally, micro-institutions refer to the institutional layer within which transactions are actually initiated, planned, and delivered, providing coordination mechanisms required to make technology operational and create value. An example would be the contract regulating the venture between Air France-KLM and Delta Airlines, which shaped a specific strategic alliance, including internal rules to allocate benefits and deficits.

The technological layers were specified in a similar way, with a differentiation made between technological architecture, technological design, and technical operation.

Technological architecture stipulates the generic technological features, embedded in physical systems, necessary to provide the services expected from the network infrastructure at stake. For example, the technological architecture of the Paris Métro system can be characterized by its generic purpose (the provision of a local rail transport service) and the establishment of nodes and links (including trains and tracks) and the arrangement of these technological components (tracks are the transport medium for the trains) needed to achieve that goal. The technological design is characterized by context-specific arrangements of technical and material components necessary, within a given generic architecture, to make up a network delivering services specific to a certain time and space. This is related to the contemporary provision of metro services in the city of Paris, its specific underground rail tracks and the homogenous types of trains required for short-distance transport. Finally, the technical operation specifies the operation of technical systems in terms of the monitoring and control of dedicated material functionalities, given a context-specific design and its underlying technological architecture. In this sense, the technical operation of the Paris Métro is characterized by a high frequency of trains, with multiple stops, low operating speed, and automated train control systems.

These concepts allowed us to specify the institutional and technological arrangements involved in the fulfillment and safeguarding of the four critical functions. For each of the three distinct layers, it provided us with the possibility to connect differently to these functions, and hence to explore with more precision and rigor than the traditional approach discussed in Chapter 1 the capacity of network infrastructures to provide expected services. Part II of this book is illustrative in that respect.

To make our analysis fully operational, we needed a third building block within our framework. We needed to characterize the interrelations between technology and institutions for each layer of the two dimensions (institutions and technology); and we needed to conceptualize the modalities of alignment required at each layer to fulfill and safeguard the critical functions.

Before returning to this last step in the development of our framework, there is a caveat about a difficulty we were well aware of. In the real world of cases such as those explored in Part II, the three layers often overlap and combine, which illustrates the need for coordination within each dimension, institutional and technological. Indeed, such overlapping precisely makes different network infrastructures distinct with respect to their institutional setting as well as their technological characteristics over time and space. This is highlighted in more detail in Section 8.3.

8.2.3 Modalities of Alignment

For our last building block, regarding the alignment issue, and consistent with our three-layered approach, we identified distinct horizontal relations between institutions and technology, respectively coined as structure, governance, and transactions. For each layer, we therefore characterized modalities of alignment through these three concepts, pointing out the existence of entities and devices designated to proceed to alignment, or to the restoration of alignment when there is misalignment (see Chapter 4).

Structure refers to the constitutive features needed to align the architecture and the macro-institutions, so as to fulfill the critical functions of the network infrastructure at stake. At this generic layer of analysis, the architecture is largely determined by the characteristics of the physical networks that interconnect complementary nodes and links. The macro-institutions define the norms and rules embedded in the entities and devices required to make the technological system operational and to provide expected generic services. The development of the Dutch natural gas system is illustrative of such structural alignment between macro-institutions and technological architecture. After the discovery of huge gas resources in the 1960s, the gas system needed to be physically developed and the institutional layout determined through rules that established the rights for the exploration and exploitation of the natural resource, and for access to transport and distribution pipelines. As illustrated in Chapter 4, the structural modalities of alignment were (among other things) related to the specific calorific value of Dutch gas, requiring generic technological and institutional arrangements for a safe and reliable provision of this energy source. This included the establishment of dedicated physical networks, and a legal framework assigning rights and responsibilities for monitoring and enforcing the specific Dutch gas quality throughout the entire grid.

Governance deals with the combination of entities and devices (procedures and protocols) through which context-specific technologies and specific meso-institutions are aligned, making the delivery of relevant services possible. At this intermediate layer of analysis, the interrelatedness between institutions and technology is determined by the framing of services in particular technological and institutional contexts. This is the layer within which the generic features of network infrastructures must be translated into specific arrangements necessary for implementing and monitoring the provision of services according to the needs expressed in a certain time and place. Related to the Dutch gas sector, meso-institutions such as the system operator Gasunie have been assigned the responsibility for operating the high-pressure transport network such that a reliable provision of natural gas will be secured. Corresponding technological devices include the pipeline grid, gas storage facilities, and gas quality monitoring devices.

Transactions are modalities of transfer of rights to use goods and services across technologically separable activities, in order to align technical operations with micro-institutions, which is needed to fulfill the critical functions of the network infrastructure at stake. Thus, transactional modalities of alignment articulate the features of the technical operation and the micro-institutions involved in the actual provision of services. A typical example is related to the monitoring and control of the pipeline pressure needed to safely transport gas. In the Netherlands, this critical function of system control was standardized to a pressure of 40 bar for long-distance transport, and 8 bar for local distribution networks. Such standardized pipeline pressures are typical of rules defined within the meso-institutional layer, but which need to be implemented at the micro layer. In the specific Dutch case, the technical operation of specific pipeline pressures to meet these standards and

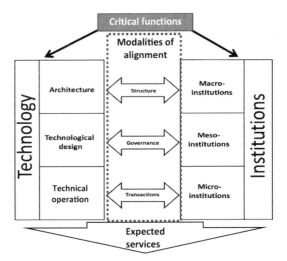

Figure 8.1 Alignment framework

secure this critical function is realized by different compressor stations throughout the network, which are operated by Gasunie.

In bringing together two worlds apart, economics and engineering, we made our framework particularly relevant for an extensive understanding of how network infrastructures work … or fail to work! The relevant characteristics of technological coordination on the one hand and institutional coordination on the other hand must be compatible in order to reach alignment. However, we recognize that alignment has multifaceted features and can be reached and/or restored in many ways. There is no simple answer to the question of which characteristics must be satisfied to make technological and institutional coordination compatible, thus guaranteeing that the two dimensions are properly aligned along their three different layers. We have already identified some universal and possibly interrelated factors determining the modalities of alignment, for example, spatial and/or temporal issues, proximity, or centralization of coordination that enable or hamper alignment (Chapter 4). More factors need to be explored in future research.

8.2.4 Our Comprehensive Framework

Figure 8.1 summarizes the alignment framework thus developed throughout the chapters of this book around its three building blocks –

the critical functions, the interdependent dimensions of institutions and technologies, and the modalities of their alignment – and the associated concepts outlined in the previous sections.

This representation captures the essence of what in our view characterizes network infrastructures and the challenges they may face with respect to the fulfillment of critical functions and the provision of expected services. We consider that the set of concepts giving flesh to this framework provides the tools relevant for an empirical analysis of the alignment of institutions and technology in network infrastructures, as was substantiated in Part II. We now turn to a short review of some lessons we have learned from this usage of our framework through these empirical explorations.

8.3 Lessons from Our Empirical Explorations

Once the conceptual framework was well established, we considered it essential to check its explanatory power through empirical investigations focusing on specific network infrastructures. This was the central motivation behind Part II. To achieve that goal, we developed "specialized" chapters, each successive chapter paying particular attention, although not exclusively, to the relevance of our framework when it comes to identifying the various components involved in the alignment issue along each of the three layers we have identified. At the same time, taken as a whole this set of chapters delivers a strong message about the generic value of our framework. Through the variety of cases we selected, from the structural energy transition at a country level, to the local governance of water and wastewater networks, to the radical transformation in the organization of transactions commanded by technological innovations in road transportation, these empirical explorations showed the capacity of our framework to identify and analyze characteristics and difficulties proper to the network infrastructures investigated. Notwithstanding this variety, we maintained consistency across the chapters by referring to the same conceptual apparatus and by using the same methodology of in-depth case studies. The underlying objectives aimed to show how our framework can be operational (Section 8.3.1); how it can help in pointing out dynamic processes, notwithstanding its static character (Section 8.3.2); and how it raises issues that allow the framing of future research (Section 8.3.3). Throughout the entire process, we addressed our core question: how can the institutional and technological dimensions of network infra-structures be aligned in order to obtain the performance that meets societal expectations?

8.3.1 Operationalization: Key Results and Lessons

Although we cannot list them all, important gains have been made and some limitations better understood by investigating the properties of the selected network infrastructures through the lenses provided by our framework. Let us emphasize three aspects that we consider of particular significance.

Grasping the Complexity of Network Infrastructures

Because they depend on relatively sophisticated technologies and on insti-tutional settings in which they are deeply embedded due to their specific societal functions, network infrastructures are often analyzed through segmented and often isolated approaches; for example, focusing on tech-nological issues, or regulatory functions, or societal impact, etc. Our empirical investigations showed the capacity of our framework to deliver a more unified view, introducing some order in what could otherwise be regarded as a mess, and disentangling the intricacy of the many compon-ents that provide the configuration for specific infrastructures.

The identification of different layers and the characterization of their respective roles in the specific network infrastructures we examined allowed for a better understanding of the complexity of the socio-technological structures at stake and their embeddedness in societal values. For instance, reference to our framework helps to better grasp the challenges that the development of smart grids pose to the existing organization of electricity systems; or to better identify and analyze how the introduction of new technologies in water and wastewater networks raises fundamental questions regarding coordination and the allocation of rights, a challenge for the existing governance of the system; or to better understand how profoundly the introduction of self-driving vehicles will affect the organization of transactions and the governance of road transportation, while recognizing the existence of major dilemmas regarding fundamental societal values such as privacy, or even more dramatic ones such as transferring the right of life or death to automated devices when almost instantaneous choices have to be made in the face of potential car accidents.

Identifying Relevant Issues and Problems with Respect to Sources of Alignment/Misalignment

If we look more specifically at the different hypotheses stated in our initial chapter and which are embedded in our framework, the empirical explorations gave substance to our core statement, which is that the alignment (or misalignment) of the institutional and technological dimensions of network infrastructures is essential in determining whether expected services can be delivered or not.

Let us illustrate by associating the three hypotheses with the three layers characterizing our framework. Hypothesis 1 suggested the need for alignment at the structural level, linking the architecture of a network and the macro-institutional setting that shape its properties. The analysis of the problems raised by the transition in electric power systems initiated by the development of alternative sustainable resources and of smart grids showed the multi-dimensional restructuring this transition would impose. Our framework allowed a precise identification of several of these needed changes. Hypothesis 2 pointed out the key role of an intermediate layer connecting specific institutional protocols and guidelines to context-specific technological features, thus characterizing a mode of governance. The case of Singapore's water network provided substance, showing how public initiative and guidance played a crucial role in the centralized mode of coordination that led to the successful development of the network, but also demonstrating the problems this centralized system faced with the introduction of new technologies involving a reallocation of rights in relation to the introduction of public–private partnerships, as well as the interference of policy makers, illustrated by the freezing of prices for almost two decades. Hypothesis 3 focused attention on the way transactions need to be reorganized and implemented to secure the interdependence between technical operations that differ substantially from pre-existing ones, and the innovative micro-institutional arrangements these changes require. Our review of the challenges raised by the development of automated and self-driving vehicles showed the importance of the organization of transactions that can secure alignment at the micro-level, but which is also compatible with other layers.

In exploring these issues through the lens of our framework, our chapters pointed out different sources of misalignment. For instance, we pointed out how the failure of one micro-institution participating in the network could unbalance the system, leading to a change in the way transactions are organized. The need for a public utility company to take over a failing private operator in the case of water and wastewater in Singapore illustrates this. The examination of the reorganization necessitated by the introduction of self-driving vehicles allowed us to go further. It showed how the transition to new modes of road transportation requires a complete realignment of transactions through a process loaded with issues that concern societal values. Finally, the case of the introduction of new sources of renewable energy led us to point out the need to find new ways to coordinate, in order to safeguard the critical functions of interconnection, system control, interoperability, and capacity management. Ultimately, such sources of misalignment would necessitate a switch to significant modalities of alignment at the three layers identified by our framework – respectively, structure, governance, and transactions – if the network under consideration is to deliver expected services. Indeed, transitions to new energy systems, to new modes of road transportation, or to different modalities of producing and delivering water and processing wastewater all pointed to the cascade effects on the three layers of our framework of changes that started in one specific dimension and/or component.

Some Limitations to Overcome
Another value added by confronting our framework with the exploration of specific network infrastructures comes from the opportunity it provides to better assess the limits this model faces, thus suggesting possibilities for future developments.

One difficulty our empirical explorations made even more explicit than the conceptual developments can be called the identification problem. In the real world, the different institutional components of the layers of our model often overlap. For example, in the traditional centralized energy sector, one utility often holds a monopoly, whether with public or private status, so that it operates simultaneously as a micro-institution, with properties of a classic integrated firm, and in many aspects as a meso-institution, since it fixes standards and protocols for the entire sector. Similarly, in the case of the centralized water and wastewater system of Singapore, the public utility (PUB) acts as a firm in producing and delivering expected services, but because of its status it also functions as a regulator, a role that became particularly significant after the introduction of public–private partnerships. If we turn to the technological side, we also find cases of ambiguities. For example, disentangling the technological design from the architecture of a specific network is not always obvious. In the case of Singapore, the combination of four substantially different technologies defines an architecture that overlaps with the technological design resulting from this combination. The same can be said of the introduction of renewable sources of energy in the electricity sector, which alters its structure and unbalances its existing technological design; or of the co-existence of traditional vehicles and self-driving ones in road transportation. To overcome these difficulties and better disentangle the different components and the layers to which they belong, we identified the specific functions ensured through each layer, so that many ambiguities can be removed. For instance, the example of the airline industry allowed us to point out the different tasks and responsibilities to be fulfilled at the different layers if the critical functions are to be secured and the different entities involved (see Table 2.1). However, there is still room for improvement in refining the criteria that could facilitate the unraveling of the different layers on both the technological and institutional sides. For example, in order to better identify the respective roles of micro- and meso-institutions, the analysis needs to examine further their very different status when it comes to the creation of value.

Filling these gaps should allow us to make progress in the transition from a framework, which is what we delivered so far, to a model that would formalize the different components identified, and would allow us to reach the conceptual level at which hypotheses could be rigorously tested, and not only substantiated through qualitative analyses (which have their own merit!). Refining the criteria for differentiating the layers and their components would also help to specify the data needed to deliver these tests. Indeed, as in the other approaches to institutions and socio-technological systems discussed in Chapter 1 as well as (less systematically) in Chapters 2 and 3, measurement remains an issue in our contribution. However, the development of empirical investigations through the lens of our framework often brought us very close to identifying and collecting data that would allow quantitative analyses. For instance, the statement about the energy transition that a structural alignment between macro-institutional rules and the emerging technologies would require to satisfy "reliability and availability under acceptable economic conditions," opened up room for indicators that could be associated with these conditions, for example, the capacity to deliver electricity with appropriate intensity continuously (reliability), the capacity to connect users and deliver under tariffs in relation to their resources (availability), or to take on board conditions to balance the costs of switching to alternative technologies with expected revenues and benefits (acceptable economic conditions). Nevertheless, much more remains to be done in this direction.

One last lesson that we have learned from our empirical investigations is the need to push further the analysis of the way societal values contribute to shape the choices and organization of the existing network infrastructures, how this permeates all three layers through different channels of transmission, and how it also frames the conditions of transition from one type of arrangement in network infrastructures to another. At the other end of the spectrum, more attention needs to be paid to the role of individual agents in the alignment process, either through their position as leaders of a firm or through their political leadership. The role of some firms in the development of self-driving vehicles, or the role of the political leadership and a few high-ranking bureaucrats in modeling the water and wastewater systems of Singapore illustrate the need to pay more attention to these aspects.

8.3.2 Can a Static Framework Lead to a Dynamic Approach?

Many of the points listed above relate to the need to move in the direction of a more dynamic model. Indeed, our framework remains static, although our empirical investigations often ran into issues that would require a dynamic approach. In many aspects, our framework provided the basis for a comparative static approach. For instance, the successive characterization of traditional energy systems, contemporary systems mixing fossil sources of energy with renewable ones, and future energy systems opened the door for the development of comparative statics. Similarly, the exploration of the consequences of the introduction of new technologies in water and wastewater systems or in road transportation led to elements of a comparative approach.

From Static to Comparative Static to Dynamic
Although we did not make the step toward a fully dynamic model, which would have required analyzing the process of change, our

empirical analyses suggested the potential for developing our model in this direction. Indeed, in pinpointing within the different network infrastructures analyzed in this book the types of misalignment that emerged and how the sources of such misalignments could initiate moves to change, in order to restore alignment and safeguard the critical functions, we introduced considerations on the verge of a dynamic approach.

First, in all three empirical chapters we paid attention to the need for vertical coordination along each of the two dimensions of technology and institutions, and the need for horizontal alignment at the three layers. For instance, considering the introduction of renewable sources of energy and the development of smart grids in traditional energy systems allowed us to question the existing modalities of coordination through a centralized and closed system, and the appropriateness of the structure, governance, and transactional arrangements for integrating the new technologies into existing systems. The introduction of self-driving vehicles in traditional road transportation systems raised similar issues. And so did the development of desalination and wastewater reuse in existing water and wastewater systems. In all cases, challenges raised with respect to interconnection between the resulting heterogeneous parts of the system, the problems they posed for existing system control, the consequences of the reallocation of rights involved on interoperability and management capacities led to a consideration of the capacity of these systems to adapt. Although we did not go further in the analysis of the adaptation process, our framework opened doors in this direction.

Second, another case in point is the attention we paid to issues of misalignment. We successively looked at the sources of structural misalignment with respect to energy transition; to sources of misalign-ment in governance with respect to the status of a public utility moni-toring a water and wastewater system, and facing the introduction of new technologies associated with private partners; and to sources of misalignment in the organization of transactions when the develop-ment of self-driving vehicles imposes radical transformation of the prevailing arrangements in road transportation, in order to satisfy the technological as well as institutional requirements of the new technology. What these cases show is the role of misalignment as a driver of change. Again, our framework allows us to identify these forces of transformation. What it does not do is provide specific tools for analyzing the adaptation process.

Embedding Dynamics: Changes in Societal Values
One last aspect we want to mention that connects to the need to extend
our framework toward a dynamic one relates to the role of societal
values in the acceptance of new institutional as well as new technological
arrangements. For instance, in the case of water and wastewater
systems, we pointed out the significance of the introduction of new
technologies to process wastewater and allow its reuse, including for
household consumption. Technology permits this solution. But we also
mentioned, although we did not develop the idea, that in order for these
technologies to be implemented with success, quite substantial changes
in societal values needed to occur; namely, the acceptance by consumers
to drink recycled wastewater. In the same vein, the development of
smart grids requires not only solving the technological problems related
to renewable energies, but also changing the valuation made by society
about the role of technology, which raises what we identified as "ethical
dilemmas," for example, the trade-off between privacy and efficiency in
the development of self-driving vehicles. While looking at these issues,
we mentioned the role of citizens' participation as a component and
sometimes an obstacle to change that interferes in all three layers of our
framework. We also referred to the role of leadership in technological as
well as institutional transformations. However, we did not push further
the analysis of these factors in the process of change.

8.3.3 Dropping White Stones, Tracing Paths for Future Research

What the discussion above suggests is that beyond its relevance for
understanding the characteristics of network infrastructures and the
modalities of interdependence between institutions and technologies,
our framework provides food for thought about its possible development and extension. Let us mention some potential paths that future
research investigations could take.

**A More Integrated Perspective on the Articulation between
Coordination and Alignment**
A central argument underlying the empirical exploration of specific
cases through the lens provided by our framework is that the
interdependence between institutions and technologies determines the
capacity of a network infrastructure to deliver the expected services.

We went further in analyzing how this interdependence operates through vertical coordination that conditions complementarities along the technological dimension as well as along the institutional one; and through horizontal alignment that conditions coherence along the three layers that interconnect institutions and technologies.

However, the modalities through which coordination and alignment operate and complement each other need a more in-depth analysis. For instance, what are the general rules and mechanisms underlying the combination of different technologies in a coordinated way, and how does this relate to structural changes in macro-institutional rules and norms? Our discussion of future energy systems or of the development of self-driving vehicles illustrates this interdependence between technological changes and the need for changes in societal values.

In that vein, the need for more "adaptability" along the two dimensions of institutions and technology in order to allow the successful implementation of these new systems requires more investigation. This issue raises many questions, for instance, what are the processes through which societal values can change in a way compatible with technological requirements? Issues of privacy, security, and safety that must accompany more open and less centralized systems still remain to be explored further. And what would the role of citizens' participation be in such a process? How can it be structured in a way that correctly expresses their views and allows their active contribution to changes? And how can misalignment in that process be avoided, for example, through the capture of participation by specific groups of interest?

Another aspect that we mentioned and which would greatly benefit from further investigation concerns the reallocation of rights that accompany the introduction of new technologies and its impact on the structure, governance, and organization of the transactions of specific network infrastructures. There is an abundant literature on the reallocation of property rights, almost entirely in the context of privatization of public utilities. But there is almost nothing on how the introduction of new technologies may push toward radical realignment of property rights as well as decision rights, for example, in the case of the development of smart grids, or of self-driving vehicles, or of the implementation of decentralized systems for providing water and processing wastewater. Again, our framework unambiguously points out the need to dig deeper into the institutional consequences of such technological changes.

The Role of Political Interference

What the issue of citizens' participation points out relates to a specificity of network infrastructures, which is that they concern all citizens. Consequently, changes in the structure, governance, and organization of transactions affect one specific subset of societal values: the status of polity and, more precisely, the role of the political process involved in the monitoring of existing networks as well as their transition to new arrangements. Again, our empirical explorations provide food for thought: the switch to smart grids requires substantial changes not only in the technological arrangement, but also in the way the electricity systems are regulated; the development and changes in the water and wastewater networks we analyzed depend on the decisions of policy makers; and the increasing predominance of self-driving vehicles will also require political intervention, with policy makers having to deal with societal choices, such as the trade-off between privacy and security in the collection and usage of the big data needed to make the new technologies operational.

Again, there is an abundant literature, all too often ideologically motivated, about the ambiguities of political interference in network infrastructures. True, these interventions often introduce biases and distortions or even corruption in those systems; but in many cases, they can also provide much needed guidance and incentives, as the example of the development of the water and wastewater system in Singapore suggested. One aspect that the "reading" of empirical cases through the lens of our framework revealed is the political transaction costs that may result from political interference and/or from switching from one technological and/or institutional arrangement to another. Political transaction costs refer to the costs of building a sustainable coalition to support transition between different arrangements (Marshall and Weingast, 1988; North, 1990b; North, Wallis, and Weingast, 2009). Switching to a radically different organization of the energy sector in Germany, or making water independence a top priority and acting accordingly provide illustrations of the capacity and political costs of building robust coalitions of interest. This issue leads on naturally to questions about leadership, an issue we mentioned but which deserves much more attention. All these aspects point to the connection of our framework to policy issues, a topic which is addressed in the next section.

Building Datasets

Before indicating more precisely how our framework could help with policy issues and offer a refreshing perspective with regard to their analysis, there is one path this opens to further investigation that we would like to emphasize: the measurement issue. Our alignment framework is instrumental in analyzing the compatibility (resp. incompatibility) of the coordination within the technological and the institutional dimension, as well as the alignment/misalignment between these two dimensions along the layers we have identified. Ultimately, the central goal of appropriate coordination and alignment is the safeguarding of the critical functions that condition the capacity to deliver expected services. Performance indicators can be associated with this that need to be quantified.

Our empirical explorations have already suggested the criteria and indicators of performance that could be implemented. Future research needs to go further and develop ways to assess the costs and benefits of different structures, modes of governance, and organization of transactions. We doubt that this can be done by calculating the absolute value. Following Coase, North, Williamson, and many others, we would argue that this can be done only in a comparative way, for example, by comparing the costs and benefits of alternative solutions. However, the appropriate answer to this problem can only be provided through further investigations based on trial-and-error approaches.

8.4 Policy Issues from the Alignment Perspective

Network infrastructures have been and will remain important public policy domains, because infrastructures are the backbone of national economies and the foundation of citizens' welfare (European Union, 2019; United Nations, 2019).[1] Public policies in different forms are common in most network infrastructures, ranging from legislation

---

[1] EU Horizon 2020 reflects the policy priorities of the Europe 2020 strategy and addresses major concerns shared by citizens in Europe and elsewhere. Funding will focus on the following challenges, showing the central position of infrastructures: health, demographic change, and wellbeing; food security, sustainable agriculture and forestry, marine and maritime and inland water research, and the bio-economy; secure, clean, and efficient energy; smart, green, and integrated transport; climate action, environment, resource efficiency, and raw materials; Europe in a changing world – inclusive, innovative, and reflective societies; secure societies – protecting freedom and security of Europe and its citizens (https://ec.europa.eu/eurostat/web/europe-2020-indicators; last accessed

listing the safety requirements for the delivery of drinking water to the nationalization of complete industries such as the railways and the electricity sector. In this section, we discuss the implications of our alignment perspective for public policies.

In Section 8.2, we summarized the conceptual core of our framework as the fulfillment and safeguarding of the critical functions. We specified that the coordination of complementary components is needed in each of the dimensions of socio-technological systems, as well as alignment between them in each of the three layers. In this section, we explore how the issues of coordination and alignment could be taken care of by private agents (consumers, firms, and other organizations) together with public policies. We argue that because of the criticality of the four functions of system control, capacity management, interoperability, and interconnection, a community needs to have a clear picture of the entities and arrangements that are involved in coordination and alignment. A community ought to have a clear picture of how these entities and arrangements perform the tasks of coordination and alignment, and how public policies could complement private agents.

Because of the great uncertainties and limited knowledge surrounding the interdependencies in network infrastructures, we suggest that government should first of all be a "learning" government (Section 8.4.1). Next, we explore two public policy issues that turned out to be central in our case studies (Section 8.4.2). First, the question of identification and monitoring. How can we identify defects in coordination in each of the dimensions, and how can we identify misalignments? How can we identify the entities and arrangements involved in coordination and alignment, and how can we monitor their performance? Second, the question of intervention. When mis-coordination and/or misalignment exist, how should interventions be best organized: as top-down or more participatory? How detailed and prescriptive should public policies be in influencing the behavior of private agents?

8.4.1 Different Types of Public Policy Learning

"Normal" On-Path Policy Learning
From the case studies, we learned that technology and institutions in network infrastructures can be well coordinated and aligned for long

December 6, 2019). United Nations sustainable development goal no. 9 concerns industry, innovation, and infrastructure (United Nations, 2019).

periods of time. In the electricity sector, for example, centralized and closed arrangements were aligned for a long time in both dimensions of the socio-technological system (Chapter 5). Over time, technology, institutions, and the coordination arrangements and modalities of their alignment evolved rather harmoniously. The agents involved learned how to adapt to small changes and incrementally improved technologies and institutions. Following Denzau and North (1994), this type of learning could be termed as "normal" policy learning (Groenewegen and van der Steen, 2007). It takes place in a well-defined institutional framework with harmonious relationships between the layers, and it is based on clear and stable shared mental maps of the agents involved (see Chapter 2). The technologies in this framework are also stable, and agents can continuously improve on them through incremental changes. The communication through which agents code and decode messages (Denzau and North, 1994) is crystal clear and provides agents with all the relevant information. Experimentation and trial-and-error are possible within the existing policy instruments, but the basic features of the architecture, contextual design, and operation are not disturbed. The existing technologies and institutions absorb innovations so that these fit well within the existing structures. This type of learning has also been referred to as "on-path learning" (Groenewegen and Künneke, 2005).

Re-description and Off-Path Learning
From the case studies, we also learned that network infrastructures can be subject to fundamental changes due to technological innovations, profound changes in institutions, and/or (radical) changes in values and norms. In Chapter 5, the change in energy policy was discussed, Chapter 6 analyzed changes due to the simultaneous introduction of new technologies and private firms in the Singaporean water sector, and Chapter 7 described fundamental changes in the transportation sector. North (2005) calls these types of changes "re-descriptions": new cognitive models and new "habits of thought" are part of a new "logic" of the socio-technological system.

Such fundamental changes can have different causes. They can result from cumulative small evolutionary changes in technologies or institutions that ultimately cause a fundamental change; they can also result from revolutionary changes, for instance, in societal values (no more fossil energy sources), or in the organization of the sector (introduction of liberalization, deregulation, and privatization). Moreover, fundamental changes can result from purposeful interventions by government or private agents based on an explicit policy design, but they can also come about as unintended consequences of such purposeful actions. Take, for example, the wave of liberalization, deregulation, and privatization that fundamentally changed the networks of the electricity, telecommunications, and public transport sectors in the final decades of the twentieth century. The introduction of competition implied the need to purposefully design supporting institutions such as competition laws and specific authorities to monitor and intervene at the meso layer. Liberalized markets need adequate supportive organizational arrangements such as vertically integrated entrepreneurial firms, long-term contracting, and/or strategic alliances to coordinate the transactions. Moreover, values and norms of economic efficiency and individual initiative are needed that support the new formal institutions and become internalized in the mental maps of the private and public agents. These changes all result from purposeful design linked to the introduction of "market-oriented" policies into network infrastructures.

However, the implementation of new institutions also had unintended consequences, due not only to a lack of knowledge among designers of the new technologies and institutions, but also due to the opportunistic behavior of interest groups, resulting in "regulatory risk and regulatory capture" (see Chapter 1). Furthermore, as Sandel (2012) pointed out, to give markets, private firms, and individual consumers a prominent position in the socio-technological system has serious long-term feedback implications for the values and norms in society. For instance, when markets are introduced into network infrastructures and individuals learn to behave in terms of economic efficiency, over time individualistic selfish efficiency-driven behavior becomes a norm and influences the societal values. More individualistic and selfish behavior then contributes to the dominance of individualistic societal values at the cost of collective values. This also holds true for the reverse situation: the introduction of non-market institutions such as democratic, participatory coordination arrangements also have a long-term impact on the norms and values in society. More collective decision-making over a long period of time, for instance, in the energy sector (Chapter 5), could contribute to the development of community values and participatory modalities in decision-making.

In sum, network infrastructures are nowadays characterized by the simultaneous presence of several public and private decision-makers, by influential interest groups, and by fundamental technological and institutional changes, all of which cause substantial uncertainties and unpredictable long-term effects between the layers of socio-technological systems. What are the implications for public policies?

8.4.2 Identification, Monitoring, and Intervention

In a certain world with incremental on-path developments, private agents and governments could formulate well-defined end states for the future and apply top-down instruments of incentives and directives to steer producers and consumers in the desired direction. Such a blueprint organization of centralized decision-making would require a fully informed government, a set of effective policy instruments, and private agents that have little room to maneuver. However, an uncertain world with innovations, segmented private agents, interest groups, and changing values and norms demands a different approach in which exploration, experimentation, and learning are central.

Identification and Monitoring
In most network infrastructures, the technological innovations that initiated the emergence of new services (e.g., electricity, telephony) first came from private entrepreneurs. When changes in societal values deemed the service important for all citizens, it became a "utility," and government stepped in to secure the expected services. Often, large vertically integrated monopolies took care of the production and distribution of the services under the direct monitoring of public authorities. After the waves of liberation and privatization in most of the network infrastructures, private agents became important decision-makers regulated by competition authorities and sector-specific regulators. Decision-making in the sector was organized in a more decentralized way, but because the provision of the expected services was deeply embedded in the societal values, private agents were tightly regulated from a public point of view. Recently, we have observed the emergence of and need for new modalities of collective decision-making,[2] due, for instance, to technological changes taking place in the electricity sector (see

---

[2] Collective decision-making is considered to be a subfield of collective behavior and is concerned with how groups reach decisions without centralized leadership (Bose, Reina, and Marshall, 2017).

Chapter 5) and in the transportation sector (Chapter 7), offering the possibility of introducing more participatory means of decision-making.

As we have just pointed out, when facing fundamental uncertainties the process of decision-making should first of all make room for learning. At stake is then not the "normal" type of learning, but a type of learning based on creativity, innovation, and exploration. In situations of "re-description," agents at all layers and in both institutional and technological dimensions could be guided and their exploration of new ways facilitated by public policies. Government could then have a special responsibility in creating the right conditions for private and public agents to innovate and to explore, while monitoring the implications for coordination, alignment, and the safeguarding of the critical functions. The creation of so-called platforms that offer all stakeholders the possibility to exchange information and to consult each other illustrates the new participatory way of collective decision-making. Such platforms provide important information to private agents, and offer government a tool to guide the expectations of different stakeholders in desirable directions. In guiding the energy transition or the widespread introduction of automated vehicles, government could play an important role in facilitating and securing conditions of realignment (see Chapters 5 and 7).

When responsible private and/or public institutions identify mis-coordination between the complementary components or misalignment between technology and institutions that endanger the fulfillment of critical functions, the responsible institutions should intervene, in order to secure the provision of expected services.

Intervention: A Matter of (De)centralization
When fundamental changes take place in one or more parts of the socio-technological system, it is of utmost importance to know about the implications for the technological and institutional coordination arrangements, the alignment between them, and the consequences for the safeguarding of the critical functions. Ideally, the responsible private and public institutions at all three layers of our framework would know about the coordination issues at stake with respect to the critical functions, about entities and arrangements involved in the coordination of the complementary components, and about entities and arrangements involved in the modalities of alignment. Ideally, the responsible institutions would know about the nature of the

fundamental changes, monitor their impact, and intervene when coordination and/or alignment is endangered. Intervention could be indirect, supplying additional information to the (private) agents on the basis of which they can adjust their decisions. Intervention can be more direct, through positive and negative incentives, and even more direct through guidelines or directives with detailed prescriptions.

Ideally, government agencies should have a clear picture of the impact of fundamental changes on the technological and institutional coordination arrangements and on the modalities of alignment. Based on that knowledge, government could then monitor and intervene, in order to safeguard the critical functions. Ideally, government would know, for instance, which transactions at the operational layer could be coordinated through contracts and organizations to safeguard critical transactions (see the Tempe case in Chapter 7).

However, because of the complexities involved, and especially since private agents have become more important decision-makers in a number of network infrastructures, it has become more and more difficult for government to know exactly about the core complementarities that need tight coordination, and about the core interdependencies between technology and institutions that need to be aligned. Nevertheless, because of the issues at stake, citizens would expect government to take responsibility and do everything in its power to identify correctly, to monitor closely, and to intervene effectively when needed.

With respect to intervention, two policy issues deserve particular attention. First, how to best organize decision-making in network infrastructures when uncertainty prevails. Should government follow a top-down centralized approach, or is a more open, decentralized participatory approach with stakeholders preferable? Second, how detailed can government be in guiding and intervening at the different layers of a socio-technological system? For instance, should a government prescribe the details of the technical devices at the operational layer? We shall explore these questions in more detail and, where possible, suggest the beginnings of answers.

(De)centralized Decision-Making

When fundamental changes in socio-technological systems take place and developments are partly the result of purposeful design (with intended and unintended consequences) and partly the result of spontaneous evolution, what would be an appropriate public policy with respect to safeguarding the critical functions? In ideal terms: how could a re-description of a socio-political system be made, and how could a switch to a new path of development be facilitated, supported, or guided by public policy? More specifically: how could a process of decision-making be organized; what kind of policy makers and leadership are required; and what would the relationship between them and the private agents look like?

When the desired direction of change becomes visible, government could trigger collective action supported by all the stakeholders, including research institutes, education and training institutes, and private producers and consumers. Investments in the "right" direction could be facilitated through preferential access to resources, while economic and political pressures could facilitate all kinds of production and consumption decisions that make changes in the desired direction possible.

This kind of government guiding role is no doubt very demanding, and includes economic, social, political, and cultural elements. No doubt such intervention would require government officials and their civil servants to be well equipped with information and knowledge, and to have full access to specific expertise. Special attention should be paid to maintaining the balance between exploitation (making efficient use of existing "ways of doing things") and exploration (initiating and implementing new "ways of doing things") (Gilsing and Nooteboom, 2006). Preferably, the new ways should have predictable effects, so agents become aware of the benefits. Also, a sense of urgency could be created, making agents feel the need to participate, to learn, and to get used to the idea that change is needed.

Good leadership is required to play a guiding role through public policies, an issue that our framework does not fully capture, although the case studies revealed its importance. In the context of the substantial technological and/or institutional changes already detailed, good leadership comes less from a top-down hierarchical model that consistently directs all agents in the direction of a specific, well-formulated end goal, but rather from a leadership that allows experiments, organizes a learning process, facilitates information exchange and consultation, organizes collective decision-making with stakeholders about desirable directions of development, and ultimately provides relevant guidance to stakeholders through information, incentives, guidelines, and directives.

General Guidelines and/or Detailed Prescriptions?
A second issue related to public policies that our empirical explorations suggested refers to the degree of specific direction public policies should prescribe. Are the policies of a general nature, or do they consist of detailed prescriptions? Are they general and do they leave much room for agents to maneuver, or do they prescribe in a detailed manner how agents should behave? In that respect, Ray and Skorup (2019) analyze an interesting case of top-down directives from federal US regulators concerning the production of technical devices in the vehicle-to-infrastructure (V2I) communication in the automated transportation sector (see also Chapter 7). In 1995, Department of Transportation (DOT) regulators prescribed the technical components of the V2I type via a "top-down systematic process, in which each component is prescribed by the regulator" (Ray and Skorup, 2019: 5). In terms of our framework, this was a closed centralized coordination arrangement, interfering at the operational layer. However, the results of this top-down approach were disappointing. In particular, the dedicated short-range communications (DSRC) devices (an important part of the intelligent transportation system, ITS) developed too slowly, and therefore the DOT itself "took a lead role in the device development process" (Ray and Skorup, 2019: 6). This further step toward a government prescribing in a detailed way the technical devices and their coordination in closed, centralized arrangements also failed; deciding about technical devices at the operational layer demands very specific knowledge of production and coordination requirements, which was simply lacking at the central level. Moreover, it was recognized that "there is a growing sense, noted by the Government Accountability Office and others, that the state and local transportation authorities will not have the personnel and funding necessary to install and maintain an extensive ITS system" (Ray and Skorup, 2019: 7). Today, the top-down approach to V2I initially adopted by the DOT has been replaced by a competition-induced, decentralized open system. Public authorities set the general standards, contract out the production of devices to private firms, and arrange through public–private partnerships rules and modalities to monitor and intervene in the case of undesirable developments.

What about government prescriptions at the macro and meso layers? All the cases described in Part II of this book converge in pointing out the importance in network infrastructures of a government providing guidance or even in some cases leading the way with respect to the architecture of the technology (the transition in the energy sector, the Four Pillars in water production, and 5G in the transportation network). Sure, such fundamental decisions should be based on broad consultations with stakeholders, on accurate information, and knowledge about values and institutions; however, all of the cases reviewed suggest the significance of a leading role played by public authorities in the organization of the decision-making, the monitoring, and the guiding/directing of the process. This active role could also hold for the meso layer. The creation of responsible meso-institutions that contribute toward organizing, monitoring, guiding, and controlling, while providing the governance needed to maintain or restore the alignment with the new technological design, could also be a core issue of public policies.

To sum up. In stable socio-technological systems that develop along a path-dependent trajectory, agents learn and adapt "spontaneously" without explicit incentives and directives from government, because the desirable decisions belong to their "normal" practices. In other words, the agents share the same mental maps (Denzau and North, 1994). The institutions that are responsible for the identification, monitoring, and intervention are in place to fulfill the critical functions needed to deliver the expected services. The components of technologies and institutions at the different layers are vertically well coordinated within each dimension, and so are the horizontal modalities of alignment between them. In the case of gradual small changes, the coordination arrangements as well as the modalities of alignment are able to adapt smoothly. Smoothly, because adaptations fit perfectly within the established technologies and institutions, as well in the shared mental maps of the agents involved.

However, technological innovations, institutional transformation, and changes in societal values create fundamental uncertainties and confront private and public agents with unknown complexities and causalities that impact the performance of socio-technological systems. We argue that government policies would then do better to take a step back and focus on policies that explore, facilitate information exchange among stakeholders through the creation of consultation platforms, and implement institutional arrangements to closely monitor the impact of fundamental changes on the fulfillment and safeguarding of critical functions.

8.5 Leading the Way

Based on the overview provided in the previous sections, wrapping up the contribution of this book is quite straightforward.

The research question stated upfront and repeated at the beginning of this chapter provided the guiding theme that underlined and linked the different chapters. We developed a set of interdependent concepts that formed a framework, allowing us to capture what we consider to be the central characteristics of network infrastructures: the four critical requirements of system control, capacity management, interconnection, and interoperability, whose fulfillment and safeguarding condition the capacity of a specific network infrastructure to deliver the services expected by its final users, ultimately all citizens.

In order to fill in the gap between these two poles – the functions to be fulfilled and the delivery of expected services – and to establish the precise links that connect them, we considered the respective roles of the two dimensions along which all network infrastructures are built: the technological dimension and the institutional dimension. We went a step further in showing that there are different layers within these two dimensions. The distinction between the architecture, technological design, and technical operation that shape the technological dimension, and between the macro- , meso- and micro layers that shape the institutional dimension allows a better understanding of the complexity of network infrastructures and the modalities through which they actually operate. The very existence of these layers raises problems of coordination in each dimension, problems that we explored throughout the empirical part of this book.

However, if we acknowledge that both institutions and technologies matter for the efficient operation of network infrastructures, that is, their capacity to deliver the expected services, we also need to understand the way these two dimensions relate to each other, making it possible to achieve this goal. Our framework captured this link between the two dimensions by considering the modalities of their alignment. Consistent with the distinction made between the three layers, we defined these modalities in relation to these layers. The concepts of structure, governance, and transactions respectively delineated these modalities of alignment between institutions and technologies. They also help to identify and understand the possibility of flaws resulting from misalignment along these three layers, a possibility that we also explore throughout the empirical chapters.

The problems of coordination and/or alignment that network infrastructures might face must be considered in relation to the expected services, expectations which are ultimately shaped by societal values. This led naturally to issues of public policy. Although our book is essentially analytical, these policy issues form the horizon of our framework. The set of concepts developed and implemented through a variety of examples and cases in the previous chapters provides powerful tools to identify and understand the sources of flaws in existing network infrastructures, as well as the problems that can emerge from technological innovation and/or institutional changes. In pointing out these issues, our framework provides potential guidance to policy makers, as suggested in the previous section.

Throughout this entire analytical exercise, we remained aware of the limitations of a framework that is essentially static, and which needs to be substantiated and enriched or potentially revised through more extensive empirical studies. We never pretended to answer the numerous questions raised along the way. Still, we remain persuaded that this framework provides a useful set of conceptual tools to go much further in the analysis of network infrastructures and in understanding the dramatic changes they all face. In that respect, we are convinced that the approach we have submitted opens the way to future, fruitful research.

Glossary

Alignment/misalignment: refers to the compatibility (or incompatibility) between technological and institutional characteristics of the coordination arrangements needed to safeguard the critical functions along each layer of our framework.

Architecture (technological): stipulates the generic technological features, embedded in physical systems, necessary to provide the services expected from the network infrastructure at stake.

Capacity management: refers to the allocation of scarce infrastructure resources needed to balance the physical capacity of the network.

Complementarity: refers to the interdependence between nodes and links that characterize a "network."

Contracts: understood as formal agreements within the micro-institutional layer, which explicitly determine binding rules for allocating and transferring rights to use goods and services among well identified entities (the "parties" to a contract).

Coordination: refers to the existence of technological and/or institutional arrangements that allow different components and/or agents to work together and to fulfill common goals while safeguarding the critical functions of specific networks.

Criticality: designates technological and/or institutional conditions needed to safeguard or restore the critical functions in network infrastructures.

Critical functions: refer to the four functions (system control, capacity management, interconnection, and interoperability) that must be fulfilled for the network to deliver the expected outcome.

Entities: configurations of complementary devices to fulfill requirements for delivering expected services. Devices are those components that constitute specific network infrastructures.

Expected services: services developed to satisfy a basic need for citizens according to their societal values.

Governance: the combination of institutional entities and devices (procedures and protocols) through which context-specific technologies and specific meso-institutions are aligned, making the delivery of relevant services possible.

Institutions: the intricate combination of norms and rules embedded in entities and devices that provide the foundations to interactions among agents and their connection to socio-technical systems in which they evolve.

Interconnection: refers to the coordination of activities and services between different segments that perform similar or complementary tasks in an infrastructure network.

Interoperability: refers to the requirements that components of infrastructure networks must satisfy to support the complementarity between different nodes and links that structure the network.

Macro-institutions: institutional layer within which "constitutive" norms and rules are established that delineate and structure the domain of possible transactions necessary to provide the services expected from the network infrastructure at stake.

Meso-institutions: institutional layer within which constitutive norms and rules are translated by specific entities into specific guidelines and protocols for allocating rights and implementing and monitoring their usage.

Micro-institutions: institutional layer within which transactions are actually initiated, planned, and delivered, providing coordination mechanisms required to make technology operational and create value.

Modalities of alignment: refers to the entities and devices that designate respectively "who" is proceeding to the alignment, "what" is aligned, and "how" the alignment is reached or restored.

Network infrastructures: socio-technical systems in which interrelated technical and institutional artefacts complement each other through nodes and links, the coordination of which determines the capacity to fulfil specific critical functions and to deliver expected services according to societal values.

Performance: relates to the fulfillment of critical functions as shaped by societal values.

Structures: constitutive features needed to align the architecture and the macro-institutions in order to fulfill the critical functions of the network infrastructure at stake.

System control: refers to the monitoring and regulation of the standards that frame the expected quality of service to be delivered.

Technical design: relates to the context-specific arrangement of technical and material components necessary, within a given generic architecture, to make up a network delivering services specific to a certain time and space.

Technical operation: refers to the operation of technical systems in terms of monitoring and control of specific material functionalities, given a context-specific design and technological architecture.

Technology: understood as the set of technical devices, procedures, and tools defining the architecture of a network infrastructure, implemented in a specific design, and made operational through interrelated nodes and links, the coordination of which is needed to satisfy the critical functions.

Transactions: modalities of transfer of rights to use goods and services across technologically separable activities in order to align technical operations with micro-institutions, which is needed to fulfill the critical functions of the network infrastructure at stake.

Valuation: specific societal values applied as criteria to decide the type of services to be implemented and the technological as well as institutional modalities of their implementation.

References

Acemoglu, D., and J. Robinson (2012). *Why Nations Fail: The Origins of Power, Prosperity and Poverty*. New York, NY: Crown Publishers

Albrechtslund, A. (2007). Ethics and technology design. *Ethics and Information Technology*, 9: 63–72

Alchian, A. A. (1965). Some economics of property rights. *Il Politico*, 30 (4): 816–819. Reprinted in *Economic Forces at Work* (1977). Indianapolis, IN: Liberty Press

Alchian, A. A., and H. Demsetz (1972). Production, information costs and economic organization. *American Economic Review*, 62 (5): 777–795

American Heritage Dictionary (2011). Boston, MA: Houghton Mifflin Company

Aoki, M. (2001). Production, information costs and economic organization. *American Economic Review*, 62 (5): 777–795

Arbib, J., and T. Seba (2017). *Rethinking Transportation 2020–2030*, pp. 143–144. Report from RethinkX. Available at www.rethinkx.com

Arentsen, M. J., and R. W. Künneke (eds.) (2003). *National Reforms in European Gas*. Amsterdam, Netherlands: Elsevier

Baker, G., R. Gibbons, and K. J. Murphy (2002). Relational contracts and the theory of the firm. *Quarterly Journal of Economics*, 117 (1): 39–84

  (2008). Strategic alliances: bridges between islands of conscious power. *Journal of the Japanese and International Economies*, 22 (2): 146–163

Barabasi, A. L. (2003). *Linked: How Everything Is Connected to Everything Else and What It Means*. New York, NY: Plume

Barnard, C. (1938). *The Functions of the Executive*. Cambridge, MA: Harvard University Press

Barzel, Y. (2002). *A Theory of the State: Economic Rights, Legal Rights, and the Scope of the State*. Cambridge, NY and UK: Cambridge University Press

Bauer, J. M., and P. Herder (2009). *Designing Socio-technical Systems*. *Handbook of the Philosophy of Science, Volume 8: Philosophy of Technology and Engineering Sciences*. Amsterdam, Netherlands: North Holland

Baumol, W., R. Willig, and J. Panzar (1982). *Contestable Markets and the Theory of Industrial Structure*. Boston, MA: Harcourt Brace Jovanovich

Bauwens, T., B. Gotchev, and L. Holstenkamp (2016). What drives the development of community energy in Europe? The case of wind power cooperatives. *Energy Research & Social Science*, 13: 136–147

Beermann, J., and K. Tews (2016). Decentralised laboratories in the German energy transition. Why local renewable energy initiatives must reinvent themselves. *Journal of Cleaner Production*, 169: 125–134

Berle, A. E., and G. C. Means (1932). *The Modern Corporation and Private Property*. New York, NY: Commerce Clearing House; New Brunswick, NJ: Transaction Publishers (1991)

Bijker, W., T. P. Hughes, and T. J. Pinch (1987). *The Social Construction of Technological Systems: New Directions in the Sociology and History of Technology*. Boston, MA: MIT Press

Birk, M., J. P. Chayes-Avila, T. Gomez, and R. Tabors (2017). TSO/ DSO Coordination in a Context of Distributed Energy Resource Penetration. Boston, MA: MIT Center for Energy and Environmental Policy Research, Working Paper Series, 2017-017. Boston: MIT

Bose, T., A. Reina, and J. Marshall (2017). Collective decision making. *Current Opinion in Behavioral Sciences*, 16: 30–34

Brandstätt, C., G. Brunekreeft, M. Buchmann, and N. Friedrichsen (2014). Information Governance in Smart Grids: A Common Information Platform (CIP). Bremen, Germany: Jacobs University Bremen, Energy Working Papers no. 18.

Braun, M., S. Krebs, F. Flohr, and D. Gravila (2019). EuroCity persons: a novel benchmark for person detection in traffic scenes. *IEEE Transactions on Pattern Analysis and Machine Intelligence*, 41 (8): 1844–1861. Available at https://doi.org/10.1109/TPAMI.2019.2897684

Brunekreeft, G., M. Buchmann, and R. Meyer (2016). The rise of third parties and the fall of incumbents driven by large-scale integration of renewable energies: the case of Germany. *Energy Journal*, 37 (special issue)

Bush, P. D. (2009). The neoinstitutionalist theory of value. *Journal of Economic Issues*, 43 (2): 293–307

Bush, P. D., and M. R. Tool (2003). Foundational concepts for institutionalist policy making. In P. D. Bush and M. R. Tool (eds.), *Institutional Analysis and Economic Policy*. New York, NY: Springer

Cabral, L. M. B. (2000). *Introduction to Industrial Organization*. Cambridge, MA and London, UK: MIT Press

Canguilhem, G. (2019). Gaston Bachelard et les philosophes. *Sciences*, 24 (mars–avril): 7–10. Reprinted in C. Limoges (ed.), *Georges Canguilhelm, Œuvres Complètes, tome 3: Écrits d'histoire des sciences et d'épistémologie*. Paris, France: Éditions Vrin

CBS Statistics Netherlands (2017). *Aardgasbaten op laagste niveau in ruim 40 jaar*. Available at www.cbs.nl/nl-nl/nieuws/2017/17/aardgasbaten-op-laagste-niveau-in-ruim-40-jaar

Chor Boon, G., and S. Gopinathan (2008). The development of education in Singapore since 1965. In S.-K. Lee, G. Chor Boon, B. Fredriksen, and J. P. Tan (eds.), *Toward a Better Future: Education and Training for Economic Development in Singapore since 1965*, pp. 12–38. Washington, DC: World Bank Group

Coase, R. H. (1938). Review: *British Experiments in Public Ownership and Control* by Terence H. O'Brien. *Economica*, 5 (20): 485–487

(1947). The origin of the monopoly of broadcasting in Great Britain. *Economica*, (n. s.) 14: 189–210

(1959). The Federal Communications Commission. *Journal of Law and Economics*, 2 (October): 1–40

(1960). The problem of social cost. *Journal of Law and Economics*, 3 (October): 1–44

(1972). Industrial organization: a proposal for research. In V. R. Fuchs (ed.), *Economic Research: Retrospect and Prospect, Volume 3, Policy Issues and Research Opportunities in Industrial Organization*, pp. 59–73. Cambridge, MA: NBER

(1998). New institutional economics. *American Economic Review*, 88 (2): 72–74

Connolly, D., H. Lund, and B. V. Mathiesen (2016). Smart energy Europe: the technical and economic impact of one potential 100% renewable energy scenario for the European Union. *Renewable and Sustainable Energy Review*, 60: 1634–1653

Correljé, A. F. (2013). *Markets for Natural Gas: Reference Module in Earth Systems and Environmental Sciences*. Amsterdam, Netherlands: Elsevier

Correljé, A. F., and J. Groenewegen (2009). Public values in utility sectors: economic perspectives. *International Journal of Public Policy*, 4(5): 395–413

Correljé, A., J. Groenewegen, R. Künneke, and D. Scholten (2014). Design for values in economics. In J. van den Hoven, P. E. Vermaas, and I. van de Poel (eds.), *Handbook of Ethics, Values, and Technological Design*. Dordrecht, Netherlands: Springer

Correljé, A. F., C. Van der Linden, and T. Westerwoudt (2003). *Natural Gas in the Netherlands: From Cooperation to Competition*. Amsterdam, Netherlands: Orange Nassau Group BV

Davis, L. E., and D. C. North (1971). *Institutional Change and American Economic Growth*. Cambridge, UK: Cambridge University Press

De Bruijne, M., B. Steenhuisen, A. F. Correljé, E. Ten Heuvelhof, E., and L. de Vries (2011). How to design a new gas bid price ladder? Exploring market design issues in the new Dutch gas balancing regime. *Competition and Regulation in Network Industries*, 12 (1): 83–97

De Carne, G., Z. Zou, G. Butuicchi, M. Liserre, and C. Vournas (2017). Overload control in smart transformer-fed grid. *Applied Sciences*, 7(2): 208

Denzau, A., and D. C. North (1994). Shared mental models: ideologies and institutions. *Kyklos*, 47(1): 3–31

Depuru, S. S. S. R., L. Wang, and V. Devabhaktuni (2011). Smart meters for power grid: challenges, issues, advantages and status. *Renewable and Sustainable Energy Review*, 15(6): 2736–2742

De Vries, P., and E. B. Yehoue (2013). *The Routledge Companion to Public–Private Partnerships*. London, UK: Routledge

Domanski, A., and C. Ménard (2011). Liberalization in the water sector: three leading models. In R. Künneke and M. Finger (eds.), *International Handbook of Network Industries: The Liberalization of Infrastructures*, chapter 18, pp. 310–327. Cheltenham and Northampton, UK: Edward Elgar Publishing

Dosi, G. (1982). Technological paradigms and technological trajectories. A suggested interpretation of the determinants and directions of technical change. *Research Policy*, 11(3): 147–162

Dutch Ministry of Infrastructure and the Environment (2017). *On our Way Towards Connected and Automated Driving in Europe*. Outcome of the first High Level Meeting held in Amsterdam, February 15. The Hague, Netherlands: MIE. Available at www.government.nl/documents/leaflets/2017/05/18/on-our-way-towards-connected-and=automated-driving-in-Europe

Dutton, K., S. Thompson, and B. Barraclough (1997). *The Art of Control Engineering*. Harlow, UK: Addison Wesley Longman

Economides, N. (1996). The economics of networks. *International Journal of Industrial Organization*, 14 (6): 673–699

ENTSO-E (2015). Towards Smarter Grids: ENTSO-E Position Paper on Developing TSO and DSO Roles for the Benefit of Consumers. Brussels, Belgium: ENTSO-E, ENTSOE-E Position Paper

ENTSOG (2019). *Transparency Platform, European Gas Transport Network*. Available at https://transparency.entsog.eu

European Commission (2008). *Modern rail modern Europe. Towards an integrated European railway area*. Luxembourg: European Commission

European Union/European Commission (2019). *2020 Targets, EU Policy, Strategy and Legislation for 2020 Environmental, Energy and Climate Targets*. Brussels, Belgium: European Commission. Available at https://ec.europa.eu/info/energy-climate-change-environment/overall-targets/2020-targets_en

Faulconbridge, I. R., and M. J. Ryan (2014). *Systems Engineering Practice*. Canberra, Australia: Argos Press

Finger, M., J. Groenewegen, and R. W. Künneke (2005). The quest for coherence between technology and institutions in infrastructures. *Journal of Network Industries*, 6(4): 227–259

Finger, M., and D. Finon (2011). From "service public" to universal service: the case of the European Union. In M. Finger and R. Künneke (eds.), *International Handbook of Network Industries: The Liberalization of Infrastructure*, pp. 54–69. Cheltenham and Northampton, UK: Edward Elgar Publishing

Finger, M., and P. Messulam (eds.) (2015). *Rail Economics, Policy and Regulation in Europe*. Cheltenham and Northampton, UK: Edward Elgar Publishing

Friedman, B. (1996). Value-sensitive design. *Interactions*, 3(6): 17–23

Funcke, S., and D. Bauknecht (2016). Typology of centralised and decentralised visions for electricity infrastructure. *Utilities Policy*, 40: 67–74

Gabert, J. (ed.) (2018). *Memento de l'assainissement: Mettre en œuvre un service d'assainissement complet, durable et adapté*, 844 pp. Paris, France: Éditions du Gret et Quæ

Gasunie Transport Services (2019). *The Transmission Network*. Available at www.gasunietransportservices.nl/en/network-operations/the-transmission-network

Geels, F. W. (2004). From sectoral systems of innovation to socio-technical systems. Insights about dynamics and change from sociology and institutional theory. *Research Policy*, 33: 897–920

Gerard, H., E. I. Rivero Puente, and D. Six (2018). Coordination between transmission and distribution system operators in the electricity sector: a conceptual framework. *Utilities Policy*, 50: 40–48

Gerxhani, K., and J. Van Breemen (2019). Social values and institutional change: an experimental study. *Journal of Institutional Economics*, 15 (2): 259–280

Gibbons, R., and R. Henderson (2012). Relational contracts and organizational capabilities. *Organization Science*, 23 (5): 1350–1364

Gilsing, V., and B. Nooteboom (2006). Exploration and exploitation in innovation systems: the case of pharmaceutical biotechnology. *Research Policy*, 35 (1): 1–23

Glachant, J.-M. (2012). Regulating networks in the new economy. *Review of Economics and Institutions*, 3 (1): 1–27. Available at https://DOI.10.5202/rei.v3il.49

Glachant, J.-M., and M. Hallack (2010). The Gas Transportation Network as a "Lego" Game: How to Play with It? Florence, Italy: European University Institute, EUI Working Paper RSCAS 2010/42

Goodman, B., and S. Flaxman (2016). European Union regulations on algorithmic decision-making and a "right to explanantion." *ArXiv e-prints* (June)

Greif, A. (1993). Contract enforceability and economic institutions in early trade: the Maghribi traders. *American Economic Review*, 83 (3): 525–547

Greif, A., P. Milgrom, and B. Weingast (1994). Coordination, commitment and enforcement. The case of Merchant Guild. *Journal of Political Economy*, 102: 45–76

(2005). Commitment, coercion, and markets: the nature and dynamics of institutions supporting exchange. In C. Menard and M. Shirley (eds.), *Handbook of New Institutional Economics,* chapter 28, pp. 725–786. Berlin-Dordrecht-New York: Springer

(2006). *Institutions and the Path to the Modern Economy: Lessons from Medieval Trade*. Cambridge, UK: Cambridge University Press

Groenewegen, J. P. M. (2011). The Bloomington School and American institutionalism. *The Good Society*, 20 (1): 15–36

Groenewegen, J. P. M., and R. W. Künneke (2005). Process and outcomes of the infrastructure reform: an evolutionary perspective. In R. W. Künneke, A. F. Correljé, and J. P. M. Groenewegen (eds.), *Institutional Reform, Regulation, and Privatization*, chapter 1, pp. 1–35. Cheltenham and Northampton, UK: Edward Elgar Publishing

Groenewegen, J. P. M., and M. van der Steen (2007). The evolutionary policy maker. *Journal of Economic Issues*, 41 (2): 351–358

Groenewegen, J. P. M., A. van Spithoven, and A. van der Berg (2010). *Institutional Economics: An Introduction*. New York, NY: Palgrave Macmillan

Hadjipaschalis, I., A. Poullikkas, and V. Efthimiou (2009). Overview of current and future energy storage technologies for electric power applications. *Renewable and Sustainable Energy Review*, 13 (6–7): 1513–1522

Helm, D. (2009a). Utility Regulation, the RAB and the Cost of capital. Working Paper. Available at www.dieterhelm.co.uk

(2009b). Infrastructure investment, the cost of capital, and regulation: an assessment. *Oxford Review of Economic Policy*, 25(3): 307–326

Hewitson, L., M. Brown, and R. Balakrishnan (2004). *Practical Power System Protection*. Amsterdam, Netherlands: Elsevier

Hines, P., and S. Blumsack (2008). A centrality measure for electrical networks. *Proceedings of the 41st Annual International Conference on System Sciences*. Hawaii: IEEE

Ho, P. (2013). In defense of endogenous, spontaneously ordered development: institutional functionalism and Chinese property rights. *Journal of Peasant Studies*, 40 (6): 1087–1118

Hodgson, G. (1988). *Economics and Institutions: A Manifesto for a Modern Institutional Economics*. Philadelphia, PA: University of Pennsylvania Press

  (2015a). On defining institutions: rules versus equilibria. *Journal of Institutional Economics*, 11 (3): 497–505

Hodgson, G. M. (2015b). *Conceptualizing Capitalism. Institutions, Evolution, Future*. Chicago, IL: University of Chicago Press

Holstein, T., G. Dodig-Crnkovic, and P. Pelliccione (2018). Ethical and social aspects of self-driving cars. *ArXiv 18*, Gothenburg, Sweden

Hurwicz, L. (1996). Institutions as families of game forms. *Japanese Economic Review*, 47: 113–133

Hurwicz, L., and S. Reiter (2008). *Designing Economic Mechanisms*. Cambridge, UK: Cambridge University Press

International Energy Agency (IEA) (2011). *Harnessing Renewables: A Guide to the Balancing Challenge*. Paris, France: OECD/IEA

  (2014). *Technology Road Map: Energy Storage*. Paris, France: O. I. E. Agency

  (2017). *World Energy Outlook*. Paris, France: OECD/IEA

  (2018). *System Integration of Renewables. An Update on Best Practice*. Paris, France: OECD/IEA

International Renewable Energy Agency (IRENA) (2018). *Renewable Power Generation Costs in 2017*. Abu Dhabi, UAE: IRENA

International Union of Railways (UIC) (2015). *High Speed Rail: Fast Track to Sustainable Mobility*. Paris, France: UIC

Jaag, C., and U. Trinkner (2011). A general framework for regulation and liberalization in network industries. In M. Finger and R. Künneke (eds.), *International Handbook of Network Industries. The Liberalization of Infrastructure*. Cheltenham and Northampton, UK: Edward Elgar Publishing

Jensen, O. (2017). Public–private partnership for water in Asia: a review of two decades of experience. *International Journal of Water Resources Development*, 33 (1): 4–30

Jensen, O., and H. Wu (2018). Urban water security indicators: development and pilot. *Environmental Science & Policy*, 83: 33–45

Joskow, P. L. (1985). Vertical integration and long-term contracts: the case of coal-burning electric generating plants. *Journal of Law, Economics, and Organization*, 1 (1): 33–80

(1996). Introducing competition into regulated network industries: from hierarchies to markets in electricity. *Industrial and Corporate Change*, 5 (2): 341–382

(2008 [2005]). Vertical integration. In C. Ménard and M. Shirley (eds.), *Handbook of New Institutional Economics*, chapter 13. Berlin-Dordrecht-New York: Springer

Joskow, P. L., A. M. Polinsky, and S. Shavell (2007). Regulation of natural monopoly. In A. M. Polinsky and S. Shavell (eds.), *Handbook of Law and Economics*, pp. 1227–1348. Amsterdam, Netherlands: Elsevier

Kessides, I. (2004). *Reforming Infrastructure: Privatization, Regulation and Competition*. Oxford, UK: Oxford University Press

Klein, P. (2008 [2005]). The make-or-buy decision: lessons from empirical studies. In C. Ménard and M. Shirley (eds.), *Handbook of New Institutional Economics,* chapter 17, pp. 435–464. Berlin-Dordrecht-New York: Springer

Kooij, H.-J., M. Oteman, S. Veenman, K. Sperling, D. Magnusson, J. Palm, and F. Hvelplund (2018). Between grassroots and treetops: community power and institutional dependence in the renewable energy sector in Denmark, Sweden and the Netherlands. *Energy Research & Social Science*, 37(supplement C): 52–64

Kroes, P., M. Franssen, I. van de Poel, and M. Ottens (2006). Treating socio-technological systems as engineering systems: some conceptual problems. *Systems Research and Behavioral Science*, 23: 803–814

Künneke, R. W. (2008). Institutional reform and technological practice: the case of electricity. *Industrial and Corporate Change,* 17(2): 233–265

Künneke, R. W., J. Groenewegen, and J. F. Auger (2009). *The Governance of Network Industries. Institutions, Technology and Policy in Reregulated infrastructures.* Cheltenham and Northampton, UK: Edward Elgar Publishing

Künneke, R. W., J. Groenewegen, and C. Ménard (2010). Aligning modes of organization with technology: critical transactions in the reform of infrastructures. *Journal of Economic Behavior & Organization*, 75: 494–505

(2018). Interrelated technical and institutional coordination: the case of network infrastructures. In C. Ménard and M. Shirley (eds.), *Research Agenda of New Institutional Economics*, chapter 8, pp. 72–79. Cheltenham and Northampton, UK: Edward Elgar Publishing

Laffont, J.-J., and J. Tirole (1993). *A Theory of Incentives in Procurement and Regulation*. Boston, MA: MIT Press

Laffont, J.-J. (2005). *Regulation and Development*. Cambridge, UK: Cambridge University Press

Lafontaine, F., and M. Slade (2007). Vertical integration and firm boundaries: the evidence. *Journal of Economic Literature*, 45: 629–685

Lemstra, W., V. Hayes, and J. Groenewegen (2011). *The Innovation Journey of Wi-Fi – The Road to Global Success*. Cambridge, UK: Cambridge University Press

Levinson, M. (2006). *The Box, How the Shipping Container Made the World Smaller and the World Economy Bigger*. Princeton, NJ: Princeton University Press

Levy, B., and P. Spiller (1994). The institutional foundations of regulatory commitment. *Journal of Law, Economics and Organization*, 9 (fall): 201–246

  (1996). *Regulations, Institutions and Commitments. A Comparative Analysis of Telecommunications Regulation*. Cambridge, UK: Cambridge University Press

Liebowitz, S. J., and S. E. Margolis (2003). Network effects. In M. E. Cave, S. K. Majumda, and I. Vogelsang (eds.), *Handbook of Telecommunications Economics*, pp. 75–96. Amsterdam, Netherlands: North-Holland/Elsevier

Long, C. (2018). The China experience: an institutional approach. In C. Ménard and M. Shirley (eds.), *Research Agenda of New Institutional Economics*, chapter 15, pp. 135–143. Cheltenham and Northampton, UK: Edward Elgar Publishing

Lund, H., P. A. Ostergaard, D. Connolly, and B. V. Mathiesen (2017). Smart energy and smart energy systems. *Energy*, 137: 556–565

Macaulay, S. (1963). Non-contractual relations in business: a preliminary study. *American Sociological Review*, 28 (1): 55–67

Maier, M. W., and E. Rechtin (2000). *The Art of System Architecting*. Boca Raton, FL: CRC Press. Available at https://doi.org/10.1201/9781420058529

Mantzavinos, C. (2001). *Individual, Institutions and Markets*. Cambridge, UK: Cambridge University Press

Marshall, A. (1908). *Principles of Economics*. London, UK: Macmillan

  (1919). *Industry and Trade: A Study of Industrial Technique and Business Organization, and of Their Influences on the Conditions of Various Classes and Nations*, 2 vols. London, UK: Macmillan

Marshall, W., and B. R. Weingast (1988). The industrial organization of congress. *Journal of Political Economy*, 96 (February): 132–163

McCloskey, D. (2016). *Bourgeois Equality: How Ideas, Not Capital Or Institutions, Enriched the World*. Chicago, IL: University of Chicago Press

McNeill, W. H. (1982). *The Pursuit of Power. Technology, Armed Force, and Society since A.D. 1000.* Chicago, IL: University of Chicago Press

Ménard, C. (2004). The economics of hybrid organizations. *Journal of Institutional and Theoretical Economics*, 160 (3): 345–376

(2008 [2005]). A new institutional approach to organization. In C. Ménard and M. Shirley (eds.), *Handbook of New Institutional Economics,* chapter 12, pp. 281–318. Boston-New York-Berlin-Dordrecht: Springer

Ménard, C., and A. Domanski-Peeroo (2011). Liberalization in the water sector: three leading models. In R. Künneke and M. Finger (eds.), *International Handbook of Network Industries: The Liberalization of Infrastructures,* chapter 18, pp. 310–327. Cheltenham and Northampton, UK: Edward Elgar Publishing

Ménard, C., and M. Ghertman (eds.) (2009). *Regulation, Deregulation, Reregulation: An Institutional Approach.* Cheltenham and Northampton, UK: Edward Elgar Publishing

Ménard, C., (2012). Risk in urban water reform: a challenge to public–private partnership. In A. Gunawansa and L. Bhular (eds.), *Water Governance: An Evaluation of Alternative Architectures,* chapter 12, pp. 290–320. Cheltenham and Northampton, UK: Edward Elgar Publishing

(2013). Hybrid modes of organization. Alliances, joint ventures, networks, and other "strange" animals. In R. Gibbons and J. Roberts (eds.), *The Handbook of Organizational Economics,* chapter 26, pp. 1066–1108. Princeton, NJ: Princeton University Press

(2017). Meso-institutions: the variety of regulatory arrangements in the water sector. *Utilities Policy*, 49: 6–19

Ménard, C., A. Jimenez, and H. Tropp (2018). Addressing the policy-implementation gaps in water services: the key role of meso-institutions. *Water International*, 43 (1): 13–33

(2019). Dimensionalizing Institutions. In F. Gagliardi and D. Gindis (eds.), *Institutions and Evolution of Capitalism: Essays in Honour of Geoffrey M. Hodgson,* chapter 8, pp. 110–126. Cheltenham and Northampton, UK: Edward Elgar Publishing

Milakis, J. D., B. van Arem, and B. van Wee (2017). Policy and society related implications of automated driving: a review of literature and directions for future research. *Journal of Intelligent Transportation Systems*, 21 (4): 324–348

Milchram, C., G. Van de Ka, N. Doorn, and R. W. Künneke (2018). Moral values as factors for social acceptance of smart grids. *Sustainability*, 10 (8): 1–23. Available at https://doi.org/10.3390/su10082703

Milgrom, P., D. C. North, and B. Weingast (1989). The role of institutions in the revival of trade: the law merchant, private judges, and the champagne fairs. *Economics and Politics*, 2: 1–23

Mockyr, J. (2014). Culture, institutions, and modern growth. In I. Sened and S. Galiani (eds.), *Economic Institutions, Rights, Growth, and Sustainability: The Legacy of Douglass North*, pp. 151–191. Cambridge, UK: Cambridge University Press

(2016). A Culture of Growth: Origins of the Modern Economy. Princeton, NJ: Princeton University Press

Murmann J. P. (2003). *Knowledge and Competitive Advantage: The Coevolution of Firms, Technology and National Institutions.* Cambridge, UK: Cambridge University Press

National Highway Traffic Safety Administration (NHTSA)/Department of Transportation (DOT) (2018). *Advance Notice of Proposed Rulemaking (ANPRM)*. October 3, Washington, DC, under authority delegated in 49 CFR part 1.95. Available at www.federalregister.gov

National Research Council (2006). *Drinking Water Distribution Systems: Assessing and Reducing Risks.* Washington, DC: National Academies Press

National Transportation Safety Board (NTSB) (2018). *Preliminary Report Released for Crash Involving Pedestrian, Uber Technologies, Inc. Test Vehicle.* May 24

(2019a). *Inadequate Safety Culture Contributed to Uber Automated test Vehicle Crash – NTSB Calls for Federal Review Process for Automated Vehicle Testing on Public Roads.* NTSB Office of Public Affairs News Release, November 19

(2019b). Testimony of the Honorable Robert L. Sumwalt, III Chairman National Transportation Safety Board, before the Committee on Commerce, Science and Transportation. *United States Senate on Highly Automated Vehicles: Federal Perspectives on the Deployment of Safety Technology.* November 20, Washington DC

Nightingale, P., T. Brady, A. Davies, and J. Hall (2003). Capacity utilization revisited: software, control and the growth of large technical systems. *Industrial and Corporate Change*, 12 (3): 477–517

North, D. C. (1968). Sources of productivity change in ocean shipping, 1600–1850. *Journal of Political Economy*, 76 (5): 953–970

(1981). *Structure and Change in Economic History.* New York, NY: Norton & Co.

(1990a). *Institutions, Institutional Change, and Economic Performance.* Cambridge, UK: Cambridge University Press

(1990b). A transaction cost theory of politics. *Journal of Theoretical Politics*, 2 (4): 355–367

(2005). *Understanding the Process of Economic Change*. Princeton, NJ: Princeton University Press.

North, D. C., J. J. Wallis, and B. R. Weingast (2009). *Violence and Social Orders. A Conceptual Framework for Interpreting Recorded Human History*. Cambridge, UK: Cambridge University Press

OECD (2011). *Water Governance in OECD Countries: A Multi-level Approach*. Paris, France: OECD

(2012). *Water Governance in Latin America and the Carribean*. Paris, France: OECD

OECD (2015a). *Principles on Water Governance* (coordinated by A. Akhmouch). Paris, France: OECD

OECD (2015b). *The Governance of Water Regulators* (coordinated by C. Kauffmann). Paris, France: OECD

OECD (2015c). *Inventory: Water Governance Indicators and Measurement Frameworks* (collected by A. Akhmouch and O. Romano). Paris, France: OECD

OECD/G20 (2015). *Principles of Corporate Governance*. Paris, France: OECD

Ostrom, E. (1986). An agenda for the study of institutions. *Public Choice*, 48: 3–25

(1998). A behavioral approach to the rational choice theory of collective action: presidential address. *American Political Science Review*, 92 (1): 1–22

(2005). *Understanding Institutional Diversity*. Princeton, NJ: Princeton University Press

(2009). A general framework for analyzing sustainability of social-ecological systems. *Science*, 325: 419–422

(2014a). Institutions and sustainability of ecological systems. In I. Sened and S. Galiani (eds.), *Economic Institutions, Rights, Growth, and Sustainability: The Legacy of Douglass North*, pp. 151–191. Cambridge, UK: Cambridge University Press

(2014b). Do institutions for collective action evolve? *Journal of Bioeconomics*, 16 (1): 3–30

Perennes, P. (2014). Use of combinatorial auctions in the railway industry: can the "invisible hand" draw the railway timetable? *Transportation Research Part A: Policy and Practice*, 67: 175–187

Pezon, C., C. Fonseca, and J. Butterworth (2011). Pumps, pipes, and promises. Costs, finances and accountability for sustainable WASH services. IRC Symposium, November 18–20, 2010, The Hague, Netherlands.

Public Utilities Board (PUB) (2019). *PUB Annual Report 2018–2019*. Available at www.pub.gov.sg/annualreports/annualreport2019.pdf

(2020). *Singapore's National Water Agency: Singaport Water Story*. Available at www.pub.gov.sg/watersupply/singaporewaterstory

Ray, K., and B. Skorup (2019). Smart Cities, Dumb Infrastructure: Policy-Induced Competition in Vehicle-to-Infrastructure Systems. Arlington, VA: Mercatus Center at George Mason University, Mercatus Working Paper

Rodrik, D. (2008). *One Economics, Many Recipes: Globalization, Institutions, and Economic Growth*. Princeton, NJ: Princeton University Press

Royal Academy of Engineering (2012). *Smart Infrastructure: The Future*. London, UK: Royal Academy of Engineering

Rubinfeld, D. L. (1998). Antitrust enforcement in dynamic network infrastructures. *Antitrust Bulletin*, 48: 859–882

Sandel, M. (2012). *What Money Can't Buy: The Moral Limits of Markets*. London, UK: Penguin

Savedoff, W. D., and P. Spiller (1999). *Spilled Water: Institutional Commitment in the Provision of Water Services*. Washington, DC: Inter-American Development Bank

Saviotti, P. P. (2005). The coevolution of technologies and institutions. In M. Weber and J. Hemmelskamp (eds.), *Towards Environmental Innovation Systems*, chapter 2, pp. 9–31. Berlin-Heidelberg, Germany: Springer

Schotter, A. (1981). *The Economic Theory of Social Institutions*. Cambridge, UK: Cambridge University Press

Selznick, P. (1948). Foundations of the theory of organization. *American Sociological Review*, 13 (1): 25–35

Shapiro, C., and H. R. Varian (1999). *Information Rules: A Strategic Guide to the Network Economy*. Boston, MA: Harvard Business School Press

Shelanski, H. A., and P. Klein (1995). Empirical research in transaction costs economics. *Journal of Law, Economics and Organization*, 11 (2): 335–361

Shelanski, H. A. (2007). Adjusting regulation to competition: toward a new model for U.S. telecommunications policy. *Yale Journal on Regulation*, 24: 55–62. Available at https://digitalcommons.law.yale.edu/yjreg/vol24/iss1/3

Shirley, M. S. (ed.) (2002). *Thirsting for Efficiency. The Economics and Politics of Urban Water Reform*. London, UK: Pergamon and the World Bank Group

Shirley, M. S. (2008). *Institutions of Development*. Cheltenham and Northampton, UK: Edward Elgar Publishing

Shleifer, A., E. L. Glaeser, R. La Porta, F. Lopez de Silanes, and S. Djankov (2003). The new comparative economics. *Journal of Comparative Economics*, 31 (4): 595–619

Siemens (2016). *Planning of Electric Power Distribution. Technical Principles*. Erlangen, Germany: Siemens AG

Singapore Post (n. d.). Anti-bribery and corruption policy. Available at www.singpost.com/sites/default/files/SingPost ABC Policy.pdf

Society of Automotive Engineers (SAE) (2014). *Levels of Driving Automation are Defined in New SAE International Standard J3016*. Available at www.sae.org/misc/pdfs/automated_driving.pdf

Spiller, P. T. (2009). An institutional theory of public contracts. In C. Ménard and M. Ghertman (eds.), *Regulation, Deregulation, Reregulation: An Institutional Approach*. Cheltenham and Northampton, UK: Edward Elgar Publishing

(2013). Transaction cost regulation. *Journal of Economic Behavior and Organization*, 89: 232–242

Stigler, G. J. (1971). The theory of economic regulation. *Bell Journal of Economics and Management Science*, 2 (1): 3–21

Tadelis, S., and O. E. Williamson (2013). Transaction costs economics. In R. Gibbons and J. Roberts (eds.), *The Handbook of Organizational Economics*, chapter 4, pp. 159–189. Princeton, NJ: Princeton University Press

Tropp, H. (2007). Water governance: trends and needs for new capacity development. *Water Policy*, 9 (S2): 19–30

UNICEF (2015). *WASH and Accountability: Explaining the Concept*. Stockholm and New York: Accountability for Sustainability Partnership, UNDP Water Governance Facility at SIWI and UNICEF. Available at http://www.watergovernance.org

United Nations (2019). *17 Sustainable Development Goals*. Available at https://sustainabledevelopment.un.org/?menu=1300

US Government Accountability Office (GAO) (2016a). *Vehicle Cybersecurity*. Report to Congressional Requesters, GAO-16-350. Available at www.gao.gov/products/GAO-16-350

(2016b). *Vehicle Cybersecurity: DOT and Industry have Efforts under Way, but DOT Needs to Define its Role in Responding to a Real-world Attack*. Available at https://bit.ly/1ruZi09

US Secretary of Energy (2004). *Final Report on the August 14 Blackout in the United States and Canada: Causes and Recommendations*. Washington, DC. Available at www.energy.gov/sites/prod/files/oeprod/DocumentsandMedia/BlackoutFinal-Web.pdf

Van der Wal, W. (2003). The technological infrastructure of the gas chain. In M. Arentsen and R. W. Künneke (eds.), *National Reforms in European Gas*, chapter 2, pp. 13–29. Amsterdam, Netherlands: Elsevier

Vazquez, M., M. Hallack, and Y. Perez (2018). The dynamics of institutional and organizational change in emergent industries: the case of electric vehicles. *International Journal of Automotive Technology and Management*, 18 (3): 187–208

Verzijlberg, R. A., L. J. De Vries, G. P. J. Dijkema, and P. M. Herder (2017). Institutional challenges caused by the integration of renewable energy sources in the European electricity sector. *Renewable and Sustainable Energy Reviews*, 75: 660–667

Villar, J., R. Bessa, and M. Matos (2018). Flexibility products and markets: literature review. *Electric Power Systems Research,* 154: 329–340

Wahaab, R. Abdel (2018). *Water and Sanitation in Egypt.* Overview Report (based on a partially updated and complemented report to the African Development Bank (AFDB), Côte d'Ivoire, 2015)

Water International (2018). The OECD principles on water governance: from policy standards to practice. 43 (1): 1–132

Williamson, O. E. (1975). *Markets and Hierarchies: Analysis and Antitrust Implications.* New York, NY: Free Press

  (1979). Transaction-cost economics: the governance of contractual relations. *Journal of Law and Economics*, 22(2): 233–261

  (1985). *The Economic Institutions of Capitalism.* New York, NY: Free Press-Macmillan

  (1996). *The Mechanisms of Governance.* Oxford, UK: Oxford University Press

  (1998). Transaction cost economics: how it works, where it is headed. *De Economist*, 146 (January): 23–58

  (1999). Public and private bureaucracies: a transaction cost economics perspective. *Journal of Law, Economics and Organization*, 15 (1): 306–342

  (2000). The new institutional economics: taking stock, looking ahead. *Journal of Economic Literature*, 37 (3): 595–613

Wolsink, M. (2018). Co-production in distributed generation: renewable energy and creating space for fitting infrastructure within landscapes. *Landscape Research*, 43(4): 542–561

World Bank (2017). *Governance and the Law.* World Bank Annual Report. Washington, DC: International Bank for Reconstruction and Development/World Bank Group

World Commission on Environment and Development (WCED) (1987). Special working session. *Our Common Future*, no. 17, pp. 1–91. Oxford: Oxford University Press

Wu, X., and N. A. Malaluan (2008). A tale of two concessionaires: a natural experiment of water privatization in Metro Manilla. *Urban Studies*, 45 (1): 207–229.

Xenias, D., C. J. Axon, L. Whitmarsh, P. M. Connor, N. Balta-Ozkan, and A. Spence (2015). UK smart grid development: an expert assessment of the benefits, pitfalls and functions. *Renewable Energy*, 81: 89–102

Yildiz, Ö., J. Rommel, S. Debor, S. L. Holstenkamp, F. Mey, J. R. Müller, J. Radtke, and J. Rognli (2015). Renewable energy cooperatives as gate-keepers or facilitators? Recent developments in Germany and a multi-disciplinary research agenda. *Energy Research & Social Science*, 6: 59–73

Zhang, F. (2018). *The Institutional Evolution of China. Government vs Market*. Cheltenham and Northampton, UK: Edward Elgar Publishing

Index of Names

Acemoglu, D., 47, 63
Albrechtslund, A., 144, 146
Alchian, A. A., 61
Aoki, M., 47, 49
Arbib, J., 22, 177, 180
Arem, B. van, 177, 198
Arentsen, M. J., 94, 98, 101
Auger, J. F., 49
Axon, C. J., 129
Ayres, C. E., 33

Baker, G., 61, 66
Balakrishnan, R., 84
Balta-Ozkan, N., 129
Barabasi, A. L., 109
Barnard, C., 63
Barraclough, B., 109
Barzel, Y., 54
Bauer, J. M., 31
Bauknecht, D., 110
Baumol, W., 64
Bauwens, T., 128
Beermann, J., 110
Berg, A. van der, 29
Berle, A. E., 62
Bessa, R., 139
Bijker, W., 32
Birk, M., 139
Blumsack, S., 110
Bose, T., 229
Brandstätt, C., 79
Braun, M., 192
Breemen, J. van, 20–21, 26
Brown, M., 84
Brunekreeft, G., 79, 128
Buchmann, M., 79, 128
Butterworth, J., 149
Butuicchi, G., 136
Bush, P. D., 23

Cabral, L. M. B., 79
Canguilhem, G., 123
Chayes-Avila, J. P., 139
Chor Boon, G., 162
Coase, R. H., 55, 63–64, 71, 225
Connolly, D., 141, 142, 143, 144, 145
Connor, N., 129
Correljé, A. F., 23, 98, 100, 106

Davis, L. E., 47–48, 50, 57, 59
Debor, S., 128
De Bruijne, M., 106
De Carne, G., 136
Depuru, S. S. S. R., 144
Devabhaktuni, V., 144
De Vries, L. J., 106, 133, 136
Demsetz, H., 61
Denzau, A., 49, 52, 227, 234
Dijkema, G. P. J., 133, 134, 136
Djankov, S., 60
Dodig-Crnkovic, G., 181, 183, 187, 191
Domanski, A., 171
Doorn, N., 144
Dosi, G., 32
Dutton, K., 109

Economides, N., 24, 28, 30, 79, 109
Efthimiou, V., 136

Faulconbridge, I. R., 80, 84, 109
Finger, M., 19, 34, 35, 36, 208
Finon, D., 19
Flaxman, S., 193
Flohr, F., 192
Fonseca, C., 149
Franssen, M., 31, 76, 80
Friedman, B., 144, 146
Friedrichsen, N., 79
Funcke, S., 110

Gabert, J., 149
Galbraith, J. K., 33
Geels, F. W., 54
Gerard, H., 140
Gerxhani, K., 20–21, 26
Ghertman, M., 49, 66, 73
Gibbons, R., 61, 66
Gilsing, V., 232
Glachant, J.-M., 79, 97
Glaeser, E. L., 60
Gomez, T., 139
Goodman, B., 193
Gopinathan, S., 162
Gotchev, B., 128
Gravila, D., 192
Greif, A., 47, 49, 50, 54–55, 60
Groenewegen, J., 29, 34, 35, 36, 49, 52, 60, 66, 67, 113, 208, 227

Hadjipaschalis, I., 136
Hallack, M., 32, 97
Hayes, V., 60
Helm, D., 27, 79
Henderson, R., 66
Herder, P. M., 31, 133, 134, 136
Hewitson, L., 84
Hines, P., 110
Ho, P., 61
Hodgson, G. M., 47, 50, 51, 54–55
Holstein, T., 181, 183, 187, 191
Holstenkamp, S. L., 128
Holstenkamp, L., 128
Hugues, T. P., 32
Hurwicz, L., 49
Hvelplund, F., 128

Jaag, C., 79
Jensen, O., 156, 175
Jimenez, A., 73, 159
Joskow, P., 65, 66, 79, 134

Ka, G. van de, 144
Kessides, I., 27, 35
Klein, P., 65
Kooij, H. J., 128
Krebs, S., 192
Kroes, P. A., 31, 76, 80
Kunneke, R., 31, 32, 34, 35, 36, 49, 66, 67, 94, 98, 101, 113, 144, 208, 227

Laffont, J. J., 30
Lafontaine, F., 65
La Porta, R., 60
Lemstra, W., 60
Levinson, M., 36
Levy, B., 60, 66
Liebowitz, S. J., 79
Linden, C. van der, 23, 99, 100
Liserre, M., 136
Long, C., 61
Lund, H., 141, 142, 143, 144, 145

Macaulay, S., 60
Magnusson, D., 128
Maier, M. W., 80, 84
Malaluan, N. A., 71
Mantzavinos, C., 49
Margolis, S. E., 79
Marshall, A., 64
Marshall, J., 229
Marshall, W., 224
Mathiesen, B. V., 141, 142, 143, 144, 145
Matos, M., 139
McCloskey, D., 47
McNeill, W. H., 48
Means, G. C., 62
Ménard, C., 34, 49, 54, 65, 66, 67, 73, 113, 159, 163, 171, 175, 208
Mey, F., 128
Meyer, R., 128
Milakis, J. D., 177, 198
Milchram, C., 144
Milgrom, P., 55
Mockyr, J., 49, 51
Müller, J. R., 128
Murmann, J. P., 32
Murphy, K. J., 61, 66
Myrdal, G., 33

Nader, R., 21
Nooteboom, B., 232
North, D. C., 47–49, 50, 52–53, 54, 55, 57, 58, 59, 112, 224–225, 227, 234

Ostergaaard, P. A., 141, 143, 145
Ostrom, E., 14, 32, 47, 50, 52–55, 58, 60, 68, 120

Oteman, M., 128
Ottens, M., 31, 76, 80

Palm, J., 128
Panzar, J., 64
Pelliccione, P., 181, 183, 187, 191
Perennes, P., 88
Perez, Y., 32
Pezon, C., 149
Pinch, T. J., 32
Poel, I. van de, 31, 76, 80
Polinsky, A. M., 79
Poullikkas, A., 136

Radtke, J., 128
Ray, K., 233
Rechtin, E., 80, 84
Reina, A., 229
Reiter, S., 49, 58
Rivero Puente, E. I., 140
Robinson, J., 47, 63
Rodrik, D., 63
Rognli, J., 120
Rommel, J., 128
Rubenfield, D. L., 79
Ryan, M. J., 80, 84, 109

Sandel, M. J., 228
Savedoff, W. D., 29–30, 66, 175
Saviotti, P. P., 32
Schleifer, A. E., 60
Schotter, A., 47, 49
Seba, T., 22, 177, 180
Selznick, P., 63, 68
Shapiro, C., 79
Shavell, S., 79
Shelanski, H. A., 30, 65
Shirley, M. M., 63, 66, 73, 175
Silanes, F. L. de, 60
Six, D., 140
Skorup, B., 233
Slade, M., 65
Spence, A., 129
Sperling, K., 128
Spiller, P., 29–30, 60, 66, 174,
    175

Spithoven, J. J., 29
Steen, M. van der, 227
Steenhuisen, B., 106
Stigler, G. J., 30

Tabors, R., 139
Tadelis, S., 65
Ten Heuvelhot, E., 106
Tews, K., 110
Thompson, S., 109
Tirole, J., 30
Tool, M. R., 23
Trinkner, U., 79
Tropp, H., 72, 73, 159

Varian, H. L., 79
Vasquez, M., 32
Veblen, T., 33
Veenman, S., 128
Verzijlberg, R. A., 133, 134, 136
Villar, J., 139
Vournas, C., 136

Wahaab, R. A., 71
Wal, W. van der, 99
Wallis, J., 50, 54, 112, 224
Wang, L., 144
Wee, B. van, 177, 198
Weingast, B., 50, 54, 55, 112, 224
Westerwoudt, T., 23, 99, 100
Whitmarsh, P. M., 129
Williamson, O. E., 5, 29, 31–32, 38–39,
    47, 50, 55, 63–64, 66, 73, 201,
    225
Willig, R., 64
Wolsink, M., 128, 144
Wu, H., 156
Wu, X., 71

Xenias, D., 129

Yew, L. K., 152
Yildiz, Ö., 128

Zhang, F., 61
Zou, Z., 136

Subject Index

Agency theory, 29
Air France-KLM, 43–45, 69
Air transportation, 44, 46, 67, 70, 73, 87–88
Airline industry, 8, 43, 46, 56, 74, 210, 219
Algorithm, 19, 37, 89, 191–192
Alignment, 48, 53, 63, 70, 72–73, 78, 92, 94–97, 106–110, 115–116, 118–121, 128, 139, 151, 155, 159, 161, 166, 168, 175, 178, 193, 198, 204, 207, 215, 217, 221, 223, 226, 230, 235
  Governance, 5–6, 95, 106, 118–119, 151, 159–160, 167, 170, 173, 175, 202, 212–213
  Horizontal, 96–97, 100, 103, 212, 221, 223, 234
  Modalities, 13, 33, 41, 75, 95, 107, 115, 140, 145–146, 177, 208, 212–214, 227, 231, 235
  Structure, 5, 95–96, 99, 106, 117, 132, 152, 207, 212
  Transactions, 5–6, 106, 119, 177, 200, 207
Alternate current technology, 133
Ancillary services, 134–135, 138, 141
Antitrust
  Authorities, 44
  immunity, 45, 57, 69–70
Architecture, 5, 10, 13, 15, 39, 49, 57, 69, 76–77, 82, 87, 90, 95, 97, 106, 116, 118–121, 126, 132–137, 139, 143–144, 151, 153, 159, 167, 177, 190, 201, 211–212, 227, 234
Arrangement
  Institutional, 17, 34, 50, 52, 67, 70, 82, 84, 95, 115, 134, 137, 140, 143, 146, 149, 159, 167, 198, 209–210, 217

Intermediate, 46, 69
Organizational, 6, 57, 64, 66, 89, 228
Technological, 25, 78–79, 84, 87, 90, 92, 95, 113, 132, 135, 143, 159, 161, 163, 198, 208, 211, 222, 224
Asset
  Specificity, 198
  Strategic, 167
Authority
  Regulatory, 160
Automated driving system (ADS), 179, 182, 188, 191
Automated train protection system (ATP), 77, 84
Automated vehicles, 177–178, 180–181, 184–185, 187, 190, 194–197, 202, 204, 230

Basic need, 20
Behavior, 25–26, 31, 50, 52, 68, 178, 189, 191, 226, 228
Beliefs, 20, 51–52, 59–60, 69
Bi-directional power flow, 116, 136
Big data, 191, 224
Blueprint, 31, 159, 229
Brundtland Commission, 127
Bureaucratic control, 26

Capabilities, 131, 199, 206
Capital
  Human, 51–52
  Physical, 51–52
Central point, 79
Centralization, 5, 110, 114, 138, 214, 230
Centralized arrangements, 10, 110, 206, 233
Citizen protection, 20

Citizens, 19–20, 22, 40, 50, 59, 134, 144, 209, 222, 224–225, 229, 231, 235
Civil Code, 60
Committee, 44–45
Common Law, 60
Common pool
  resource, 61
Communication, 3, 15, 28, 36, 57, 67, 173, 181–182, 227, 233
  5G, 182, 191
Comparative static, 33, 147, 204, 220
Competition, 27, 45–46, 57, 67, 69–70, 127, 137, 172, 179, 198, 228, 233
Complementarity, 1, 5, 13, 24–25, 36, 40, 83, 110, 208
  Institutional, 25
  Technological, 24
Complexity, 48, 65, 92, 176, 178, 191, 198, 216, 235
Consumer protection, 19
Contract, 6, 16, 19, 27, 30, 44–45, 50, 55, 165, 168, 178, 195, 198
  bilateral, 94
  Design-build-own-operate (DBOO), 172
  law, 59
  Relational, 66, 201
Contractual arrangements, 105, 202
Control systems engineering, 108–110, 194–195, 199–200
Coordination
  adequate, 17, 26, 34, 37
  arrangement, 37, 40, 64, 83, 95, 132, 135, 147, 186, 198–202, 227–228, 230, 233–234
  compatibility, 18, 38–39, 110, 140, 147, 225
  lack of, 39, 72, 139
  mechanism, 63, 65, 211
  modality, 140
  open and closed, 38, 110, 112–113, 137, 139–140, 146, 233
  spatial, 110, 113
  tight, 8, 17, 19, 24–25, 40–41, 57, 66, 93, 153, 165, 174, 200, 231
Critical function, 1, 3–4, 6, 8, 10, 13, 24, 34–41, 46, 56, 61, 63, 67, 72, 76, 90, 96–97, 100–101, 104, 108–110, 115, 117, 119, 133, 135,

138, 145–147, 159, 161, 167, 188, 193, 200, 208–214, 230
  Capacity management, 33–35, 56, 79, 87, 89, 94, 99, 116, 133, 136, 145, 161, 165, 208, 218, 226, 235
  Interconnection, 8, 33, 36, 80, 86, 94, 99, 101, 104, 112, 116, 145, 160, 162, 171–172, 188, 209, 221, 226
  Interoperability, 3, 8, 34, 36–37, 82, 99, 112–113, 145, 152, 162, 166, 171, 176, 188, 209, 221
  System control, 80–81, 84, 99, 104, 112, 133, 136, 145, 161, 163, 168, 193, 196, 208, 218, 235
Criticality, 3, 226
Culture, 70, 168, 192, 196

Decentralization, 5, 110, 116, 118, 129, 168, 172
Decision rights, 53, 61–62, 65, 67, 82, 134, 137, 158, 167, 172, 178, 195, 198, 210, 223
Deep Tunnel Sewerage System (DTSS), 154
Delta Airlines, 43, 211
Demand
  pattern, 130–131, 142
Desalination, 155–156, 165, 167, 173, 221
Design
  purposeful, 228, 231
  technical, 116, 192
Devices
  institutional, 26, 83, 200
  material, 89
  Technological, 25–26, 72, 79, 82, 90, 93, 97–98, 108, 112, 128, 200, 208
Digitalization, 127–128
Directorate-General for Directorate-General for Competition (EU), 45
Dispute resolution, 72
Disruption, 3, 46, 67, 160, 163, 196
Distribution network operator, 118
Dutch gas system, 100, 106, 111, 114–116

Economics of networks, 79
Economies of scale and scope, 79

Efficiency, 16, 22–23, 26, 51, 73, 143, 146, 177, 181, 198, 201, 222, 228
Electric power, 36, 104, 128–129, 131–132, 134, 137, 142
  Distribution, 139
  Network, 139, 141
  Production, 2, 5, 7, 84, 128, 131, 135
  Transport, 2, 5
Electricity system, 3, 8, 123, 127, 132–133, 135, 137, 139, 216, 224
  contemporary, 126, 131, 135, 137–139, 147
  future, 140–142, 147, 220
  traditional, 130, 132–133
Embeddedness, 29, 43, 54, 77, 216
Energy
  community, 128
  New York blackout, 1, 84, 210
  Policy Act, 2
  service, 141, 145
  transition, 125, 127, 146, 215, 219, 230
Engineering system, 4, 7, 13
Entity (entities), 6, 56–58, 61, 69, 96, 100, 106, 110, 151, 167, 199, 212, 226, 230
  governmental, 29
  institutional, 7, 23, 26, 35, 68, 70, 72, 108
  material, 79
  technological, 78, 108, 112, 135, 194, 209
ENTSO-E, 139, 143, 209
ENTSOG, 94
Environment
  constraints, 31
  institutional, 46, 48–49, 54, 57, 104, 163
  protection, 22
  values, 22–23
Ethical dilemma, 183, 192, 222
EU High Level Meetings on Connected and Automated Driving, 186
European
  gas system, 101
  gas transmission network, 93, 95
  Railway Agency (ERA), 113
  railways, 67, 92, 113
European Union, 19, 44, 57, 68, 225

Expectations, 4, 9, 17, 39, 48, 51, 59, 77, 85, 88, 92, 96, 99, 101, 104, 128, 143, 145, 206, 209, 216, 230, 236
Expected services, 1, 3, 6–7, 10, 13, 17, 19, 23–24, 26, 34, 41, 46, 64, 67, 76, 79–81, 87, 93–94, 98, 115, 119, 132, 144, 146, 155, 160, 175, 202, 207–208, 210, 215, 222, 229–230, 235–236
Externality, 29
Exxon, 100, 103

Federal Motor Vehicle Safety Standards (FMVSS), 187, 189
Firms
  integrated, 16, 64, 193, 195, 218
  private, 19, 28, 35, 134, 168, 177, 179, 227–228, 233
  state-owned, 22
Fixed trajectory, 184, 198–199
Fossil fuel, 101, 125, 128, 131, 134, 144
Four National Taps strategy, 153, 159
Framework, 3, 9, 13–15, 17, 32, 40, 114, 120, 123, 125, 143, 146–147, 156, 175–178, 190, 202, 204, 206–208, 212, 214, 216–217, 220–221, 223, 232, 235–236
Frequency, 8, 85, 133, 138, 198, 211

Gas quality, 99, 108, 117–118, 208, 213
  Groningen-gas, 99, 101–102, 104, 106, 108
  H-gas, 102, 104–106, 108, 114
  L-gas, 99
Gasunie, 100–105, 111–112, 213–214
Generic layer, 96, 119, 210, 212
Governance, 6, 11, 29, 33, 38, 72, 96, 100, 102, 123, 148, 150–151, 156, 159, 163–164, 168, 171, 176, 207, 216, 223, 234

Handshake agreements, 60
Hierarchies, 64, 66, 93
High-speed rail system, 76–77, 81, 85–87, 92
Household, 7, 30, 93, 117, 128, 140, 144, 170, 206, 222

Hubs, 93–94, 97
Human capital. *See* Capital, human
Hybrid, 65, 70, 93, 163, 165, 173
Hydrogen, 132, 142

IAD framework, 53
Incentive(s), 29–30, 35, 64, 67, 71,
    103, 140, 162, 168, 190, 224, 229,
    232
Information, 4, 16, 37, 44, 184, 190,
    230, 232, 234
  Information and communication
    technology (ICT), 57, 79, 87, 128,
    181
Infrastructure(s)
  airports, 56, 67
  automated vehicles. *See* Automated
    vehicles
  concept, 1, 3–4, 7, 18–26, 43, 46, 63,
    66, 77–78, 90
  internet, 1, 5, 73, 112, 197
  Natural gas, 93, 97–99, 101, 104,
    125, 208, 212
  Railway, 57, 69, 79, 83, 87, 89, 92,
    226
  Road, 15–16, 19, 22, 24, 31, 34, 36,
    178, 180, 182, 186–187, 191
  sanitation, 1, 73, 148–149,
    169
Innovation, 8, 61, 182, 230
  and growth, 51
  institutional, 206
  technological, 87, 127–129, 137,
    215, 227, 234
Institution(s)
  concept, 4, 25, 29, 46–57, 108,
    208–209
  Macro-institutions, 39, 58, 62, 95,
    126, 134, 137, 157, 181–182
  Meso-institutions, 39, 68–69, 71, 95,
    100, 102, 118, 151, 159, 164, 168,
    183, 186, 190
  Micro-institutions, 39, 63, 67, 87,
    100, 104, 165, 190, 193, 200–201
Institutional
  arrangement. *See* Arrangement,
    institutional
  artefacts, 31, 52, 80
  dimensions, 13, 15, 24, 32, 38, 40,
    108, 110, 202

embeddedness. *See* Embeddedness
environment. *See* Environment,
    institutional
  layers, 16, 39, 46–47, 52, 56–57, 67,
    74, 150, 165, 175, 204
  modalities, 9, 111, 115
Interconnection. *See* Critical function,
    interconnection
Interdependence, 1, 3, 9, 11, 14, 33, 47,
    49, 54, 56, 72, 95, 156, 179, 202,
    207, 217, 222
Intermittency, 131, 146
International Energy Agency (IEA),
    127, 131, 133–134, 137–138, 143
International Renewable Energy
    Agency (IRENA), 125
International Union of Railways (UIC),
    77, 86, 88–89, 92
Interoperability. *See* Critical function,
    interoperability
Investment, 27, 48, 103, 137, 163, 232
  private, 27
  public, 28
  specific, 64
  sunk, 27, 30, 79

Johor River, 153

Laws and decrees, 61
Layer of analysis, 76–78, 81, 83, 87,
    96–97, 100, 102, 146, 207, 213
Learning, 197, 227, 229–230
  learning-by-doing, 187, 203
  policy learning, 226
  technology, 192
Legitimacy, 45
Load balancing, 8, 133

Maatschap Groningen, 100, 103
Malaysia, 150, 152–153, 158, 161, 171
Market
  arrangements, 64, 66, 108
  economy, 49, 58, 61
  structure(s), 30, 79
Microeconomics, 18, 27–28, 30, 40
Monitoring, 56, 66, 69, 77, 87, 89, 99,
    102, 104, 106, 108, 117, 128, 138,
    152, 159, 163–164, 168, 174, 177,
    195, 208–209, 211, 213, 226, 229,
    234

Monopoly (monopolies), 166
  monopolistic, 33, 79, 127, 135
  natural, 27, 29, 64, 66, 128
  natural, 134

National Highway Traffic Safety
  Administration (NHTSA), 39, 180,
  187, 201
National Transport Safety Board
  (NTSB), 178
Nederlandse Aardolie Maatschappij
  (NAM), 100
Netherlands (the), 7, 95, 98, 101, 104,
  114, 213
Network
  configuration, 135
  effect, 28, 64
  operator, 82, 97
New Institutional Economics (NIE), 18,
  26, 29, 40, 55
New York blackout, Northeast
  blackout. *See* Energy, New York
  blackout
NEWater, 154–155, 160, 165,
  170–171
Nodes and links, 7, 17, 24, 34–36, 40,
  110, 119, 160, 208–209, 211–212
Norms, 5–6, 10, 25, 31, 52–55, 57–58,
  60–61, 97, 151, 159, 172, 207,
  209–210, 228–229
North American Electric Reliability
  Corporation (NERC), 2, 71

One-directional power flow, 117
Open Skies policy, 44–46, 61, 210
Operational design domain (ODD),
  184, 199
Organization, 6, 25, 29, 50, 67, 70, 207
  organization theory, 63
Organizational modalities, 95, 102,
  104, 106, 156, 195, 200
Ownership, 28, 98, 144, 173

Paris Agreement, 125, 127
Paris Métro, 82, 92, 211
Participation, 224
  citizens. *See* Citizens' participation
Passenger transportation, 123
Path dependency, 7, 32, 77, 92, 234
People's Action Party, 157

Performance (parameter)
  comfort, 85, 89
  efficiency, 17, 26, 177
  privacy, 17, 39, 190, 201
  punctuality, 88–89
  safety, 89, 108, 177, 187, 200–201
  security of supply, 97, 105
Performance network infrastructure, 1,
  4, 17, 26, 39, 41, 67, 82, 115, 124,
  175, 206, 208
Physical capital. *See* Capital, physical
Physical laws, 15, 43, 80
Pipelines, 83–84, 93–94, 97, 108, 213
Platform, 230
Political
  choice, 29, 150, 155, 162
  decision, 7
  interferences, 167, 175, 224
  leadership, 220
  party, 157
  system, 51, 60, 152, 232
Price(s), 28, 30, 140, 170
Principal-agent
  problem, 62
  theory, 29
Procedure, 6, 58, 72, 93, 119, 165, 172,
  213
Property rights, 58, 60–61, 64–65, 67,
  134, 210, 223
Prosumer, 128, 140
Protocol, 151, 172, 183, 187, 193, 207,
  218
Proven-in-use, 187, 203
Public
  ordering, 29, 201, 204
Public Utilities Act, 158, 162
Public Utilities Board (PUB), 157, 164,
  166
Public–private partnership, 16, 27, 100,
  102, 155, 165, 167, 193, 217

Regulation, 28–30, 79, 182, 198
  deregulation, 44, 95, 111, 115,
  228
  laws and regulation, 16, 177
  laws and regulations, 25
  physical, 79
  self-regulation, 108
Regulatory
  agency (agencies), 68–69, 71–72

Regulatory (cont.)
  authority (authorities). *See* Authority,
    regulatory
  capture, 30, 228
  institutions, 30
  risk, 30, 228
Residual claimant, 61
Responsibility, 25, 139, 160, 213, 230
Retail competition, 128, 137
Right-to-use, 58, 61
Risk, 20, 27, 162–163
Road transportation system, 221
Royal Academy of Engineering, 128
Rules, 68–73, 186–190, 207, 210
  and rights, 93, 119
  constitutive, 95, 97
  formal, 59–60
  functions, 53, 69
  general, 112, 165, 175, 203
  informal, 59–62
  of the game, 45, 49–50, 52, 58,
    70–71, 189

Self-driving vehicles, 3, 11, 22, 37, 59,
    177, 180, 183, 186–187, 192, 196,
    198, 202, 216, 220, 223
service(s)
  essential, 19, 23, 34, 76, 84
  expected. *See* Expected services
  quality, 34, 177, 200, 208
  universal, 19, 23
Shanghai Maglev, 86
Shell, 100, 103
Shinkansen, 85, 91
Signaling
  devices, 76, 80, 83
  system, 25, 65, 81, 92
Singapore, 150, 152–156, 158,
    169–170, 174–175, 190, 217
Singapore's National Water Agency, 164
Sky Team, 44
Slot allocation, 8, 44, 83, 209
Smart grid, 60, 116–118, 137, 206,
    216, 222–223
Social order, 52
Socio-technological system, 1, 15, 20,
    31, 43, 57, 80, 194, 207, 227–228,
    234
Solar panels, 8, 128, 138

Solar power, 129, 133, 135
Spanish power system, 138
Sri Lanka, 192
Storage, 84, 93, 104, 132, 136, 142,
    145, 213
Strategy, 153, 159, 171
Structure(s), 31, 97, 102, 126, 212,
    219
Subsidiary principle, 57, 69
Sustainability, 39, 127, 141, 144–145,
    149, 167, 177
  Sustainable energy, 10, 111, 123,
    125, 128–129, 136, 141, 143, 146
System
  boundary (boundaries), 81–82
  socio-technological. *See* Socio-
    technological system
  technological, 82, 90, 97, 155, 169,
    212
Systems engineering, 31, 80, 82, 90,
    109

Tariffs, 35, 163, 167, 170, 175,
    220
Taxes, 28–29
TCP/IP standard, 112
Technological
  change, 2, 11, 79, 127, 223, 229
  dimension, 4, 15, 17, 33, 37–38, 49,
    52, 90, 96, 115, 119, 124, 175,
    181, 194, 206, 223, 235
  layer(s), 78, 82, 92, 156,
    211
  lock-in, 92
Technology
  architecture. *See* Architecture
  technical design. *See* Design,
    technical
  technical operation, 14, 76, 87, 90,
    104–105, 117, 179, 190, 199, 201,
    211, 235
Tempe (Arizona), 177–178, 193–195,
    201
Thalys, 82, 86, 89
TomTom, 197
Traffic
  control center, 79
  flows, 79
Transaction cost economics, 29, 38

Transaction(s), 15, 29–30, 38, 55, 57,
    63–67, 95, 102, 177–178, 196,
    203, 211, 217
  costs, 29, 38, 171, 201, 224
  critical, 179, 190, 193, 203–204,
    231
Transport-as-a-Service (TaaS), 180
Trolley problem, 183

Uber, 177–180, 196
UN Committee on Economic, Social
    and Cultural Rights, 148
Uncertainty, 58, 65, 198, 231
Urban roads, 15, 182, 199
US Department of Transportation, 210

Valuation, 53, 149, 222
Value
  conflicting values, 23
  Societal values, 9, 16, 20, 22, 100,
    127, 143, 177, 182, 216, 222
Volvo, 177–178, 196

Wastewater treatment, 148–149, 155,
    168
Water
  resources, 148, 150, 158
  system, 32, 71, 84, 113, 152, 157
Waymo, 197
Wind power, 60, 138, 142
World Health Organization, 148

Printed in the United States
by Baker & Taylor Publisher Services